BEYOND BERGSON

SUNY series, Philosophy and Race
―――――――
Robert Bernasconi and T. Denean Sharpley-Whiting, editors

BEYOND BERGSON
EXAMINING RACE AND COLONIALISM THROUGH THE WRITINGS OF HENRI BERGSON

EDITED BY

ANDREA J. PITTS AND MARK WILLIAM WESTMORELAND

FOREWORD BY

LEONARD LAWLOR

On the cover: *Night Journey* by artist Frank Bowling (British, born Guyana, 1936)
Date: 1969–70
Medium: Acrylic on canvas
Dimensions: H. 83³/₄ × W. 72¹/₈ in. (212.7 × 183.2 cm)
Metropolitan Museum of Art, NY. Accession number 2011.590.2.
Gift of Maddy and Larry Mohr, 2011.
© 2018 Artists Rights Society (ARS), New York/DACS, London

Published by State University of New York Press, Albany

© 2019 State University of New York

All rights reserved

No part of this book may be used or reproduced in any manner whatsoever without written permission. No part of this book may be stored in a retrieval system or transmitted in any form or by any means including electronic, electrostatic, magnetic tape, mechanical, photocopying, recording, or otherwise without the prior permission in writing of the publisher.

For information, contact State University of New York Press, Albany, NY
www.sunypress.edu

Library of Congress Cataloging-in-Publication Data

Names: Pitts, Andrea J., editor. | Westmoreland, Mark William, 1983, editor.
Title: Beyond Bergson : examining race and colonialism through the writings
  of Henri Bergson / edited by Andrea J. Pitts and Mark William Westmoreland.
Description: Albany : State University of New York Press, [2019] | Series:
  SUNY series, philosophy and race | Includes bibliographical references and index.
Identifiers: LCCN 2018020075 | ISBN 9781438473512 (hardcover) |
  ISBN 9781438473529 (pbk.) | ISBN 9781438473536 (ebook) Subjects: LCSH:
Bergson, Henri, 1859–1941.
Classification: LCC B2430.B43 B479 2019 | DDC 194—dc23
LC record available at https://lccn.loc.gov/2018020075

10 9 8 7 6 5 4 3 2 1

Contents

Foreword: The Hope for this Volume: Sympathy   vii
    Leonard Lawlor

Acknowledgments   xv

Introduction
Creative Extensions   1
    Andrea J. Pitts and Mark William Westmoreland

Part I
Bergson on Colonialism, Social Groups, and the State

Chapter 1
Decolonizing Bergson: The Temporal Schema of the Open and the Closed   13
    Alia Al-Saji

Chapter 2
The Language of Closure: Homogeneity, Exclusion, and the State   37
    Martin Shuster

Chapter 3
The Politics of Sympathy in Bergson's *The Two Sources of Morality and Religion*   57
    Melanie White

Part II
Bergsonian Themes in the Négritude Movement

Chapter 4
Bergson, Senghor, and the Philosophical Foundations of Négritude: Intellect, Intuition, and Knowledge   79
Clevis Headley

Chapter 5
The Spectacle of Belonging: Henri Bergson's Comic Negro and the (Im)possibility of Place in the Colonial Metropolis   121
Annette K. Joseph-Gabriel

Part III
Race, Revolution, and Bergsonism in Latin America

Chapter 6
Racial Becomings: Evolution, Materialism, and Bergson in Spanish America   143
Adriana Novoa

Chapter 7
Bergsonism in Postrevolutionary Mexico: Antonio Caso's Theory of Aesthetic Intuition   171
Andrea J. Pitts

Chapter 8
Antagonism and Myth: José Carlos Mariátegui's Revolutionary Bergsonism   193
Jaime Hanneken

Bibliography   211

List of Contributors   227

Index   231

Foreword

The Hope for this Volume: Sympathy

LEONARD LAWLOR

It is an honor for me to write the foreword to this volume, which extends Henri Bergson's thought into areas of research that Bergson himself probably would have never imagined. It is in fact gratifying for me to see a volume like this appear. It is a good sign for those of us who see in Bergson a model for philosophical work. Over the twenty years or so that I have worked on Bergson, three ideas have appeared to me to be fundamental in his thinking and fundamental for genuine philosophical work: the starting point in an intuition, the idea of qualitative multiplicity, and the idea of creative emotions. This last idea comes from Bergson's *The Two Sources of Morality and Religion*. *The Two Sources*, appearing in 1932, may be Bergson's greatest work. It is also, however, the most controversial. I will turn to what is controversial in *The Two Sources* at the end of this foreword. The problem of what Bergson says about "the primitives" in *The Two Sources* will disclose my hope for this volume.

The first idea that is fundamental is the starting point for all philosophical thinking in an intuition. In Bergson, the word *intuition* has two senses. On the one hand, for Bergson, intuition refers to a method.[1] Negatively, in intuition one does *not* remain outside of the thing one is considering. The positive formula for the method of intuition is to enter into the thing.[2] Bergson provides the image of either standing outside of a city in order to look at it, or walking around within the city to experience it. Of course, one learns more about the city from within the city than from outside the city. Therefore, in Bergson, unlike the psychologist who observes a patient's inner life from the outside, one must enter into the continuous, inner flow of time that defines consciousness. As is well known, Bergson called the inner flow of time "the duration" (which, as we shall see in a moment, is defined by qualitative multiplicity). When one has entered into the duration, one is able to learn how the continuous flow is differentiated (and even seems to be an opposition between, for instance, the soul and the body), and one is able to learn how to integrate the differences back into the continuity. Bergson's second sense of intuition takes us to *The Two Sources*. In *The Two Sources*, Bergson shows that, on the other hand, intuition means a mystical vision.[3] The meaning of *intuition* as a mystical vision is part of the controversy surrounding this book. It is controversial because the mystical vision seems to resemble madness. Likewise, the mystic seems to resemble a madman because both undergo a disequilibrium in the mind.[4] However, Bergson at length tries to distinguish the vision from madness.[5] Madmen and mystics who are actually mad, Bergson says, are "charlatans"; they speak and speak, but make no sense. They remain in the disequilibrium.[6] In contrast, the true mystic overcomes the disequilibrium resulting in a new and different equilibrium. Responding to the vision, the true mystic speaks, makes sense, and creates changes in the world. Bergson's example of a great mystic is of course Joan of Arc.[7] It is precisely the expression of the experience in meaningful words and actions that distinguishes the mystic from the madman. I think the identification of intuition with a mystical vision is important because it seems that philosophy must maintain its traditional aim of being presuppositionless. If philosophy indeed aims to be presuppositionless, then only an encounter like the mystical vision allows us to eliminate presuppositions. As philosophers, we need to be thrown into disequilibrium. But is this encounter enough to free us from the prejudices relative to our times? As we shall see at the end, the answer is probably not.

The second idea that is fundamental for philosophical thinking in general is Bergson's idea of qualitative multiplicity. In his first book, *Time and Free Will*, published in 1889, Bergson distinguishes (through the method of intuition) qualitative multiplicity from quantitative multiplicity. As the name suggests, a quantitative multiplicity enumerates things or states of consciousness by means of externalizing one from another in a homogeneous space. In contrast, a qualitative multiplicity consists in a temporal heterogeneity, in which "several conscious states are organized into a whole, permeate one another, [and] gradually gain a richer content."[8] Bergson even insists that the word *several* is inappropriate to qualitative multiplicity because it suggests numbering. In *Time and Free Will*, Bergson provides examples of a quantitative multiplicity; the example of a flock of sheep is perhaps the easiest to grasp.[9] When we look at a flock of sheep, what we notice is that they all look alike. But also, we notice that we can enumerate the sheep. We are able to enumerate them because each sheep is spatially separated from or juxtaposed to the others; in other words, each occupies a spatial location. Therefore, quantitative multiplicities, as Bergson says, are homogeneous and spatial. Bergson also provides examples of qualitative multiplicity. Let us consider the example of a moral feeling, namely, sympathy.[10] Our experience of sympathy begins, according to Bergson, with us putting ourselves in the place of others, in feeling their pain. But, if this were all, the feeling would inspire in us abhorrence of others, and we would want to avoid them, not help them. Bergson concedes that the feeling of horror may be at the root of sympathy. But then you realize that if you do not help this poor wretch, it is going to turn out that when you need help, no one will come to your aide. There is a "need" to help the suffering. For Bergson, these two phases are "inferior forms of pity." In contrast, true pity is not so much fearing pain as desiring it. It is as if "nature" has committed a great injustice and what we want is not to be seen as complicit with it. As Bergson says, "The essence of pity is thus a need for self-abasement, an aspiration downward."[11] But, this downward aspiration develops into a sense of being superior. One realizes that one can do without certain sensuous goods; one is superior over them since one has managed to dissociate oneself from them. In the end, one feels humility, since one is now stripped of these sensuous goods. Bergson calls this feeling "a qualitative progress." It consists in a "transition from repugnance to fear, from fear to sympathy, and from sympathy itself to humility."[12] The genius of Bergson's description is that there is a heterogeneity of feelings here, and yet no one would be able to juxtapose them. The feelings are continuous with one another; they interpenetrate one another, and there is even an opposition between inferior needs and superior needs. A qualitative multiplicity is therefore heterogeneous, continuous, oppositional at the extremes, and progressive or temporal, an irreversible flow, which is not given all at once. Bergson's idea of qualitative multiplicity is important for philosophical thinking not only because it allows us to see how complicated psychic life is, but also because it provides us with the foundation for a new kind of social collectivity, one that is at once heterogeneous and interpenetrating, or, more simply, one that is sympathetic.

The third idea that is fundamental for philosophical thinking in general is the idea of creative emotions. Creative emotions elaborate on the idea of intuition with which we started, and therefore we turn back to *The Two Sources*. The difference between creative emotions and normal, uncreative emotions consists in this: in normal emotions, we first have a representation that causes the feeling (I see my friend and then I feel happy); in creative emotion, we first have the emotion that then creates representations.[13] While normal emotions and feelings are determined by their object, creative emotions are not based on their objects. Bergson's example is Rousseau's creation of the feeling of innocence experienced when in the mountains.[14] Rousseau, according to Bergson, used the "notes" of the sensations that mountains arouse in all humans since time immemorial to compose a new and original emotion. Rousseau gave to mountains "the principal tone" that only Rousseau could compose.[15] Another example Bergson provides is the composition of a symphony; he mentions Beethoven.[16] Outside of all the intellectual work of selecting and arranging, the composer was in search of inspiration, "an indivisible emotion which intelligence helped to unfold into music." Thanks to the two examples, we see that creative emotions are themselves created (Rousseau), but also creating (Beethoven). The idea of creative emotions is important for philosophical thinking because a creative emotion, like an intuition and a mystical vision, throws one out of the habitual mode of thinking. It requires the abandonment of common sense and customs. Within *The Two Sources*, creative emotions are important because they open an individual's soul, transforming the person into a "hero," who in turn opens society through the creation of new values, and the hero being a mystic makes religion dynamic. Dynamic religion is the religion of love. In *The Two Sources*, Bergson advocates this sort of openness and dynamism, which of course he places in opposition to closedness and stasis.

For Bergson, closed societies and static religions aim only at social cohesion. The static, moral values one finds within closed societies, while presented as universal, have the sole function of making individuals conform to that particular society. The phenomenon of war shows clearly that these values are not universal; in war, the fair becomes the foul when it comes from the enemy, and the foul becomes the fair when it comes from the friend.[17] Despite their lofty appearance, our moral duties do nothing more than provide us with an attitude of "discipline in the face of the enemy."[18] We can see that while dynamic religion is the religion of love, static religion seems to point in the direction of hatred. Now Bergson explains the values and duties of closed societies and their static religions by means of habits.[19] The habits themselves or the rules of conduct of a society might be contingent, but the habit of contracting habits is instinctual. Like any instinct, the habit of contracting habits serves the need to survive; it serves social cohesion in the face of the enemy. Thus, based in the instincts for survival, closed societies and static religions are those societies and religions that are closer to nature.

It is in the context of closed societies and their static religions that Bergson speaks of the "primitives."[20] One must not misread these pages. Bergson is arguing that primitive societies and modern societies have a kind of equality in status.[21] No matter how "spiritualized" a society becomes, the need for social cohesion and thus the habit of moral duties are still there at the base.[22] No matter how civilized a society may become, it still "fundamentally resembles" primitive societies.[23] In short, Bergson is arguing that all of us are still primitive. Bergson is even arguing that primitive societies resemble modern ones because the primitives have indeed emerged from nature and have their own accretion of culture.[24] Nevertheless, Bergson speculates that primitive societies have remained closer to nature and have never developed science, "probably" because they have had no neighbors and therefore no enemies. Consequently, never having had their survival threatened, "they were not called upon to make the initial effort."[25] Not being called on, through war, to develop more sophisticated and useful forms of knowledge, the primitives have remained under the sway of magic, which has the effect of "encouraging laziness."[26] The primitives "abandon themselves," as Bergson says, "to a certain laziness."[27] What a stereotype of aboriginal peoples! There can be no question that the attribution of laziness to the primitives of "the Cameroons" reveals that Bergson was unaware of his own prejudices. We can claim in his defense that he is a product of his times, but certainly we cannot call him enlightened in regard to the diversity of cultures. Bergson's attribution of laziness to the primitives is especially unfortunate in light of the themes of this volume.

Yet, even if we conclude, as we must, that Bergson's comments about the primitives in *The Two Sources* are based in European ethnocentrism and thus based in an unexamined and probably unconscious prejudice, we equally have to recognize that no philosopher, no matter how hard she or he tries, is able to reach the absolute. No philosopher is able to reach a position that is entirely free of relativity. No philosopher is able to be responsible completely for her or his ideas. The inability—whether conceived as a weakness or as a strength—is of course based in finitude. But this finitude is not merely human. It is the finitude of the absolute level, which is time; it is based in an absolute finitude. The openness and dynamism of time makes it so that the absolute cannot be given all at once, even to the absolute itself. To put this idea simply, the openness of the future implies that no one is able to see very far. But the very idea of futurity implies that this finitude is fundamentally connected to an infinitude. It is the infinity of time—the duration—that produces hope, even the hope I have for this volume. My hope for this volume lies not only in disclosing the unconscious prejudices of this great philosopher, but also in the extension of what is infinite in his thought. May these extensions be open and dynamic. At bottom, for Bergson, and this we must never forget, genuine philosophy must be creative.

Notes

1. Gilles Deleuze, *Bergsonism*, trans. Hugh Tomlinson and Barbara Habberjam (New York: Zone Books, 1988), 13–35.
2. Henri Bergson, *The Creative Mind*, trans. Mabelle L. Andison (Mineola: Dover, 2007), 135.
3. Henri Bergson, *The Two Sources of Morality and Religion*, trans. R. Ashley Audra, Cloudesley Brereton, and W. Horsfall Carter (Notre Dame, IN: University of Notre Dame Press, 1977), 212, 230. Hereafter referred to as "*TSMR*."
4. *TSMR*, 245.
5. See Jean-Christophe Goddard, *Mysticisme et folie: Essai sur la simplicité* (Paris: Desclée de Brouwer, 2002), 23–79.
6. *TSMR*, 246.
7. Ibid., 228.
8. Henri Bergson, *Time and Free Will*, trans. F. L. Pogson (Mineola, NY: Dover Publications, 2001), 122.
9. Ibid., 76–77.
10. Ibid., 18–19.
11. Ibid., 19.
12. Ibid.
13. *TSMR*, 43–44.
14. Ibid., 41.
15. Ibid., 43.
16. Ibid., 252–53.
17. Ibid., 31.
18. Ibid.
19. Ibid., 26.

20. Ibid., 24, 26–27.
21. Alexander Lefebvre, *Human Rights as a Way of Life: On Bergson's Political Philosophy* (Stanford, CA: Stanford University Press, 2013), 29–30.
22. *TSMR*, 27.
23. Ibid., 145–46.
24. Ibid., 127.
25. Ibid., 172.
26. Ibid., 149.
27. Ibid., 150.

Acknowledgments

Andrea J. Pitts

I would like to first extend thanks to my coeditor, Mark William Westmoreland, who has been a wonderful philosophical interlocutor and a tremendously supportive colleague throughout our work together on this volume.

Many thanks also to my friend and mentor, Dr. Adriana Novoa, who I am delighted to be featuring in this collection. Were it not for Adriana's critical insight about the importance of studying Bergsonism within the context of Latin American philosophy, this project would not have come to fruition. I am sincerely grateful for all the resources she has sent me over the years, and for our many late-night conversations about history, culture, and life.

Alex Levine has also been an important interlocutor in my thinking through this project as well. Alex has remained a steadfast supporter of my work and has enriched my thinking about process, time, and history.

Many thanks to Ash Williams, who put in many hours formatting the bibliography for the volume, and to Heather Dubnick for completing the index. Their work has been invaluable in this project. Thanks also to Andrew Kenyon, Chelsea Miller, and the staff at SUNY Press. Their editorial support has been greatly appreciated. Sincere thanks as well to Frank Bowling for granting us permission to reprint his painting, *Night Journey*, for the cover image of this book. I am immensely grateful for his generosity.

Additional thanks especially to my friends and colleagues Geoffrey Adelsburg, Alejandro Arango, Adam Burgos, Denise Callejas, Natalie Cisneros, Joseph Jordan, José Medina, Mariana Ortega, Stephanie Rivera Berruz, Elena Ruíz, Muhammad Velji, and Elizabeth Victor. They were the extended community of scholars who enabled my early work in Latin American

Philosophy, and I am forever indebted for their support, kindness, and constructive criticism. Many thanks as well to the organizers and participants of the many venues in which I was able to engage in rich discussions and learn from others about a number of themes in the volume, including meetings of the Caribbean Philosophical Association, the Latin American Studies Association, philoSOPHIA, the Annual Philosophy Conference at Villanova University, the Roundtable on Latina Feminism, and the Society for Phenomenology and Existential Philosophy.

Last, I am eternally grateful to my family, Maria Guzman Pitts, Jay Pitts, James Pitts, Pilar Pitts, Isabela Pitts, and Cesar Guzman for their encouragement, humor, and unending support. Without their love and guidance, I would not be the scholar I am today. Finally, my most heartful thanks to my partner in life, love, and friendship, Elisabeth Paquette, who has taught me so many things about philosophy, politics, and how to strive for a better world. Her eye for detail and her enduring belief in the value of my research has made it possible for me to do this work. For that, I can never thank her enough.

Mark William Westmoreland

I would like to begin by thanking my coeditor, Andrea J. Pitts, who has shown remarkable insight and perseverance throughout the process. They are the sort of colleague that makes our profession worthwhile. It has been a pleasure to work with them.

Many thanks go to the editorial staff with whom we worked. Andrew Kenyon was gracious and supportive from the very beginning. Chelsea Miller, Ryan Morris, and the other SUNY staff did a wonderful job bringing the volume to completion.

Frank Bowling's artwork is both inspiring and challenging. Having his work on the cover of this volume is an honor. Leslie Knight and David Acosta have my gratitude for helping me with questions regarding translations. Alexandre Lefebvre has been a generous and kind colleague on more than one occasion. Also deserving of thanks is Ash Williams, who helped us with the bibliography, and Heather Dubnick, who compiled the index for this volume.

Two mentors are especially deserving of thanks. For several years, Sally J. Scholz has offered words of wisdom about the profession, philosophy, and life. Sally has repeatedly given advice when I've sought it (and sometimes even when I have not). In many ways, she has been a rock amid the stormy sea of graduate school. George Yancy never ceases to amaze me in his philosophical acumen, hard work, and generosity. I have much respect for George's pen and his voice—his humble but playful tone warms one's heart with a realistic hope. Both Sally and George have guided me through some of the most difficult decisions in my career. I am indebted.

I owe my introduction to the philosophy of Bergson to two people. I first read Bergson in a graduate seminar taught by Leonard Lawlor at the University of Memphis in 2005. In the years following, Len and I have remained in touch, and I am honored to have him involved with this volume. Brien Karas and I have spent more than a decade conversing about Bergson. It was listening to Brien talk about Bergson that made me realize just how underappreciated Bergsonism had been, and yet how interesting it was and remains to be.

Last, I would like to thank my family. Over the years, they have been encouraging despite their not fully understanding what it is we philosophers do. They have watched our children so that I could have more time to write. They have cooked meals when things became too busy. Our children, Brynne Loucille and Adeline Rubye, remind me every day what trust, hope, and love mean. These two sidekicks of mine bring more joy than I could ever express. To Laura Berkemeyer Westmoreland, I owe the greatest amount of gratitude. She has never wavered in her support of my work.

Introduction

Creative Extensions

ANDREA J. PITTS AND MARK WILLIAM WESTMORELAND

Henri Bergson (1859–1941) did not write a book of political philosophy or one that dealt specifically with race or colonialism. "What interest[ed] him," Philippe Soulez writes, "[were] problems, rather than a subject matter or discipline."[1] After a cursory read through Bergson's works, one might conclude the problems that concerned Bergson most were consciousness, memory, temporality, and freedom. To consider Bergson a philosopher of race and/or colonialism might seem to be a stretch for many. Nevertheless, Bergson's work did carry tremendous influence for many thinkers grappling with these sociopolitical phenomena. As we highlight throughout this volume, while Bergson's writings were not themselves directly attuned to the themes of race and colonialism, prominent philosophical traditions within Latin America, Africa, and Black Europe were analyzing and extending his work within distinct geopolitical contexts.[2] It is thus our hope that this volume will demonstrate and justify why thinking with and beyond Bergson is useful for diagnosing and challenging our thinking about race and colonialism.

Regarding the status of *Beyond* in our title, we mean that this book is not an apology for a distinguished philosopher, nor is it a return to philosophy bound up within a sociohistorical context different from our own without adapting that philosophy to meet the changes that have occurred over the last century. Rather, we have something in mind akin to Gilles Deleuze's concluding words in *Bergsonism*: "A 'return to Bergson' does not only mean a renewed admiration for a great philosopher but a renewal of his project today, in relation to the transformations of life and society."³ In this vein, we want to reconsider some old problems, a few with which Bergson was familiar, by extending his thought in new and creative ways. Likewise, we want to apply Bergson's thought to questions unknown or not discussed by the philosopher. And, we hope, like Alexandre Lefebvre and Melanie White, "To show that Bergson does not just offer a new solution to already established problems, but, in keeping with the methodological privilege he gives to them, he dissolves or reconfigures the formation of the problem itself."⁴ Thus, our aim in this volume is to shed light on systems of oppression such as racism and colonialism, and on the creative possibilities for resistance to these forms of oppression from the theoretical influences of Bergsonism. In what follows, we highlight some relevant biographical details of Bergson's political career, and then connect his work to the topics of race and colonialism. Finally, we close with an outline of the chapters in this volume and some suggested pathways to move through the text.

Bergson's Political Career

Bergson left his mark on early twentieth century internationalism. For instance, John Humphrey, one of the main authors of the United Nations' *Universal Declaration of Human Rights* (1948), was significantly influenced by Bergson. According to Clinton Curle, "Humphrey kept a journal of his private thoughts during his early tenure at the United Nations. From these journals, it is apparent that he came to view the *Universal Declaration* in terms of Bergson's book *The Two Sources of Morality and Religion*."⁵ Years earlier, during World War I, particularly in 1916, Bergson became a French emissary to Spain and delivered lectures at the Ateneo de Madrid. In February 1917, Bergson (unofficially) visited the United States, and through this visit, French Premier Aristide Briand had hoped that Bergson would passionately encourage Woodrow Wilson to enter the war.

After war ceased toward the end of 1918, the Paris Peace Conference provided the blueprint for peace between the Allied victors and the Central Powers. During the conference, which lasted from January 18, 1919 to June 28, 1919 (the fifth anniversary of the assassination of Archduke Franz Ferdinand), Bergson took on the role of liaison between France and the United States. The Conference resulted in five peace treaties, including the Treaty of Versailles, and the creation of the League of Nations, which was officially founded on January 10, 1920, with the purpose of maintaining international peace. Bergson served as chair of the League's International Commission for Intellectual Cooperation (ICIC) from the summer of 1922 until 1925, when he resigned due to illness. The ICIC had a joint goal, namely, to cultivate both scientific cooperation and moral fraternity and solidarity.[6] Bergson later wrote in *The Two Sources* that "anyone who is thoroughly familiar with the language and literature of a people cannot be wholly its enemy. This should be borne in mind when we ask education to pave the way for international understanding."[7] Looking back, it is clear that Bergson had thought for many years about how to establish and maintain a peaceful internationalism. The League and its aim of peace were not solely political in origin but, at least for Bergson, were mystical and religious. The League of Nations was rooted in and buttressed by mystical intuition—something very distant from the mechanical rationalization of the factory (and of the gas chamber). The ICIC more specifically sought to increase communication between nations by creating a network of shared projects through which scholarship could be translated from one language to another, students and researchers could participate in the scientific and artistic life of different countries via exchange programs, and knowledge could be more readily and accessibly disseminated. These new networks, it was thought, held the potential for fostering a strong sense of community and belonging among the member states of the League.[8] Sadly, by 1939, Hitler's invasion of Poland inaugurated the second Great War, bringing with it another holocaust.[9]

Race and Colonialism

In *Humanism and Terror*, Maurice Merleau-Ponty highlights the extent to which our species is capable of both profound beauty and sublime violence: "The human world is an open or unfinished system and the same radical contingency which threatens it with discord also rescues it from the inevitability of disorder and prevents us from despairing of it, providing only that one remembers its various machineries are actually men and tries to maintain and expand man's relations to man."[10] In one line of thought, we might consider how modernity began with the hunting of Black peoples and continued with the atomic bomb.[11] It wears the mask of progress while hiding its thanatocratic nature, that is, its capacity for killing all human lives—both friend and foe. The modern era is one of contradiction. On the one hand, it lifts up the ideals of freedom, equality, and justice. On the other hand, it requires of itself unjust habits of, including but not limited to, ethnocentrism, xenophobia, racism, sexism, gender discrimination, and colonial violence. Racism, for example, is, as Soulez claims, "the flipside of the refusal to 'know' the other, namely to acknowledge or 'recognize' him [*sic*]. Naturalizing the difference (by biologizing it) opens the way to extermination."[12] As Bergson notes, a "veil of ignorance, preconceptions and prejudices" exists between one and the other, and this veil leads to all manner of injustice.[13]

The notion of justice brings to the fore other related ideas such as equality and, more recently, rights.[14] Justice, as it relates to equality, involves determining the proper relation of one thing to another by appealing to a third thing. Take, for instance, the rights of citizens within a so-called free society such as the United States. In a formal sense, affluent white men and poor Women of Color are equal with regard to a third, namely, the neutral deraced and desexed citizen of the U.S. Constitution. Much work has already been done to show how this "anonymous citizen" figure reinforces white supremacist and sexist values in so far as white men with material resources are implicitly (and often explicitly) the paradigmatic citizen. It is worth noting for our present purpose how this third category is predicated on the social norms of (closed) society. In short, the closed society can only support a relative justice. Bergson writes,

> Justice has always evoked ideas of equality, or proportion, of compensation [. . .] The idea [of justice] must have already taken shape as far back as the days of exchange and barter; however rudimentary a community may be, it barters, and it cannot barter without first finding out if the objects exchanged are really equal in value, that is to say, both exchangeable for a definite third object.[15]

Such an economy of exchange will have all things reduced to their value in the market. At some point, and we have already been at this point for some time, human life will be valued with regard to one's economic value, which will be based on one's productivity while also leaving room for any one particular person to be expendable. This is the fate of neocolonial finance capitalism of the twenty-first century.

Absolute justice, however, exceeds the social determination of the third thing—a constitution or money. Rather than affirming a person's value (citizen or not) by tying this value to an equality of rights, absolute justice affirms the incommensurate value of every person.[16] Absolute justice is none other than the love for all persons. This is not the same as, for example, the color-blindness approach to racism defended by some liberals. Color-blindness obfuscates the failures of systemic racism and addresses (perhaps) the intentions of whites while ignoring the consequences of whites' actions. Absolute justice bypasses the problems of identity politics. One can respect persons in their particularity without having this particularity be a condition for equal rights. Bergson appears to have in mind here that one ought to be affirmatively indifferent to difference. This suggests that one acknowledges differences among persons and, at the same time, defends the equality of all persons regardless of these differences. In practice, this means to begin with the social conditions in which people find themselves—such conditions are in no way equitable—and strive for what Aimé Césaire describes as "a humanism made for the measure of the world."[17] Put differently, absolute justice must be "[drawn] out to infinity."[18] There will always be more injustice to alleviate. Every society is a mixture of tendencies toward closure and openness. Put differently, there are no purely closed or purely open societies. Nevertheless, our world would be better off if the tendency toward openness were actualized much more often.

This volume seeks to unsettle the sedimentation of unjust binaries—white/black, male/female, colonizer/colonized, friend/enemy, primitive/civilized, self/other—and cast doubt on the oft held belief that Western rationalization and industrialization will bring about human flourishing on a global scale.[19] The key to human flourishing, however, lies not in walled sovereignties and nation-states, not in sexist patriarchy or racist white supremacy, but rather in the tendency toward the open—that is, the indeterminate, inclusive, and welcoming—society. Bergson writes, "Between the nation, however great it might be, and humanity there exists the distance that separates the finite from the indefinite, the closed and the open."[20] Nations are grounded in a logic of exclusion, which in turn keeps us from embarking on the fecund adventure of our proper humanity, that is, of actualizing the tendency toward an open society.

Structure of the Volume

Part I, "Bergson on Colonialism, Social Groups, and the State," begins the volume with an analysis of Bergson's treatment of conceptions of social group cohesion, history, and the formation of modern nation-states. The authors collected here demonstrate that Bergson's writings help to provide clarity for long-standing debates within political philosophy that pertain specifically to race and colonial violence. Chapter 1 by Alia Al-Saji, "Decolonizing Bergson," brings readers to the theme of temporality in Bergson's work in an attempt, in her words, to *decolonize* his writings. Taking *The Two Sources on Morality and Religion* as a primary text, Al-Saji proposes that the concept of the "half-open," rather than an open/closed dichotomy, bypasses liberalist conceptions of temporality that frame the history of colonial oppression. Chapter 2, "The Language of Closure," by Martin Shuster, analyses the political foundations of state formation, and offers Bergson's conception of language as a means to interpret the relationship between homogeneity and difference among state populations. Chapter 3, "The Politics of Sympathy in Bergson's *The Two Sources of Morality and Religion*," by Melanie White, further interrogates threads of group cohesion through an analysis of sympathy in *The Two Sources of Morality and Religion*. In this vein, White argues that Bergson's conception of sympathy may offer a fruitful theoretical site from which to explore systemic forms of racism and exclusion.

Part II, "Bergsonian Themes in the Négritude Movement," examines the influence of Bergsonism on that movement. In chapter 4, titled "Bergson, Senghor, and the Philosophical Foundations of Négritude," Clevis Headley maps out several aspects of Bergson's thought, particularly the notions of intellect, intuition, and duration and the role of science with regard to knowledge production. After providing the reader with the necessary scaffolding for understanding Bergsonism, Headley explores the status of Négritude as presented by poet, politician, and culture critic Léopold Sédar Senghor. Many critics of Négritude have prematurely denounced Négritude as being guilty of endorsing various unsavory notions: racism, essentialism, nativism, and naive ideological mystification. Headley pushes against such critics by claiming that it is only in the context of acknowledging Senghor's debt to Bergson and his involvement with African art forms that his positive assessment of emotion and his limiting of the scope of reason make philosophical sense. In chapter 5, "The Spectacle of Belonging," Annette K. Joseph-Gabriel considers how Bergson's *Laughter*—with its unique discussion of how the sight of the Black body provokes laughter from whites—was reconsidered by the editors of the renowned Négritude movement journal *La revue du monde noir*. For Haitian doctor Leo Sajous and Martinican journalist Paulette Nardal, *Laughter* became a tool used for scrutinizing the connection between nationalism and racial performativity. In short, Joseph-Gabriel argues that Négritude writers rethought Bergson's comical Negro trope—foregrounding the adverse effects of colonialism on the Black psyche—by highlighting the link between colonial ideology and comedy.

Finally, part III, "Race, Revolution, and Bergsonism in Latin America," highlights the tremendous influence that Bergson had in the context of nationalist, socialist, and antipositivist movements throughout the Americas. Chapter 6, Adriana Novoa's "Racial Becomings," demonstrates how uses of Bergsonism within recent developments by feminists within the Anglophone discourse of "New Materialisms" has rich historical precursors in nineteenth- and early-twentieth-century Latin American thought. Novoa provides a substantial overview of the scientific and philosophical debates during these periods in Argentina, Chile, Cuba, Mexico, Peru, and Uruguay, and the means by which authors in these geopolitical contexts utilized, extended, and critiqued Bergson's views on vitalism, evolution, and temporality. Chapter 7, "Bergsonism in Postrevolutionary Mexico," by Andrea J. Pitts, focuses more specifically on the writings of Mexican philosopher and educator Antonio Caso. Pitts analyzes the influence of Bergson's conception of intuition on early-twentieth-century postrevolutionary Mexican philosophy, and more specifically, the significance of his thought on Caso's articulation of aesthetic intuition. The book concludes with chapter 8, "Antagonism and Myth," by Jaime Hanneken, who analyzes the influence of Bergsonism on Peruvian socialist theorist José Carlos Mariátegui. Matiátegui, Hanneken argues, drew from a Bergsonian thread of thought found within George Sorel's writings to develop a political role for mythmaking within revolutionary struggle. "The myth of the general strike," according to Hanneken, creates the conditions of collective memory and struggle necessary to mobilize indigenous peasant workers in Peru. The conclusion of Hanneken's chapter also brings the volume back to themes from the foreword of this volume—namely, the optimism in a creative capacity within philosophical thinking that we find in Lawlor's remarks on Bergson surfaces again in Hanneken's articulation of community transformation and political mythmaking. From these distinct discursive contexts we glean hope for future extensions, critiques, and elaborations of the many philosophical questions regarding race and colonialism that can framed through the writings of Bergson.

Creative Pathways through the Volume

We close our introduction here by offering some suggested pathways by which readers of this volume can navigate the many themes, contexts, and sources discussed in this collection. For readers who are interested in Bergson's writings on humor and the social imagination, the chapters by Shuster, White, Joseph-Gabriel, Pitts, and Hanneken offer extensive analyses of these themes.

With respect to theme of Bergsonian temporality, the chapters offered by Headley, Al-Saji, and Novoa focus specifically on the relationship between history, time, and duration. Regarding philosophical questions about the formation of racial group identities and collective resistance, the works by White, Headley, Joseph-Gabriel, Novoa, and Hanneken each provide distinct perspectives that highlight how Bergsonism may be used to address such questions. A number of works in the volume also bring to light themes within the recent philosophical discourse of New Materialisms, including the chapters by Al-Saji, Novoa, and Pitts. Additionally, for readers interested in Bergson's conceptualization of sympathy, Lawlor, White, and Headley all address this concept at varying lengths. Last, with respect to attention to Bergson's *The Two Sources of Morality and Religion*, we offer here a number of chapters exploring the dynamics of that text, such as those by Al-Saji, Shuster, White, and Pitts. From these many perspectives we hope that our readers are able to creatively explore the many options available through Bergsonism, and that our readers find new and dynamic ways of approaching questions of race and colonialism through and beyond his work.

Notes

1. Philippe Soulez, "Bergson as Philosopher of War and Theorist of the Political," trans. Melissa McMahon, in *Bergson, Politics, and Religion*, ed. Alexandre Lefebvre and Melanie White (Durham, NC: Duke University Press, 2012), 109.

2. Although we do not offer analyses of these genealogical threads in the volume, Bergson's work has also had a significant impact on writings within Muslim and Asian philosophical thought, including in the work of authors such as Zaki al-Arsuzi (1899–1968), Allama Muhammad Iqbal (1877–1938), and Liang Shuming (1893–1988). Japan, in particular, has a long history of Bergson scholarship including Kiyoshi Miki (1897–1945), Kitarō Nishida (1870–1945), and Hajime Tanabe (1885–1962), as well as more recent scholars such as the founders of Project Bergson in Japan: Hisashi Fujita (1973–), Tatsuya Higaki (1964–), and Naoki Sugiyama (1964–). See, for example, Yanming An, "Liang Shuming and Henri Bergson on Intuition: Cultural Context and the Evolution of Terms," *Philosophy of East and West* 47, no. 3 (1997): 337–62; Hisashi Fujita, "Bergson's Hand: Toward a History of (Non)-Organic Vitalism," *Substance* 114, 36, no. 3 (2007): 115–30; Saleh Omar, "Philosophical Origins of the Arab Ba'th Party: The Work of Zaki Al-Arsuzi," *Arab Studies Quarterly* 18, no. 2 (1996): 23–37; Susan Townsend, *Miki Kiyoshi 1897–1945: Japan's Itinerant Philosopher* (Boston: Leiden, 2009).

3. Gilles Deleuze, *Bergsonism*, trans. Hugh Tomlinson and Barbara Habberjam (New York: Zone Books, 1988), 115.

4. Alexandre Lefebvre and Melanie White (eds.). *Bergson, Politics, and Religion* (Durham, NC: Duke University Press, 2012), 5. This is an excellent resource for considering Bergson's views on politics and religion.

5. Clinton Curle, *Humanité: John Humphrey's Alternative Account of Human Rights* (Toronto: University of Toronto Press, 2007), 6.

6. See Henri Bergson, *Mélanges* (Paris: Presses Universitaires de France, 1972), 1351.

7. Henri Bergson, *The Two Sources of Morality and Religion*, trans. R. Ashley Audra and Cloudesley Brereton (Notre Dame, IN: University of Notre Dame Press, 1977), 286. Hereafter referred to as "*TSMR*."

8. See Philippe Soulez, *Bergson politique* (Paris: Presses Universitaires de France, 1989).

9. Following decolonial theorists such as Aimé Césaire, we refer to "another holocaust" because European colonial powers, for several centuries, had already committed acts of mass genocide and mechanized extermination outside of Europe.

10. Maurice Merleau-Ponty, *Humanism and Terror: An Essay on the Communist Problem*, trans. John O'Neill (Boston: Beacon Press, 1969), 188.

11. According to Marx, capitalism began with the "hunting of black skins," that is, with the dehumanization and commodification of Black peoples. See Karl Marx, *Capital: A Critique of Political Economy*, vol. I. Introduced by Ernest Mandel, trans. Ben Fowkes (New York: Penguin Books, 1990), 915.

12. Soulez, "Bergson as Philosopher of War and Theorist of the Political," 110.

13. *TSMR*, 285.

14. For Bergson's discussion of rights in *TSMR*, see pp. 74–81 and 281–83.

15. *TSMR*, 69.

16. Ibid., 74.

17. Aimé Césaire, *Discourse on Colonialism*, trans. Joan Pinkham (New York: Monthly Review Press, 2000), 73.

18. *TSMR*, 74.

19. For a criticism of how the market serves as a rubric for flourishing, see *TSMR*, 306.

20. *TSMR*, 32.

Part I

Bergson on Colonialism, Social Groups, and the State

Chapter 1

Decolonizing Bergson

The Temporal Schema of the Open and the Closed

ALIA AL-SAJI

The remnants and legacies of colonialisms—from geographical and spatial orders to material exploitation and cultural imaginaries—often continue, in refracted modes, in postcolonial contexts. Underlying and sustaining these ways of knowing (and hence of constituting meaning) are temporal frameworks, economies of time, that persist largely unquestioned. The dichotomy of the open and the closed is one such schema; it not only plays a structuring role in colonial ways of knowing, but it also continues to be assumed in some theories of development in postcolonial settings. That colonized societies have a tendency to closure (being resistant to progress and to inclusivity and otherness) is taken to justify colonial and neocolonial paternalism.

In this chapter, I propose to attend to this well-worn temporal schema of open/closed by examining its elaboration in the philosophy of Henri Bergson and by critically parsing the possibilities his philosophy offers for its destabilization. Though Bergson wrote in a colonial context, this context barely receives acknowledgment in his work; at best, it could be read obliquely and ambiguously from his examples.[1] That Bergson was politically self-aware, having engaged in diplomatic missions and polemics for France during the First World War and having been instrumental in the establishment of the League of Nations, has been well documented.[2] His wide-ranging influence, including on the *Négritude* movement, means that this omission—or "colonial aphasia," to borrow Ann Stoler's term—must be attended to.³ For this masks the uncomfortable resonances between Bergson's philosophy of time (especially in his late work, *Les deux sources de la morale et de la religion*, published in 1932) and the temporal narratives that accompany and justify French colonialism. This is doubly important given Bergson's uptake by more recent French philosophers, such as Gilles Deleuze, and by contemporary feminist and political theorists, especially some who identify under the umbrella of "new materialism" (including such diverse thinkers as Elizabeth Grosz and William Connolly).

I mean for the project of this chapter—that of *decolonizing Bergson*—to have relevance both to Bergson studies, then, and to contemporary scholars of race and colonialism, who may wonder whether and how such questions could be addressed from within Bergson's philosophy. Rather than attend simply to Bergson's examples, I believe that a methodological approach can reveal how colonizing and racializing frames may be implicitly at work, no matter his explicit intentions. More importantly, I aim to show how questions about colonialism and racism are not simple afterthoughts, but can gain traction by attending to the structuring assumptions and methodologies of Bergson's own texts. In this regard, I not only attend to Bergsonian philosophy critically, but I mine that philosophy for the critical resources and generative tools from which such decolonizing critique finds its impetus. Thus, I understand the project of *decolonizing Bergson* to have two sides—to be at once a critical and a creative reconfiguration of Bergsonian philosophy. What is at stake in decolonizing Bergson is, in my view, the very Bergsonian recognition of the weight of the past—the pressure it exerts on, and the difference it makes for, the present. Our pasts are structured by colonial durations and imperial formations. This is the past as a whole, the past as unconscious and multiplicitous, coexistent with the present. This past is not transcended and gone, but forms the invisible glue that makes itself felt in the present, even when selectively disregarded and unattended to in so-called *postcolonial* and *postracial* presents. I understand the past as atmospheric or thalassic; it can submerge us, buoy us up, or bog us down; it ebbs and flows. Without a critical mapping and recollection of this past, the weight of the past will only lead to confirmed and habitual routes being followed through. Creative reconfigurations of Bergson hence need this critical ground, but decolonizing critique of Bergson also requires a generative rereading of his philosophy. I aim to hold together both sides of this decolonizing project in my chapter, turning to Bergson's last monograph in order to do so.

In *Les deux sources de la morale et de la religion*, Bergson theorizes social life through the lens of what he considers a grounding difference: between the open society, on the one hand, and closed societies, on the other.[4] While the first aspires to include all human beings, linking them through love, the latter is based on need and obligation, defensively and antagonistically closing in on itself. Most contemporary critics of Bergson focus on the inclusiveness and "fraternity" of the open society, its borderless love and vision of humanity, finding there a justification for Bergson's schema.[5] In my view, however, it is the dichotomy of open/closed itself that is troubling. Though Bergson clarifies that these are tendencies, so that all existing societies are mixtures of openness and closure, the dichotomy nevertheless provides the tools for constructing a hierarchy of societies and a teleological vision of civilization. It is this logic that we see in contemporary cultural racism, where discrimination against so-called illiberal cultural-religious minorities (in particular, Muslims, but often also Hasidic Jews) is justified based on their supposed intolerance and closure to change.[6] More precisely, this logic is often used to distinguish groups *within* a religion or a society, to mark out those who are tolerant or moderate from those who are fundamentalist.[7] But what if we were to begin with a different conceptual schema, that of the "half-open or ajar [*entr'ouvert*]" (as Vladimir Jankélévitch suggests in his reading of Bergson)? Could we then theorize the mixture that is society as more than compromise and negation? Thus, a different way of seeing and understanding social life might emerge: one that attends to multiplicity and difference without opposition and hierarchy.

I will proceed in four steps. I begin with the recent resurgence of interest in Bergson, examining how *Les deux sources* has been taken up and what has been elided or made visible in those readings. Second, I look more closely at *Les deux sources*, asking how colonial formations may be on the horizons of this text and what hesitations they may call into being. Third, rather than focusing on particular examples, I ask what Bergson's method is in *Les deux sources* and how the schema of open/closed—and more deeply, the couple of "primitive" and "mystic"—undergird this method. Finally, it is this question of method that will allow us to see the divergence between *Les deux sources* and the rest of Bergson's philosophy; for *Les deux sources* not only introduces a new and definitive distinction into Bergson's philosophy—that of open and closed—it also puts an end to the movement of that philosophy by defining its possibilities *as if they had already been given*. It is by turning the tools of Bergsonian critique onto *Les deux sources* that I aim to provide an alternative to the dichotomy of open/closed—that of the half-open or ajar—creating in this way the (uncertain) condition of possibility for its decolonization.

Reading *The Two Sources*

Suzanne Guerlac remarks that *Les deux sources* "can produce a distinct feeling of estrangement, even in admirers of Bergson's earlier works."[8] I would describe this feeling as one of disappointment. The reception of the book at the time of its publication was mixed, but the disappointment that has been expressed around it has had to do, in large part, with Bergson's appeal to Christian mysticism (taken as the actualization of the "pure" tendency to openness).[9] On the one hand, this was because Bergson's account of mysticism removed it from both theology and faith—making the mystic into an "auxiliary," albeit a "powerful" one, of philosophy.[10] On the other hand, the appeal to mysticism was taken to establish, once and for all, Bergson's spiritualism and antirationalism (his affective and intellectual allegiance to Catholicism, despite being Jewish). Either way it was suspect. It is, hence, around the figure of the mystic that much prior critique has centered.

In contrast, at the limit of the closed tendency lies the figure of the "primitive." While there have been a number of critical studies of Bergson's use of this figure, these discussions have generally been limited to the French literature on Bergson and almost always pivot on Bergson's critique of Lucien Lévy-Bruhl.[11] Such a focus sheds some positive light on Bergson's account, since Bergson argues against Lévy-Bruhl that there can be only differences of degree between "primitive" and "civilized" humanity, both sharing a common nature.[12] While the contrast with Lévy-Bruhl is significant for understanding *Les deux sources*, the lack of typology in Bergson's account of humanity has often meant that other ways in which Bergson constructs the difference between "primitive" and "civilized" go unnoticed (see the section on "Open/Closed"). By comparison, Bergson's "primitive" is rarely mentioned in the recent English-language resurgence of Bergsonism, so much so that it is a different *Les deux sources* that seems to be reflected back in these readings. Not only are large sections of Bergson's text disregarded—in particular in the long second chapter of *Les deux sources* on static religion—avoiding the unease produced by, or the need to confront, Bergson's secondhand stories of "primitives." But it is sometimes *Les deux sources* as a whole that is avoided, as in for instance new materialist readings of Bergson. We stop with the methodological essays that later became *La pensée et le mouvant* (published in 1934, but the majority of which were written in the period 1903–23).[13] I believe that the rest of my chapter will, at least indirectly, explain this avoidance.

But in case this seems like a facile criticism of contemporary Bergsonian interpretation, I want to include my own work in this self-critical gesture (having for some time avoided directly addressing the book). *Les deux sources* today tends to produce a form of discomfort that is not yet sufficiently self-reflective to call itself disappointment—an *aphasia* to recall Stoler's term. In my view, this discomfort is not simply about the use of the term *primitive* in the text (which often designates, for Bergson, "the primitive [*le primitif*]" in humanity, and so what is "natural," to be distinguished from "*les primitifs*"). It has to do, more broadly, with the way in which colonial formations seem to saturate the horizons and interstices of the text, while absent from the analysis. What runs across the contemporary literature on Bergson—whether English or French with a few exceptions—is an avoidance of this colonial question: the difference that colonial horizons and colonial durations might make in reading Bergson.

In this vein, Bergson's critique of imperialism and militarism in *Les deux sources* may do more to obscure, rather than clarify, what he thinks of French colonialism.[14] While imperialism and colonialism are often thought to be coextensive, this cannot be assumed in Bergson's theory. In a 1915 interview (later published in his *Correspondances*), Bergson remains uncritical of French colonial politics, even while he condemns German imperialism. He is able to hold such an aphasic position by distinguishing nations (France, Germany) from tribes (French colonies). Bergson argues: "[i]t cannot be said that these [colonies] were nations. They are warring tribes. [. . .] They had not proved to the world the usefulness, even to themselves, of their turbulent condition. So our theory [. . .] does not apply to bands of individuals in the state in which the inhabitants of Algiers, Morocco and our other possessions were before France took charge of them."[15] While the polemical and "circumstantial" character of his wartime texts mean that we must treat them with caution (and not on a par with his *œuvres* as set out in his will), the distinction Bergson draws is nevertheless telling. When they consider the colonial question, even exacting readers of *Les deux sources* assume that what Bergson says of imperialism carries over to colonialism and that, as Suzanne Guerlac argues, his reference to "colonies" in the conclusion of *Les deux sources* constitutes a critical gesture aimed at French colonial politics.[16] Indeed, Bergson notes that "people consider that life is not worth living if they cannot have comforts, pleasures, luxuries [. . .] a country considers itself incomplete if it has not good ports, colonies, etc. All this may lead to war."[17] But since the reference to "colonies" is embedded in a larger critique of how nations come to see their well-being and comfort as dependent on territorial expansion in the age of mechanization, Bergson's critique points to how luxuries come to be felt as necessities (becoming a secondary cause of war) and does not, in my view, problematize colonization as such. The critique of the luxury of spices later in the conclusion—ginger, clove, pepper, and cinnamon—focuses on the energy of navigation put at the service of acquiring these spices and glosses over the consequences that this navigation had for non-European peoples and the violence of colonization that it facilitated.[18] And while Bergson sees colonial rivalry as destructive, this remains within the perspective of an intra-European problem of rival nations and intra-European wars.[19] This means that we must look elsewhere in *Les deux sources* to uncover Bergson's views of colonized peoples and to find a foothold for decolonizing critique.

It may be time for Bergson studies to address the difficult question of the colonial horizons of *Les deux sources*, and by extension Bergson's philosophy of time. Two recent books open the way for such a questioning, and provide opposing responses. Donna Jones, in *The Racial Discourses of Life Philosophy*, sees in Bergsonism the source for racialist narratives of the early twentieth century, including those taken up by the Négritude movement,[20] whereas, in *Bergson postcolonial*, Souleymane Bachir Diagne finds Bergson to be the common inspiration for the postcolonial philosophies of Léopold Senghor and Muhammad Iqbal.[21] While neither of these works closely examines the open/closed dichotomy, or asks after its role in colonial formations of time, they address questions to Bergson that contemporary scholarship does not seem ready to take up.[22] Though Jones rightly criticizes Bergson's discussion of "primitive" life, she focuses on his troubling examples and misses the methodological troubles this figure creates for his philosophy.[23] Jones's analysis also tends to misrecognize the forms of racialism that Bergson's work displays, reading it by "imbrication," sometimes biologically, sometimes "noumenally," rather than culturally, as hints in *Les deux sources* imply.[24] More seriously, however, Jones focuses her critique on the conservation of the past in Bergson's thought, missing in my view the creativity and half-openness of the Bergsonian past and undermining the import of her own critique.[25]

This dynamic conception of the past, to which I will return below, is more productively and accurately taken up by Muhammad Iqbal in *The Reconstruction of Religious Thought in Islam*, and it is emphasized in Diagne's reading of Iqbal.[26] In reading Bergson and Islam through one another, intertwined with his exegesis of Quranic verse, Iqbal says:

Pure time, then, as revealed by a deeper analysis of our conscious experience, is not a string of separate, reversible instants; it is an organic whole in which the past is not left behind, but is moving along with, and operating in, the present. And the future is given to it not as lying before, yet to be traversed; it is given only in the sense that it is present in its nature as an open possibility. It is time regarded as an organic whole that the Qur'an describes as *Taqdir* or the destiny—a word which has been so much misunderstood both in and outside the world of Islam. [. . .] In one word, it is time as felt and not as thought and calculated.[27]

But more than this, Iqbal draws from the Qur'an and finds in Bergson arguments that the whole is not already given and, hence, that "[reality] is a growing universe and not an already completed product which left the hand of its maker ages ago."[28] That the past *moves* along with the present, that it is not only preserved but supplemented, is a vital thread by which Iqbal thinks the question of interpretation and *ijtihad* as open in Islamic thought.[29]

While I find Iqbal's and Diagne's readings of Bergson more fruitful, I recognize the colonial context that motivates Jones's critique, despite the shortcomings in her interpretation. I should note that such opposing readings of Bergson are not surprising, given the ways in which his philosophy transforms itself between texts, attempting to create ideas that fit the phenomena at stake (e.g., inner consciousness, memory, evolution) rather than apply ready-made concepts. But Bergson not only rejected system-building; he also refused to adjudicate the opposing interpretations of his thought that arose under the label "Bergsonism." In this chapter, I focus on Bergson's writings and method rather than the historical Bergsonisms to which they gave rise and whose markedly divergent interpretations and political tendencies have been well documented.[30]

The Two Sources of Morality and Religion

In what follows, I argue that decolonizing Bergson means questioning not merely this or that passage of *Les deux sources*—correcting dated accounts or tired images and stereotypes—but rather asking after the method that Bergson employs. The method of *Les deux sources* is grounded in the dichotomy of open/closed. But if, as Bergson seems to suggest, this distinction is not possible without the mystic-primitive couple, then their role becomes one that haunts any reading of Bergson's text. To clarify what is at stake, I will briefly present the structure of the book, and point to cracks where background assumptions, colonial, imperial, or otherwise, may have forced the argument, before turning my attention to method.

Les deux sources begins with an account of the sociality of life, not simply in human life but also in animal and insect life—hence appearing to continue and supplement the philosophy of life from *L'évolution créatrice* (1907).[31] Society is, in this sense, immanent to its members;[32] it is "natural" or "biological" (in Bergson's broadened sense of biology).[33] In human societies, cohesion is maintained through obligation, which Bergson describes as a force of pressure and likens to a *virtual* instinct.[34] Although the content of obligation is contingent and varies, what holds together society is "the whole of obligation," in other words, the necessity of having obligations or the habit of contracting habits.[35] It is through the force of obligation that we first see what Bergson means by a "closed society": Bergson introduces the case of war (which he argues is neither abnormal nor exceptional) to show that social obligations *always already* applied only to the members of a given society, to the exclusion of others.[36] Bergson thus conceives of the tendency to closure as both constitutive of social wholes—in an inward and circular movement of conservation and identity-formation[37]—while, at the same time, oppositional, defensive, and exclusionary.[38] It is in this sense that love as charity, "love of humanity" without limits, is incomparable to love of family or attachment to nation, requiring Bergson to search for a second source of morality, as we shall see.[39]

Here, I note two limitations of this account that should make readers of Bergson hesitate. First, that obligation functions like a virtual instinct should already inscribe it within a movement of duration that is *opening*, just as it is being instituted and closing in on itself; instinct in *L'évolution créatrice* was vital movement and sympathy with life from within, not simply the sedimentation of quasi-automatic mechanisms.[40] Second, the tendency to closure describes the materialization of social life by turning inward to form self-reflexive, organized, and cohesive wholes. That such wholes are *oppositional* groupings does not seem to follow immediately. This would imply conceiving social groups in the abstract and through negation, a mode of understanding that Bergson had previously criticized (arguing instead that living wholes, forms of order, and ways of becoming should be understood on their own terms, and not as privations).[41]

The second source of morality also comes from life, but indirectly through the mediation of particular individuals: "mystics" who, through creative emotion, take the *élan* of life farther by "partial coincidence with the creative effort which life manifests."[42] The second source takes the form of a "call" or "aspiration" rather than pressure.[43] It involves a teleological pull, transcendence, or "virtual attraction" toward—not a defined end point, but a form of movement that Bergson glimpses in the creative emotion of love.[44] For Bergson, this movement is *modeled* by mystics' actions and lives, not explicated in doctrine.[45] This second source can transfigure morality into an open form of love that includes not only humanity, but "may extend to animals, to plants, to all of nature."[46] This is what defines the tendency to openness, which, for Bergson, breaks the circle of habit and communal or national obligation to make a leap in a "forward movement."[47] But, paradoxically, it is neither the specific direction that emotion takes in escaping the circle of self-regard and interest,[48] nor the object of love that matters here; "its form is not dependent on its content."[49] Indeed, though this love goes *through* humanity, it is ultimately objectless ("humanity" being more than the assemblage of all human beings, for Bergson, and hence not an object that can be aimed at). By "forward movement [*marche en avant*]," Bergson is not evoking the idea of gradual or developmental progress;[50] rather, he points to a qualitative change that makes a "difference in kind," so that one is no longer turning around in place (hence, he also says "leap [*saut*]"). Thus, while there is a concept of progress in *Les deux sources,* Bergson explicitly localizes it *within* closed societies (though some seepage will occur, as we shall see).

Two aspects of this account should make us hesitate. But they find limited critical discussion in the literature (since they are generally taken as complements, completing rather than undermining Bergson's philosophy). First, *aspiration* in *Les deux sources* is a new, teleological force for Bergson's philosophy—one that assigns an end goal that "completes" the movement of the famous *élan vital*. While this end should not be read as a state of rest, it does define a form of movement as that which we should performatively (and normatively) aspire to. Though Bergson is ambiguous as to whether pure aspiration is a virtual limit or could be actualized,[51] his method in *Les deux sources* will require the existence of actualized models, taking the Christ of the Gospels as complete exemplar.[52] In contrast, *L'évolution créatrice* puts aside the possibility of aspirational force, leaving the push of the *élan* to differentiate and diverge contingently and without finality (at the cost of impasses and failures on its way). In *L'évolution créatrice*, he says:

> Harmony, therefore, does not exist in fact; it exists rather in principle [. . .] Harmony (or rather "complementarity") is revealed only in the mass, in tendencies rather than states. In particular (and this is the point on which finalism has been most seriously mistaken) harmony is rather behind us than ahead. It is due to an identity of impulsion and not to a common aspiration. It would be futile to try to assign to life an end, in the human sense of the word. To speak of an end is to think of a pre-existing model which has only to be realized. It is to suppose, therefore, that all is given, and that the future can be read in the present.[53]

It should be clear from this that there can be no immanent aspiration or goal to life. The aspiration of the mystic individuals of *Les deux sources* is a supplement that takes up life but also transcends it. The conditions of possibility of this aspiration are not immanent to life, rather they need to be created through the performative actions of mystics themselves. It is, in this sense, that *Les deux sources* describes the way aspiration proceeds as follows (here, the example is the transition from relative to absolute justice):

> The method consisted in supposing possible what is actually impossible in a given society, in imagining what would be its effect on the soul of society, and then inducing some such psychic condition by propaganda and example: the effect once obtained, would retroactively complete its cause; new feelings, evanescent indeed, would call forth the new legislation seemingly indispensable to their appearance, and which would then serve to consolidate them.[54]

Leaving aside the worries a democratic sensibility may have about this passage (while Bergson is describing justice, the procedure itself is neither deliberative nor necessarily democratic), I want to point to a second problem with the account of openness in *Les deux sources*. While Bergson uses the terms *open* and *closed* in his previous texts, they are neither guiding nor framing concepts there. In *L'évolution créatrice*, for instance, to be open means to be, at once, unpredictable and incomplete. Anything for which time makes a difference—living bodies of all sorts, the whole material universe, as well as any parts of matter that are not artificially isolated within this universe—is open.[55] Although life has a *tendency to closure*, by materializing into species and individuating into separate organisms, this does not stop them from becoming and aging.[56] In this account, what are closed are artificially isolated systems of matter that can be treated as inert and reversible—although Bergson's famous example of having to *wait* for the sugar to dissolve in a sugared-water mixture is supposed to show that such isolated systems are matters of perceptual closing and theoretical construction.[57] Thus to be open is to become, to have duration.[58] It would not make sense to ask, here, what this might be an opening *to*. In contrast, the openness of *Les deux sources* is both too much and too little. Too much, because it posits an aspirational openness that is measured according to a prospective limit or end—that *to* which it is supposed to be open. Too little, because the concept of "open to" is left empty and contentless, while normatively weighted. It appears to wait to be retrospectively filled, but already anticipates and prefigures what is to come, since Bergson sees this emptiness actualized as objectless and mystical love. At the same time, closure comes to be defined by *indifference* to this aspiration or lack of effort in following it through. The borders of open/closed have thus shifted, as has the sense and usage of the terms; they become even more sharply and normatively distinguished once the difference between static and dynamic religion comes into focus. With this I will turn to the central chapters of *Les deux sources* and the question of method.

Open/Closed: Questions of Method

It is in the central chapters of *Les deux sources*, on static and dynamic religion respectively, that the method of the book becomes clear. Static and dynamic religion are not extensions or foundations of the two moralities, but run in parallel, bolstering the closed and open ways of life.[59] Specifically, it is because intellect hesitates and resists in cases of obligation—through both self-interest and fear—that a social counterweight is needed to assure against this hesitation, "disorganization," or "depression."[60] This is the role of the "*fonction fabulatrice*" that defines static religion for Bergson, a defensive reaction of nature against the "dissolvent power" and risks of reflective consciousness.[61] Static religion creates ideas that have the force of perception ("*idéo-motrices*"), that structure and make sense of the world, and that strengthen the attachment to life.[62] It is in this context that Bergson criticizes Lévy-Bruhl for assigning to "primitive mentality" a different logic.[63]

For Bergson, both "civilized" and "non-civilized" societies have in common not only the ground of obligation (the obligation to have obligations), but also the risks of reflective consciousness and the "*fonction fabulatrice*," which is needed to assure against these risks. Static religion, like the structure of obligation in general, is hence "natural" to human societies; it is not only a means of social conservation, but also a tendency to closure.

Thus, for Bergson, both so-called primitive and civilized societies are on the side of closure. But lest we think all difference is dissolved, Bergson introduces a way of measuring the difference of degree between coexistent social formations. This relies on distinguishing, on the one hand, "*le primitif* [the primitive]" of humanity—which is taken to underlie cultural acquisitions and points to a *virtual* foundation or origin that can only be probabilistically described—from "*les primitifs*," who are *actually* coexistent societies.[64] While much more can be said about this distinction, Bergson's argument proceeds in three steps. First, he insists that "we are only acquainted with humanity as already evolved, for the 'primitives' we observe today are as old as we are."[65] As soon as coexistence is established, however, it is forestalled and deferred. For, second, this means that they "have had plenty of time to exaggerate and to aggravate, as it were, the possible irrationalities contained in elementary tendencies, natural enough though they are."[66] "Marking time [*piétinant sur place*]," Bergson continues, "they ceaselessly add and amplify. Through the double effect of repetition and exaggeration the irrational passes into the realm of the absurd, and the strange into the realm of the monstrous."[67] Humanity, it seems, has aged equally but differently; and this differential way of living the same interval of duration marks an irreversible threshold from which one cannot recover. Third, though partly accidental, this also shows a lack of effort or "*paresse*," which deepens the effects of irrational practices, so that "[s]ubsequently, it was too late; the society could not advance, even if it wanted to, because it was contaminated by the products of its own laziness [. . .] the practices of magic."[68] It is no wonder that Donna Jones sees an implicit justification for colonial (and missionary) intervention here.[69]

Little by little, after dissolving any difference in nature, Bergson shores up the difference of degree between "civilized" and "primitive," so that it is finally their very duration that works against "the primitives." Within closed societies, then, there are degrees of progress with a new distinction at play: that between stagnating societies ("*piétinant sur place*") and "societies in movement."[70] Their actual difference owes to the degree and form of accumulation of cultural acquisitions, and hence to the *thickness* of layering that covers over the same nature.[71] Since Bergson has already rejected any inheritance of acquired traits, it is through social milieu that he explains how acquisitions are transmitted, arguing that they accumulate superficially in one case and intensify in depth in another.[72] Moreover, while mystics emerge in all societies, according to Bergson, the mystic call will find an easier foothold and greater receptivity in societies that are already in movement; there will be a more fluid acceptance of changing habits.[73]

Given that "*les primitifs*" only differ in degree, it may appear that they are unnecessary to Bergson's method in *Les deux sources*. Indeed, Bergson suggests early on that "the observation [. . .] of civilized man of the present day" may be sufficient; all one would need is an introspective method, what Bergson has elsewhere called intuition, to get at "*l'humanité primitive*" (i.e., nature) within everyone.[74] Yet if we read deeper, Bergson seems to need "the primitives," just as he needs actual mystics, to make his method work. What is this method and what use are "the primitives" put to in this method? Bergson describes his "probabilistic" method in *Les deux sources* as one that begins in experience, but also extends the tendencies of experience to their virtual extremes, in order to find their intersections or conditions. The method is at once empirical and metaphysical. Here is his most succinct description:

> We have alluded elsewhere to those "lines of fact [*lignes de fait*]" each one indicating but the direction of truth, because it does not go far enough: truth itself, however, will be reached if two of them can be prolonged to the point where they intersect. A surveyor measures the distance to an unattainable point by taking a line on it, now from one, now from the other, of two points which he can reach [*L'arpenteur mesure la distance d'un point inaccessible en le visant tour à tour de deux points auxquels il a accès*].[75]

The analogy to the surveyor makes us see that Bergson needs two accessible points of experience to which he can move (at least imaginatively), in order to triangulate from them the desired point of intersection (the conditions of both experiences in duration). The experience of mystics provides one such point, allowing Bergson to imagine, or more precisely "intuit," a tendency to openness that he calls "*élan d'amour*."[76] But the second point is provided by "primitives." Since Bergson believes that theirs is a thinner layer of cultural acquisitions, "the road may be shorter" to arrive at the tendency to closure that grounds social life, the pressure that explains not only obligation but also static religion.[77] Indeed, this method instrumentalizes both "primitives" and "mystics" in order to guide introspection to find the natural and mystical tendencies within the self.[78] That this introspection requires *external* support or auxiliaries is key. The tendencies, Bergson explains in *Les deux sources*, need to be grasped at their culmination or completion, "*à son terme*," in order to be understood.[79] These end points are inexistent; for all we have is the mixture or composite which is experience.[80] But both mystics and "primitives" come closer to the extreme, and hence trace out the angle of the direction at which the surveyor can aim.

This is what Vladimir Jankélévitch has called "*le maximalisme bergsonien*" (though he did not mean this critically).[81] *Les deux sources* inscribes a teleology of life, which the rest of Bergson's philosophy had disavowed (at most we can find an "inverted" or retrospective finalism in *L'évolution créatrice*). Bergson is able to claim this teleology, while remaining (relatively) consistent with his previous work, because it is a teleology that is not immanent to life, but emerges from the resumption of its creative effort by the actual mystics whose experience he relies on. According to Bergson, the mystic is situated "at a point that the spiritual current, in its passage through matter, probably wanted to reach but could not [*aurait probablement voulu, jusqu'où il n'a pas pu aller*]."[82] The mystic here delineates a future, an aspirational end.

But I would add that there is also a *minimalism* in *Les deux sources*. Although the extreme that lies at the end of the other tendency, "primitive humanity," is just as inexistent a limit as that of the pure mystic, Bergson thinks that its direction, too, can be externally traced through descriptions of actual "primitives." While this "nature" is supposed to follow the same vital schema as in *L'évolution créatrice*, there are important differences in its conception of closure. The closure of the organism was always also an opening—becoming, aging, and undoing—whereas the closure of obligation goes to an extreme and takes the form of a virtual instinct that has become quasi-automatic. That both the tendency to openness and the tendency to closure go to the extreme is confirmed by Bergson in the final chapter of *Les deux sources*, when he articulates this as a law, "*la loi de double frénésie*."[83] Whereas in biological life, tendencies divide and diverge in order to develop into coexistent species, he posits that in psychological and social life tendencies develop successively and go as far as possible, "*comme s'il y avait un bout* [as if there was an end]."[84] In other words, these tendencies proceed to completion—a strange turn for a philosophy that had always defined duration by its incompleteness and unpredictability.

At first glance, the method of *Les deux sources* seems to be a continuation of that outlined in *Matière et mémoire* (1896), almost forty years earlier.[85] Bergson certainly presents it as such, a gesture that may have misled his readers. But a closer reading of the method of *Matière et mémoire* shows us the elided possibilities of Bergson's philosophy: "It would be to take experience at its source, or rather above that decisive *turn* [*au-dessus de ce tournant*] where, taking a bias in the direction of our utility, it becomes properly *human* experience."[86] While this may look like the same method, it is conceived *differentially* in *Matière et mémoire*, according to a different calculus than the linear geometry of the surveyor. In other words, the tendencies of experience are extended to their limit, but this is a limit that remains virtual and whose actuality can only ever be grasped within the mixture of experience. Tendencies are extended according to their curves (differentially by taking the tangent), and not in a geometrical projection from two points. To follow through the movement of a tendency, its directionality must be grasped *in process*, neither at the beginning nor at its end, if end there be. In *Matière et mémoire*, the intersection of tendencies at their "source" is likened to the crossing of two railway lines that never fully coincide, but where we can cross imperceptibly from one to the other. This does not mean that one can make do without external support. *Matière et mémoire* relies heavily on the psychological studies of aphasia of its time, but it does so in order to exclude theoretical interpretations of memory as localized in the brain, not as positivist experiences.

How does this help us parse, or even decolonize, the Bergsonian distinction of open/closed? I have shown that this distinction needs to assume the actual existence of mystics and "primitives" as points of departure for its methodology, so that readers of Bergson's *Les deux sources* cannot elide his discussion of "primitives" in the text, as I believe they have done in the literature. But there is a deeper problem. *Les deux sources*, as its title indicates, sets up a dichotomy between open and closed that, I think, Bergson's philosophy cannot sustain. In *Les deux sources,* Bergson takes the open and closed tendencies as conditions of possibility, as guiding concepts, with which to search out actual experiences that can provide their confirmation: the mystic and "the primitives" provide such empirical mirrors. Yet these were already prefigured in the way the problem of sociality was posed in *Les deux sources*, so that Bergson's method is skewed toward one of linear projection from assumed, external experiences.

Conclusion: Half-Opening or Decolonizing Bergson?

It is by employing Bergsonian methods that the Bergsonian distinction of open/closed can be destabilized. Bergsonian intuition (read through Deleuze's *Bergsonism*, but also through what Bergson says in the last chapter of *Matière et mémoire* and in *L'évolution créatrice*) is a method of discerning "pure" conceptual elements within any actual mixture.[87] But the method does not rest with these virtual elements; rather, it understands these elements not as static states but as *tendencies*, and it traces them back to a multiplicitous and self-differentiating virtuality (duration) that links them and shows their interpenetration. This addition is crucial, for the originality and promise of Bergson's method lies therein. Thus, memory (mind) and matter form a mitigated and interactive dualism that is traced back to different rhythms of *duration* in *Matière et mémoire*. Matter is an inversion, slowing down and undoing of the *élan* of life in *L'évolution créatrice*. To my mind, *Les deux sources* sets itself apart from Bergson's other works by getting stuck in the distinction of open/closed that it presents. This despite Bergson's warnings that there are no "pure" open or closed societies.[88] This is because the open and the closed, while tendencies, are also sources; rather than tracing them back to a common virtual source, they are presented as a dichotomy. Yet we only need to recall *L'évolution créatrice* to find a common theme and explanation for these two tendencies: openness and closure are tendencies of life as it both evolves/creates and conserves; forms of life reflexively turn in on themselves and materially sediment but also age, grow, and become otherwise. Time (*durée*) is then, as it is in the rest of Bergson's philosophy, the key to understanding openness (change, becoming-other) and closure (stasis, materialization, habit, and form). When open/closed are understood in this way, we perceive how they are, in fact, inseparable sides of temporal becoming. Openness and closure are here relative tendencies; both are necessary, neither is normative nor moralized. Moreover, *tendency* is not a teleology in this picture, but itself changes orientation and direction as time passes. Tendencies, whatever their directionality, are themselves half-open.

But how is a tendency half-open? Tendency connotes not simply movement, but "*nascent change of direction*."[89] Its course is structured at once by hesitation and delay and by elaboration as invention. To hesitate is to feel one's way tentatively and receptively. Tendency is "*tâtonnement*," to use Bergson's term; it is a search without finality, an experimentation and elaboration that does not dictate the future it will find.[90] But neither is the past a self-same or congealed idea, on this account. Though the past as a virtual whole pushes on each present, actualizing itself there, this past is dynamically reconfigured through the passage of events and through the creation of possibility that ripples back from these events (their virtualization). The past is not a container that accumulates events, but the continuous immanent transformation of directionality and sense that is tendency.[91] This implies, for Bergson, that the whole is not given, that there is no completion or closure for an enduring reality—whether in terms of the future or at the level of the past.

Rather than understanding the social realm in terms of the open and the closed, I would suggest that a more productive, and more difficult, concept would be that of the *half-open* (*entr'ouvert*). Jankélévitch, in his reading of Bergson, suggests that this is precisely what Bergson has missed about Judaism; that the gesture of opening is what we should attend to, and that to be completely open is to be nothing at all.[92] If we recall Walter Mignolo's criticism that opening is not yet decolonizing, then more would be required.[93] Is it possible to find a way of thinking the mixture of experience as more than a mixture, but as different temporalities and tendencies that run across each other as vortices?

I think that Bergson's early texts preserve the possibility for such a decentered and decolonizing temporality, a possibility that is foreclosed in *Les deux sources*. This possibility requires thinking temporal multiplicity: the nonhierarchal coexistence of rhythms of becoming and ways of life, their *coevalness* to use Johannes Fabian's term.[94] Most importantly, it presupposes a nonlinear theory of time, where the past coexists and is *reconfigured* with the present; as a whole or network of relations that includes the present, the past is not determinately closed or gone, but "half-open," capable of being inscribed with new structures of possibility.[95] It is this opening of the past that grounds the unpredictability of the future. And it is this that allows other ways of being and thinking to make a difference for, and to reconfigure, our sedimented conceptual schemas themselves.

This conceptual shift from the open/closed to the half-open means that, in the social sphere, we can understand how people who share a history of oppression may wish to conserve their identity, without being subsumed to the cosmopolitan ideal of a shared humanity, or "love of humanity," in which they are asked to renounce their *resentiment*. Openness is no longer the equivalent of progressiveness or perfectibility, and closure is no longer a moral or political failure, as they are in our common liberal parlance; neither openness nor closure can be used to justify assimilation or domination.

One last note. Bergson opens *La pensée et le mouvant* with a discussion of the abstraction and lack of precision of philosophical systems that apply ready-made concepts to all the phenomena they encounter. He proposes, instead, a method of local knowledge that takes its point of departure in the realities it engages with and that creates concepts as responses to these calls. These concepts, which he calls "intuitive," will not be immediately understood but may, with time, uncertainly, create their own conditions of intelligibility, as their mobile sense is reflected back from the phenomena they seek to illuminate.[96] I would suggest that the open and the closed are the kinds of ill-fitting concepts that Bergson describes. Whether the *half-open* will fare better depends on the nuance and complexity it makes perceptible, how it allows us to perceive differently. But in making us think and questioning complacency, it fulfills one criterion of Bergsonian local and situated thinking: to judge concepts by what they enable us to do and the conditions of possibility they help create.

Notes

I wish to acknowledge the support of the Social Sciences and Humanities Research Council of Canada.

1. Suzanne Guerlac is one of the few readers who attempts to critically gauge Bergson's stance on colonialism in *Les deux sources de la morale et de la religion* (hereafter "*DS*"). But I believe she is overgenerous in attributing an anticolonial stance to Bergson based on the reference to "colonies" in the conclusion of the book (see my argument in the next section). Suzanne Guerlac, "Bergson, the Void, and the Politics of Life," *Bergson, Politics, and Religion*, ed. Alexandre Lefebvre and Melanie White (Durham, NC: Duke University Press, 2012), 40–60.

2. See Philippe Soulez, *Bergson politique* (Paris: Presses Universitaires de France, 1989).

3. Ann Laura Stoler, "Colonial Aphasia: Race and Disabled Histories in France," *Public Culture* 23, no. 1 (2011).

4. Henri Bergson, *Les deux sources de la morale et de la religion* (Paris: Presses Universitaires de France, 1932); *The Two Sources of Morality and Religion*, trans. R. Ashley Audra and Cloudesley Brereton (Notre Dame, IN: University of Notre Dame Press, 1977). Cited as "*DS*" with French, then English pagination.

5. See Alexandre Lefebvre on the "open love" that, for Bergson, defines the open tendency of society and upon which the survival of humanity depends in *Human Rights as a Way of Life: On Bergson's Political Philosophy* (Stanford, CA: Stanford University Press, 2013), 83–109. And Alexandre Lefebvre, "Bergson and Human Rights" in *Bergson, Politics, and Religion*, ed. Alexandre Lefebvre and Melanie White (Durham, NC: Duke University Press, 2012), 193–214. See also Frédéric

Worms on the imbrication of love and creation in *Bergson ou les deux sens de la vie* (Paris: Presses Universitaires de France, 2004), 329–35.

6. When I began writing this chapter, I was thinking of the example of Quebec, where in 2013 the provincial government proposed a "charter of values" aimed explicitly at excluding the wearing of conspicuous "religious signs" by public service workers. The backdrop for this was not only a desire for secular "neutrality," but also an assumption that such workers would themselves be prejudiced and intolerant in their dealings with the public. Etienne Balibar describes this form of racism (which he argues is not new) in "Is There a 'Neo-Racism'?" in *Race, Nation, Class: Ambiguous Identities* (London: Verso, 1991), 17–28.

7. Indeed, this is taken by principle readers of Bergson to be the positive import of his distinction. Frédéric Worms writes, "First, in the religious domain: more than ever, the distinction between the closed and the open seems to us to cut like a sword—not between religions but within each religion" in "The Closed and the Open in *The Two Sources of Morality and Religion*: A Distinction That Changes Everything," trans. Alexandre Lefebvre and Perri Ravon, in *Bergson, Politics, and Religion*, ed. Alexandre Lefebvre and Melanie White (Durham, NC: Duke University Press, 2012), 25–39.

8. Guerlac, "Bergson, the Void, and the Politics of Life," 40.

9. See Ghislain Waterlot, "Penser avec et dans le prolongement des *Deux Sources de la morale et de la religion*" in *Bergson et la religion: nouvelles perspectives sur les Deux Sources de la morale et de la religion*, ed. Ghislain Waterlot (Paris: Presses Universitaires de France, 2008), 1–42.

10. Bergson, *DS*, 266/250. For one of the best instances of this form of critique, see Camille De Belloy, "Le philosophe et la théologie" in *Bergson et la religion: nouvelles perspectives sur les Deux Sources de la morale et de la religion*, ed. Ghislain Waterlot (Paris: Presses Universitaires de France, 2008), 303–19.

11. For two excellent studies, see Brigitte Sitbon-Peillon, "Bergson et le primitif: entre métaphysique et sociologie" in *Annales bergsoniennes I: Bergson dans le siècle*, ed. Frédéric Worms (Paris: Presses Universitaires de France, 2002), 171–94. And Frédéric Keck, "Le primitif et le mystique chez Lévy-Bruhl, Bergson et Bataille," *Methodos: Savoir et textes* 3 (2003). Robert Bernasconi's incisive study of the influence of Lévy-Bruhl on French phenomenology does not include a discussion of Bergson. See "Lévy-Bruhl among the Phenomenologists: Exoticisation and the Logic of 'the Primitive,'" *Social Identities* 11, no. 3 (2005): 229–45.

12. *DS*, 149–59/143–52.

13. Henri Bergson, *La pensée et le mouvant* (Paris: Presses Universitaires de France, 1938); *The Creative Mind: An Introduction to Metaphysics*, trans. Mabelle L. Andison (Mineola, NY: Dover, 2007). Henceforth cited with French, then English pagination.

14. *DS*, 331–32/310–11.

15. Bergson says this in an interview with A. J. Beveridge, the manuscript of which is included in "Bergson à A. J. Beveridge (4 mars 1915)" in Henri Bergson, *Correspondances*, ed. André Robinet (Paris: Presses Universitaires de France, 2002), 623–24. I thank Ghislain Waterlot for pointing me to the location of this interview. The interview is also mentioned in Soulez, *Bergson politique*, 60. That Bergson's position on French colonialism is uncritical, and generally positive, is reinforced by Bergson's 1923 "Rapport sur 'Le Maroc, école d'énergie' d'Alfred de Tarde" in *Mélanges*, ed. André Robinet (Paris: Presses Universitaires de France, 1972), 1395–96, where he positively interprets "l'effort colonisateur" in line with his philosophy of life.

16. Guerlac, "Bergson, the Void, and the Politics of Life," 51. Soulez also assumes this, despite recognizing that Bergson had earlier distinguished the two (*Bergson politique*, 292). See also Mark Sinclair in an otherwise critical account of Bergson's early attitude to imperialism, in "Bergson's Philosophy of Will and the War of 1914–1918," *Journal of the History of Ideas* 77, no. 3 (2016): 486–87.

17. *DS*, 308/289.

18. Ibid., 323/303.

19. While I believe she takes this in a less critical sense than I do, Yala Kisukidi reads *Les deux sources* as dependent on its context, inscribing a moment of European historicity and European empires. Nadia Yala Kisukidi, *Bergson ou l'humanité créatrice* (Paris: CNRS Éditions, 2013), 219–20.

20. Donna V. Jones, *The Racial Discourses of Life Philosophy: Négritude, Vitalism, and Modernity* (New York: Columbia University Press, 2010).

21. Souleymane Bachir Diagne, *Bergson postcolonial* (Paris: CNRS Éditions, 2011). See also "Bergson in the Colony: Intuition and Duration in the Thought of Senghor and Iqbal," *Qui Parle* 17, no. 1 (2008): 125–45.

22. Diagne's work has been better received in Bergson studies than Jones's. While this might be attributed to Diagne's comparatively sympathetic reading of Bergson, I think it also reflects the productive potential of the links Diagne forges. I should note that Diagne's reading deals mainly with Bergson's metaphysical concepts prior to *Les deux sources*, concepts with which Iqbal and Senghor engaged. See Yala Kisukidi's excellent analysis in "Présentation: Penser un Bergson postcolonial?" in *Annales bergsoniennes V: Bergson et la politique, de Jaurès à aujourd'hui*, ed. Frédéric Worms (Paris: Presses Universitaires de France, 2012), 49–59, introducing Diagne's "Bergson dans les colonies: Intuition et durée dans la pensée de Senghor et Iqbal," trans. Yala Kisukidi, *Annales bergsoniennes V*, 61–84. Sometimes, however, Diagne's reading has been taken as a confirmation of Bergson's affinity with postcolonial philosophies, rather than a call to search out or create such affinities, which I think it represents. See, for instance, Vincent Peillon, "Préface: Du renouveau des études philosophiques en France," *Annales bergsoniennes V* (2012): 9–27.

23. For example, Jones takes Bergson to task when he uses his childhood memory of visiting the dentist (he thought the dentist enjoyed pulling out teeth, so much so that he paid for it) to explain away the difference in

kind that "mentalité primitive" has for Lévy Bruhl (Jones, *Racial Discourses of Life Philosophy*, 125–126). But Bergson's point is that a kind of magical thinking exists in the "civilized" mind, not that "primitives" are like children (*DS*, 158–59/151–52). While Jones is right that the examples Bergson gives from "*[l]es récits des missionaires*" are highly problematic, the problem is not that Bergson describes "primitives" as "*ayant vécu autant de siècles que nous*," but that he sees their duration as stagnating (*DS*, 142–43/136–37). For Bergson, there is nothing essentially "biological" or "noumenal" (having to do with the deep self) about this, as there is no inheritance of acquired traits.

24. Jones argues that an internalist or "noumenal" metaphor of race is made possible by Bergson's idea of the deep self, a self that can be made to carry occult qualities that are the cause of race. She proposes that Bergson's philosophy contributes to a reconceptualization of race as "dynamic essence" (Jones, *Racial Discourses of Life Philosophy*, 101, 117–19). Yet a reading of *Les deux sources* tells us that if there are differences between societies for Bergson, it is on the level of cultural acquisitions and not in any essence (*DS*, 133/127).

25. Jones, *Racial Discourses of Life Philosophy*, 102–10.

26. Muhammad Iqbal, *The Reconstruction of Religious Thought in Islam* (Stanford, CA: Stanford University Press, 2012), 40, 43–44. See Diagne, *Bergson postcolonial*, 109–10, 112. It is important to note that most of Iqbal's lectures, which make up this book, were delivered in 1930, before *Les deux sources* was published; he met Bergson in Paris in 1931 (Diagne, *Bergson postcolonial*, 65).

27. Iqbal, *Reconstruction of Religious Thought in Islam*, 39–40.

28. Ibid., 44, 8.

29. Ibid., 131–33; Diagne, *Bergson postcolonial*, 84–88. In this vein, Iqbal conceives of Islam as a "social experiment" (*Reconstruction of Religious Thought in Islam*, 133).

30. See Mark Antliff, *Inventing Bergson: Cultural Politics and the Parisian Avant-Garde* (Princeton, NJ: Princeton University Press, 1993).

31. Henri Bergson, *L'évolution créatrice* (Paris: Presses Universitaires de France, 1907); *Creative Evolution*, trans. Arthur Mitchell (Mineola, NY: Dover Publications, 1998). Henceforth cited as "*EC*" with French then English pagination.

32. *DS*, 3/11.

33. Ibid., 102–3/100. For a critique of this enlarged concept of "biology," see Philippe Soulez, "Bergson as Philosopher of War and Theorist of the Political," trans. Melissa McMahon, *Bergson, Politics, and Religion*, ed. Alexandre Lefebvre and Melanie White (Durham, NC: Duke University Press, 2012), 99–125.

34. *DS*, 23/28.

35. Ibid., 21/26–27.

36. Ibid., 26–27/31–32.

37. Ibid., 49/51.

38. Ibid., 28/33.

39. Ibid., 28–29/33.

40. Vladimir Jankélévitch also makes the point that instinct becomes a conservative principle in *Les deux sources*. See Jankélévitch, *Henri Bergson* (Paris: Presses Universitaires de France, 1959), 194–95.

41. See *EC* 224/223, 298/299.

42. *DS*, 233/220. I will not be translating *élan*, since I want the reader to hear multiple senses in the term, which Bergson plays on: both impetus and momentum.

43. Ibid., 30/34, 48/50.

44. Ibid., 85/84.

45. Ibid., 99/97.

46. Ibid., 34/38.

47. Ibid., 50/52.

48. Ibid., 285/267.

49. Ibid., 34/38.

50. Ibid., 286/269.

51. Ibid., 85/84.

52. Ibid., 254/240.

53. *EC*, 51/51, translation modified.

54. *DS*, 78–79/78.

55. "*Partout où quelque chose vit, il y a ouvert quelque part un registre où le temps s'inscrit*" (*EC*, 16/16).

56. Ibid., 128/127–28.

57. Ibid., 9/9.

58. Suzanne Guerlac notes that the origin of Bergson's open/closed distinction lies in thermodynamics, but whereas this may be its starting point, it is clear that the concepts change over the course of Bergson's texts. See *Thinking in Time: An Introduction to Henri Bergson* (Ithaca, NY: Cornell University Press, 2006), 9.

59. See Worms, "The Closed and the Open," 33–34.

60. *DS*, 127/122, 137/131.

61. Ibid., 127/122, 144/139.

62. Ibid., 223/211.

63. Ibid., 106/103, 149–59/143–52.

64. Ibid., 131–32/126–27.

65. Ibid., 113/110.

66. Ibid., 142/136.

67. Ibid., 143/137.

68. Ibid., 180/172.

69. Given also that the accounts Bergson relies on here are "missionary stories," a circular justification is put in place (ibid., 142/136).

70. Ibid., 134/129, translation modified.

71. Ibid., 133/127.

72. Ibid., 133/128.

73. Ibid., 180/171.
74. Ibid., 132/127.
75. Ibid., 263/248.
76. Ibid., 98/96.
77. Ibid., 170/162.
78. Ibid., 185/176, 170/162.
79. Ibid., 241/228.
80. Ibid., 85/84.
81. Jankélévitch, *Henri Bergson*, 199.
82. *DS*, 226/213, translation modified.
83. Ibid., 316/296.
84. Ibid.
85. Henri Bergson, *Matière et mémoire: Essai sur la relation du corps à l'esprit* (Paris: Presses Universitaires de France, 1896); *Matter and Memory*, trans. Nancy Margaret Paul and W. Scott Palmer (New York: Zone Books, 1991). Henceforth cited with French, then English pagination.
86. Ibid., 205/184.
87. Cutting nature at its joints rather than according to an artificial grid, says Bergson citing Plato (*EC*, 157/156).
88. See essays in the volume *Bergson, Politics, and Religion*, for this insistence, especially Lefebvre, "Bergson and Human Rights."
89. Bergson, *La pensée et le mouvant*, 188/211.
90. Ibid., 93/101.
91. *EC*, 4/4.
92. Jankélévitch, *Henri Bergson*, 274–75.
93. Walter D. Mignolo, "The Geopolitics of Knowledge and the Colonial Difference," *South Atlantic Quarterly* 101, no. 1 (2002): 80.
94. Johannes Fabian, *Time and the Other: How Anthropology Makes Its Object* (New York: Columbia University Press, 1983).
95. I have developed the concept of the *reconfiguration* of the past in Alia Al-Saji, "SPEP Co-Director's Address: Hesitation as Philosophical Method—Travel Bans, Colonial Durations, and the Affective Weight of the Past," *The Journal of Speculative Philosophy* 32, no. 3 (2018): 331–59.
96. Bergson, *La pensée et le mouvant*, 12/1, 36/31.

Chapter 2

The Language of Closure

Homogeneity, Exclusion, and the State

MARTIN SHUSTER

Empirical historical research increasingly suggests that the global system of states according to which we organize ourselves is deeply problematic, accounting not only for deep inequalities across the globe, but even more horrifically, for the consistent recurrence of genocide.[1] Genocide is thereby "a systemic dysfunction and cannot be simply or solely dismissed as the aberrant or deviant behavior of rogue, revolutionary or totalitarian regimes or *for that matter ones with particular, one might say peculiar, types of political culture or social and ethnic configuration.*[2] In this chapter, I accomplish two tasks. First, I situate the themes of race and colonialism amid this state framework, stressing how they might be seen as tied to the state (avoiding the question of whether they are tied as inputs or outputs, for, as will become apparent, the question is not one of either/or). Second, I situate Henri Bergson as an important critic of the state system. This second goal might be especially puzzling given Bergson's own efforts at diplomacy,[3] and also given the fact that one of the most impressive recent readings of the work I intend to focus on, *The Two Sources of Morality and Religion* (1932),[4] has alleged its deep connection to human rights theory,[5] and thereby to something like the international state system (at least to the extent that the latter, as Hannah Arendt had stressed, is necessary for the enforcement of the former).

Genocide, as Theodor W. Adorno remarked,[6] might be seen as a method of integration: it is a way of homogenizing state populations, and in this way it exists among a spectrum of other practices, ranging from genocide and ethnic cleansing, on one end, to the construction of a fixed state identity, on the other.[7] International relations theorist, Heather Rae, has termed the bloodiest of such processes "pathological homogenization." Here is how she puts it:

> These processes [of pathological homogenization] are an integral part of the state system, and practices of pathological homogenisation have, in part, *constituted* the states system, for it has been constructed in large measure on the exclusionary categories of insider and outsider. This is not to assert that the most extreme forms of mistreatment are in some way inevitable, only that they remain a possibility in a system which is based on a sharp distinction between insiders and outsiders. The assertion that the boundary of the state constitutes the only legitimate moral boundary (and hence it is logical that those who are outside the moral community, however defined, are owed no moral duties and may be removed from the state) only makes sense, and is only morally acceptable, if the "state monopoly over the right to define identity" is accepted.[8]

The global network of states impels each state to construct a fixed identity in order to distinguish itself from others and also, more importantly, to compete among them, economically, socially, politically, and otherwise. Constitutive of such a drive toward development and/or empowerment is the construction of state identity, and such identity involves fundamentally the construction of a "people." Identity and peoplehood can thereby be seen as two sides of the same coin (and importantly, *society* ought to be interchangeable here with *people*). In modernity especially, states serve as the chief locus around which "people" or "societies" are organized; indeed, as Michael Mann notes, "states are central to our understanding of what society is. Where states are strong, societies are relatively territorialized and centralized."[9] Unlike prior eras, where notions like "Christendom" or "European" might have been central, the construction of a "people" is oriented now, and seemingly for the foreseeable future, around state identity (and this despite the existence of the European Union or despite exceptions which, in virtue of a drive *toward* statehood, chiefly prove the point, as in, say, the Kurd nation or the existence of groups of people who are fundamentally classified as interstate persons).[10] Exactly because of such state drives, in conjunction with the existence of a state system, it is in "the twentieth century," Rae writes, "as the state system has spread across the globe and there are fewer safe exits for targeted minority groups, that genocide and politicide have become a 'standard technique.'"[11]

Rae's proposal is astute and suggestive. Yet, in a philosophical register, one might ask whether the categories of "insider/outsider" that are essential to her account are contingent categories, or something akin to transcendental categories, that is, categories necessary for human thought, or perhaps less strongly, at least categories necessary for human (political) association. Furthermore, one might ask: if "pathological homogenization," as Rae alleges, is not itself sufficient for "the most extreme forms of mistreatment" (i.e., that such forms of mistreatment are not "in some way inevitable"), then what is the exact explanatory force of her account? Rae's account implies that a deeper level of explanation is available.

There are several ways to reinforce her account, and I specifically want to look at four that link to race and colonialism. At the same time, as will become obvious, looking at them in turn shows, in fact, how they are deficient and how they would benefit from a dialogue with Bergson's *The Two Sources*. While significantly more might be said about any of these options, I limit my discussion of all of them solely to the extent that it can be shown how they are incapable—on their own—of satisfying the sort of questions raised about pathological homogenization in the previous paragraph.

1. *Capitalism*: What accounts for the drive toward homogenization is the global market in which the state system is itself embedded. On both the demand side and the supply side, the drive for profit inherent to the capitalist economic order requires expansion into new territories (on the demand side, profits would be lost without expansion since more is produced than can be bought domestically, while on the supply side, profit maximization forces expansion abroad for more resources, in the form of raw materials as much as human labor). As Rosa Luxemburg put it, "Capital cannot accumulate without the aid of non-capitalist organisations, nor, on the other hand, can it tolerate their continued existence side by side with itself. Only the continuous and progressive disintegration of non-capitalist organisations makes accumulation of capital possible."[12] This drive toward profits within a global state system therefore leads to colonialism and other terrors,

deep global inequalities (and tensions),[13] frequent warfare, and thereby, often, genocide.[14] Some argue that global capitalism itself is ultimately genocidal.[15] Furthermore, as with all of the options mentioned, the effects are not solely, say, "structural" (where what is meant by that is the idea that the global market affects how humans organize themselves), but also explicitly "agential," in that it also additionally affects the ways in which humans exist in, perceive, and experience the world.[16] As a corollary to this point, and also echoing a point that will emerge in all of the options to be considered, capitalism itself, locally but just as much globally, is a normative project, not somehow simply baldly "natural" or given.[17] That is, the existence of capitalism requires a wide array of normative commitments, from property rights, to individualism, to markets, to human freedom, to group identity, and so forth.

2. *White Supremacy*: With Charles W. Mills, the drive toward homogenization might be seen as driven by a "racial contract,"[18] wherein what drives homogenization and the global system of states is the bifurcation of the world into races (I use the term *bifurcate* exactly to highlight that even in the case of a conceptualization of *races*, the important distinction is between the "master" race and the one(s) opposed to it).[19] Global injustice is "embedded in the basic structures of these societies," and is not merely an anomaly "within a structure essentially just."[20] Citing the influence of Rousseau, Mills stresses the formal analogy between his project and Rousseau's. Where Rousseau locates the origins of class inequality to human convention,[21] exposing thereby the normative origins of such inequality, Mills does the same with respect to race.[22] Race is fundamentally "sociopolitical rather than biological,"[23] and thereby "whiteness is not really a color at all, but a set of power relations."[24] And this without denying that race is still "nonetheless real,"[25] and also without suggesting that the racial contract somehow precedes the social one (the two are rather equiprimordial). The impetus for the racial contract idea is the suggestion that it presents us with a "useful model" for "thinking about things, with claims

neither to literal nor hypothetical (in the sense of possible) representation of the past."[26] In this way, the racial contract does not denote a factual occurrence or even an idealized or invented version of a factual occurrence, but rather offers a way to contextualize a variety of human actions across time and space.[27] This also accounts for and allows for the construction of an "epistemology of ignorance,"[28] where an agent's uptake of the world, and thereby their very experience, is affected.[29] What counts as a fact or an experience or a value comes to be determined by the terms of the racial contract, and so the potential arises for the exclusion of experience of certain humans, even without explicit intent on the part of those doing the excluding, since such exclusion occurs by virtue of how one is constituted as an agent (and not necessarily by any conscious choice).

3. *Patriarchy*: The drive toward homogenization is part and parcel of what Carole Pateman calls a "sexual contract," wherein "men's domination over women, and the right of men to enjoy equal sexual access to women" is what orients the original social contract that, in turn, establishes the state structure.[30] The sexual contract, like the racial contract, takes many forms and cuts across large swathes of society. Importantly, it must be noted that patriarchy does not require the actual existence of "paternal rule," but rather, from the beginning, vivifies liberal contract theory in the form(s) of marriage contracts and labor contracts.[31] Above all, it is the *form* of contracting itself that signals patriarchy, and thereby creates a "relation of subordination."[32] In this way, the sexual contract, like the racial contract, is also a fundamentally normative proposition in the sense that the terms of the *actual social contract* could have been different (i.e., it could have been women not men that dominated, and thereby present discussion would be about "matriarchy"). The problem, according to Pateman, is the relationship of subordination that "contracting" as such ultimately implies and creates. Nonetheless, it simply is a fact that "the sexual contract was integral to the historical changes that led to the consolidation of the modern state and its institutions."[33] And, again, to the extent that contracting

seemingly forms the basis of all our contemporary institutions, from even marriage and family up to the state itself, patriarchy infects agency to the core.

4. *Nationalism:* Homogenization is a necessary byproduct of the fact that people conceive of themselves as belonging to communities organized around a "fictive ethnicity,"[34] that is, the idea that communities are organized around both a natural shared past and a natural shared future, which ultimately suggests "an identity of origins, culture and interests which transcends individuals and social conditions."[35] What accounts for this conceptualization of communities is variable,[36] from the suggestion that it is material forces that drives such conceptions (notably industrialization),[37] to the idea that it is cultural forces (the invention of the printing press),[38] to the suggestion that it is psychological or ontological facts about humans (above all, mortality),[39] or simply to the thought that it is the invention of an idea itself (one attributed, say, to Kant and the Germans).[40] Importantly, as in the prior cases, the nation is a fundamentally *normative* concept—it is not a natural kind, and involves normative commitments by people for its maintenance (a fact apparent in the importance of names to nations).[41]

The issues are more complex than this quick sketch suggests, since the divisions are largely heuristic (especially to the extent that these options are normatively and materially implicated with each other). So, for example, racism might be seen as a "supplement" of nationalism, where the former "is constantly emerging out of nationalism."[42] In turn, racism itself can be seen as connected to sexism (at the very least, in the social, political, and/or aesthetic valorization of a "certain type of man"),[43] and similarly for the nation-state and sexism.[44] In a similar vein, capitalism can be seen as intimately connected to a division of the world into nation states.[45] And, of course, the connection between colonialism and nationalism cannot be ignored. My aims are not to settle or even elaborate these matters, but instead to suggest two points. First, none of these options—whether individually or in combination—are actually capable of explaining the homogenization involved in the state system at its *most fundamental* level. And, that is because, second, such homogenization is *normative* in character, and its *fundamental* basis—if it has one—can only be found at the level at which normativity is itself constructed, a topic that has been insufficiently explored in this context. Note the extent to which every option above rests on a normative component—might there perhaps be something about the construction or function of norms, of normativity itself, that requires such homogenization?

Vis-à-vis the first point, also note that these explanations, even in the minds of those advancing them, do not appear to be sufficient to account for the homogenization in question. So, for example, nationalism and capitalism are often linked in order to forge a more convincing account, as are, obviously, nationalism and white supremacy and patriarchy (in this sense, the extent to which both Mills and Pateman explicitly link their theories to social contract theory must be stressed).[46] Yet, again, for example, with the alleged link between capitalism and the nation-state, it remains a fact that other, nonnational forms of political organization are possible within the same capitalist order.[47] Given enough space, similar procedures could be performed with permutations of all of the examples above. This is because these accounts are not underwritten by any natural facts, but rather by normative claims and structures. Nothing more underwrites them (even, for example, in the case of white supremacy or patriarchy: there is no biological fact at bottom that might justify the claims of white supremacists or misogynists). All (of these) ways of organization and/or categorization are socially constructed. Every one of them might have been different, and each thereby admits of variation, evolution, and contingency. This is one way to highlight that it is in fact irrelevant whether my former point, about the insufficiency of the explanations in combination or in isolation is accepted, since this broader point is inescapable. Normativity—the process of how normative authority is established (and especially in the context of the establishment of peoplehood)—must be the site of inquiry, explicitly oriented around the question of whether there is a relationship between normativity and homogenization.

Bergson offers two important trajectories in this regard. First, a biographical point: *The Two Sources* was written in the early 1930s, when many of the problems that still trouble the global order of the world arose (notably in the form of the First World War, but also in the form of the modern, national state structure). Second, more substantively, Bergson is intimately interested in exactly how it is that societies organize themselves, in how and whether that organization might be understood and justified, and—especially crucial for present purposes—with the problem of war, and what "deeper" or more "fundamental" issue it reveals.

Bergson on Norms

In *The Two Sources*, Bergson engages with the question of "peoplehood," and thereby implicitly with the homogenization question that has been raised thus far. Here is how Bergson broaches the topic:

> Whether human or animal, a society is an organization; it implies a co-ordination and generally also a subordination of elements; it therefore exhibits, whether merely embodied in life or, in addition, specifically formulated, a collection of rules and laws [*règles ou de lois*]. But in a hive or an ant-hill the individual is tied to his task by his structure, and the organization is relatively invariable, *where the human community is variable in form, open to every kind of progress*. The result is that in the former each rule is laid down by nature, and is necessary: whereas in the latter only one thing is natural, *the necessity of a rule*.[48]

The latter point is a familiar philosophical point about agency: human action in order to be taken as a properly *human* act must accord, potentially, with some rule (it cannot be merely random),[49] but, importantly, in the case of humans, these "rules" are not merely given, not simply prescribed by nature (as in "rules" or *laws* of nature), but rather instituted and maintained socially and historically by human activity. The discussion of rules, and thereby obligation, is what drives Bergson's discussion throughout, and it is in this sense that the book is "about morality." But this sense is quite different from contemporary philosophical discussions of morality, where the desire is often to derive a *particular* and prescriptive stance. Bergson's aims, depending on where one stands, are either significantly more ambitious, or more modest, but regardless, more general: to understand the origin of morality—obligation, normativity—as such. What is the fundamental origin and thereby perhaps significance of this fact about humans?

Bergson's claims are throughout governed by his distinct approach to philosophy, one that is thoroughly naturalistic, yet entirely nonreductionistic.[50] In this way, he frequently pursues an analogy to insect society in *The Two Sources*, especially to stress the idea that thinking about what human society "*would have been*" like if it were organized in ways akin to insect society:

> We must perpetually recur to what obligation *would have been* if human society had been instinctive instead of intelligent: this

will not explain any particular obligation, we shall even give of obligation in general an idea which would be false, if we went no further; and yet we must think of this instinctive society as the counterpart of intelligent society, if we are not to start without any clue in quest of the foundations of morality.[51]

This heuristic is meant to help understand normativity and obligation. It is not, by itself, sufficient for explaining them; in fact, it would "give of obligation in general an idea which would be false"—and that is because normativity requires the possibility of *not* acting according to the rule(s) in question. In an instinctive society, such a possibility does not exist (at least not for the actors—it may be that outside contingencies impinge and, say, destroy the insect life-form and prevent *any* action). Bergson's strategy is to describe initially an intermediate position, one that he terms "habit,"[52] which denotes exactly the idea that as humans we are initiated into a form of life that we occupy largely unreflectively, and wherein our actions resemble exactly that of insect society, the difference being that those habits, although arising naturally, are not "merely" natural.[53] Habit allows for modification. In fact, as humans, we have the possibility of taking a reflective stance toward our habits and working to modify them. As Bergson puts it, "What is therefore, strictly speaking, obligatory in obligation does not come from intelligence. *The latter only supplies the element of hesitation in obligation.*"[54] "Hesitation" ought to be seen exactly as a marker of or shorthand for reflection.

Bergson is thereby framing the "homogenization" problem in an interesting way. According to Bergson, we are impelled toward being part of a people *naturally*: we are born and raised amid people, and, in this way, we are social creatures.[55] Bergson points out,

> To whatever school of philosophy you belong, you are bound to recognize that man [*sic*] is a living creature, that the evolution of life along its two main lines [instinct and intelligence] has been accomplished in the direction of social life, that association is the most general form of living activity, since life is organization, and that, this being so, we pass by imperceptible transitions from the relation between cells in an organism to the relation between individuals in society.[56]

Bergson, much akin to Hegel and segments of the German philosophical tradition, sees a direct analogy between the organic unity of the organization of cells and the (alleged) organic unity of a people. War—or, alternatively, how a people comes to be delineated, possibly to the point of violence—becomes an important site of investigation. Unlike Hegel, however, Bergson sees war as a problem rather than as a solution. For Hegel, war might be seen as the "solution" to set of problems that surround the rise of atomism among individuals—what Hegel terms the problem of the "ethical" (*sittlich*) health of the state. As modern forms of individuality and modern forms of economic (market) organization develop, individuals are prone to lose social cohesiveness, not to mention to lose sight of the (alleged) value of such cohesion. In times of war, then, according to Hegel, individuals "learn to appreciate the value of their state."[57] Because war presses individuals together, creating an opposition group to the foreign state, citizens, as a whole, allegedly gain greater cohesion, and perceive the importance of the state toward their everyday existence. For Bergson, however, war raises a significant *problem* about normativity and group coherence: "In fact, when we lay down that the duty of respecting the life and property of others is a fundamental demand of social life, *what society do we mean?* To find an answer we need only think what happens in time of war. Murder and pillage and perfidy, cheating and lying become not only lawful, they are actually praiseworthy."[58] Note how Bergson explicitly asks what we mean by people (the homogenization question), as he stresses that the answer to that question will involve understanding more deeply the way in which norms themselves are established and maintained ("how can certain formerly unlawful and blameworthy norms suddenly become lawful and praiseworthy?").

Bergson on Community

For Bergson, there are two ways to view our belonging to a community with others. The first he terms "closed," highlighting that it "does not include *everyone*, that it marks a spatial limit, a frontier, an exclusion," while the second he terms "open," stressing that "there is a sense in which we can [. . .] perceive, articulate, and, in any case, *denounce* this closure from another point of view."[59] Bergson associates the former with the tendency of society to become rigidified and codified in order to maintain social cohesion and allow for the undertaking of human projects and lives in the form of a *background* (of norms, comportments, saliences, and so forth) on which they can base their existence. The latter Bergson associates with moments, emblematically by him instantiated in mystical feeling, where the

The Language of Closure 47

boundaries between people (and things) are abandoned.⁶⁰ When adopted, such attitudes lead to an openness to *all* of existence, to a fundamental orientation that stresses above all the inapplicability of *all* categories of demarcation and thereby separation. As Bergson puts it, "What, in that case [in the case of the open attitude], is allowed in? Suppose we say that it embraces all humanity: we should not be going too far, *we should hardly be going far enough*, since its love may extend to animals, to plants, to all nature."⁶¹ In this way, Bergson is building on his work in *Creative Evolution* (1907), where he showed that the tendency of all life is toward change, and thereby already cemented the radical contingency of all forms of "closure."⁶²

How is the limit between these two orientations marked and *what* accounts for that limit? Bergson suggests the following: "Who can help seeing that social cohesion is largely due to the necessity for a community to protect itself against others, and that it is primarily as against all other men that we love the men with whom we live?"⁶³ And, generally, commentators on *The Two Sources* have taken Bergson at his word, stressing that Bergson "starts from the premise—uncontroversial for most of us—that war is natural and ineradicable."⁶⁴

This is insufficiently nuanced, however, especially when one takes stock of the discussion thus far and also of Bergson's other remarks. Bergson stresses that these limits *must* exist and are *necessary*. Does necessity here rest simply on a contingent fact of nature: that "war is natural and ineradicable? Note that some now think that the idea of war as 'natural and ineradicable' " is false.⁶⁵ Regardless of the plausibility of such a claim,⁶⁶ it is undeniable that we can easily imagine things might have been otherwise: humans might have been the sort of creatures who consistently *avoided war*.⁶⁷ Even in the face of such possible contingency, though, Bergson maintains that the limits between closed and open *must* exist. Here are two representative and striking examples:

> Now, a mystic society, embracing all humanity and moving, animated by a common will, towards the continually renewed creation of a more complete humanity, *is no more possible of realization in the future than was the existence in the past of human societies functioning automatically and similar to animal societies.*⁶⁸

> For between the nation, however big, and humanity there lies the whole distance from the finite to the indefinite, from the closed to the open. We are fond of saying that the apprenticeship to

civic virtue is served in the family, and that in the same way, from holding our country dear, we learn to love mankind [*sic*]. Our sympathies are supposed to broaden out in an unbroken progression, to expand while remaining identical, and to end by embracing all humanity [. . .] between the society in which we live and humanity in general there is, we repeat, the same contrast as between the closed and the open; the difference between the two objects is one of kind and not simply of degree.[69]

The first limit—the one between the closed and open—is easy enough to *begin* to understand: the specifications of a closed society, whatever they may be (even a cosmopolitan society or a properly "global" one), are finite: they have a fixed object, while the limits of the open society are exactly *indefinite*, admitting of no object (we do not know, nor will we ever, what *forms* life will take).

Yet, the question arises: why is a mystic *society*, that is, per Bergson's own definition, one that embraces all of *humanity*, impossible? Note that this would be a sort of intermediary between "closed" and "open" to the extent that it would be far beyond what we typically think of a "closed" society, but nonetheless not fully "open" to the extent that it is a *society*, in other words, focused on all of *humanity*, that is, not concerned (necessarily) with nonhuman life-forms. Why think *this* is impossible, *especially* given Bergson's own stress on the unknowability of the future and the constancy of change?

Community and Language

The answer lies in a remark that Bergson makes early in *The Two Sources*. He claims that "the morality of a human society *is in fact comparable to its language*."[70] This is a striking remark, and unpacking its full implications, in directions that Bergson himself likely did not intend, allows for traction on some of the questions of the last section. To the extent that both society and language rely on a sort of pragmatics of language, the easiest way to unpack this remark is to see Bergson's conception of language as underwritten by a conception of language akin to that developed by Stanley Cavell.[71] In *The Claim of Reason* (1979), Cavell stresses that "the philosophical appeal to what we say, and the search for our criteria on the basis of which we say what we say, *are claims to community*. And the claim to community is always a search for the basis upon which it can be or has been established."[72] Cavell is highlighting that it is what we *say* that determines with whom we stand in community. And, importantly, there is always the possibility that "my conviction isolates me, *from all others*."[73] In such a case, we might learn that "there is no us (yet, maybe never) to say anything about."[74] So, rather than coming premade or referring to a context outside of the present one (say, a contextless dictionary), meaning is specific and located solely in a particular speech at a particular time, established entirely by the meeting of minds (or the failure of the same). Language is a *mark* of community, or a failure of having achieved community (and in this sense, it is one among others).

Because of its normative nature, language always carries the possibility for agreement and thereby the possibility of instituting community, society, and peoplehood. At the same time, again, exactly because of *this same nature*, the risk of refusal, of disagreement, and, indeed, importantly, disagreement to the point of murder,[75] is always inherent to its possibilities and operations. Loneliness is a perpetual possibility within language, without which the phenomena of language could not exist.[76] Taking seriously, then, Bergson's idea that "the morality of a human society is in fact comparable to its language," means above all understanding that normativity, morality—indeed thereby society, peoplehood—always admits of the possibility of dissolution, and that this possibility is essential to its existence, and its possibilities. An open *community*, in other words, a truly *open* society, is an impossibility exactly *because* its impossibility is in fact essential to *any community*. (At a very high altitude: a version of this problem emerges in the all-too-common liberal problem of how states ought to deal with political actors and parties that are actively working to undermine the mechanisms that allow liberal states to function, actors who are working actively against its core values.)

It is this fact about language that accounts for any construction of community, and that underwrites, at the deepest level of analysis, the constellation between, on one hand, pathological homogenization, and, on the other hand, the four foci mentioned above (capitalism, white supremacy, patriarchy, and nationalism). As the latter interact with each other, they also feed into various homogenizing tendencies (the homogenization—commodification—of markets and persons; the whitewashing of peoples and histories; the masculinization—and thereby the bifurcation and heteronormativization—of sexuality; and the construction of nation). As homogenization proceeds, it involves these various domains, reinforcing the structures and rigidities that develop in each, pursuing across all of them a conglomerated unity of economic, racial, sexual, and national integration. What Bergson's comparison between language and the morality (or normativity or construction) of a society makes clear is that any such integration or homogenization is, at least while language has a function and continues to function, perpetually prone to failure. The operations of language—that there is a meaning to words, and that thereby there are agents capable of agreeing or disagreeing about any meaning—guarantees that any community faces, perpetually, the possibility of closure, indeed of dissolution, outright destruction, all simply in virtue of its possession and continued use of speech.[77]

Conclusion

Remember, Bergson stressed that "between the society in which we live and humanity in general there is [. . .] the same contrast as between the closed and the open; the difference between the two objects is one of kind and not simply of degree."[78] In this way, despite his own statist leanings and experience as a diplomat, Bergson suggests that any approach that relies on an international state order is doomed to failure, because it fundamentally mistakes what is at stake—for again, "between the nation, however big, and humanity there lies the whole distance from the finite to the indefinite, from the closed to the open."[79] In other words, the state structure is a structure of *states*, thereby of *closed* entities, which will always be suspicious of novel forms of life (and, so, novel forms of *living*, i.e., experiments in living—think recently of marriage law debates in the United States, but now also think of the variety of remaining queer issues that are unresolved and unlikely to be resolved soon). At its root, all versions of this suspicion are grounded in the fact of language (that language itself must have a "closed" component).[80] In this way, our political problems are both self-caused and yet not entirely political.

Pathologies like capitalism, white supremacy, patriarchy, nationalism, and others are pathologies as much because of the fact that they themselves produce human suffering as the fact that they warp and deform the very operations of language, thereby making it more difficult for some to be heard or even to speak. These pathologies leverage a basic fact about language, using it to artificially shrink its boundaries even further, thereby closing and narrowing those boundaries far beyond what language "naturally" requires. In short, the problems with these pathologies is as much that they lead to the suffering inherent to closed societies that have turned brutal, as that these pathologies close off sites for speech and expressivity, thereby barring even the possibility of an opening or of a lessening of closure. At the same time, to the extent that the possibilities of and for any human existence are presently, and likely for the foreseeable future, intimately bound up with the operations of language (broadly conceived), a truly open society is possible only at the cost of this humanity, for all language requires the existence of closure; and this for better or for worse. Importantly, then, it will still be language that offers us solace (or does not), for it is only by means of its use that we can broaden our conceptions of what counts enough and in the right ways as "like us" or "like me."

Notes

1. Mark Levene, *Genocide in the Age of the Nation State*, 2 vols. (London: I. B. Tauris, 2005).

2. Ibid., 205. Emphasis mine.

3. For Bergson's political biography, see Philippe Soulez, *Bergson Politique* (Paris: Presses Universitaires de France, 1989).

4. Henri Bergson, *Two Sources of Morality and Religion*, trans. R. Ashley Audra, Cloudesley Brereton, and W. Horsfall Carter (Notre Dame, IN: University of Notre Dame Press, 1977). Henceforth cited as "*TSMR*." The French consulted is *Œuvres*, trans. F. L. Pogson (Paris: Presses Universitaires de France, 1959). If I have modified the translation, I noted it.

5. Alexandre Lefebvre, *Human Rights as a Way of Life: On Bergson's Political Philosophy* (Palo Alto, CA: Stanford University Press, 2013).

6. "Genocide is the absolute integration." See Theodor W. Adorno, *Negative Dialectics*, trans. E. B. Ashton (New York: Continuum Publishing Company, 1973), 362.

7. In between are notable phenomena like "social death." In this context, see Claudia Card, *The Atrocity Paradigm: A Theory of Evil* (Oxford, UK: Oxford University Press, 2005).

8. Heather Rae, *State Identities and the Homogenisation of Peoples* (Cambridge, UK: Cambridge University Press, 2002), 14.

9. Michael Mann, "The Autonomous Power of the State: Its Origins, Mechanisms and Results," *European Journal of Sociology* 25, no. 2 (1984): 136.

10. While Mann's thesis is not pitched in this tenor, it is most plausible as a set of claims about *identity* not explicitly about *actual* sites of power and so is entirely compatible with the account in Wendy Brown, *Walled States, Waning Sovereignty* (Cambridge, MA: MIT Press, 2010).

11. Rae, *State Identities and the Homogenisation of Peoples*.

12. Rosa Luxemburg, *The Accumulation of Capital*, trans. Agnes Schwarzschild (London: Routledge, 2003), 397.

13. This point is often conveniently overlooked in discussions of inequality, so, for example, even in Piketty's book, there is only passing mention of global inequality. On this point, see Tony Smith, "A Category Mistake in Piketty," *Critical Sociology* 41, no. 2 (2014). See Thomas Piketty, *Capital in the 21st Century* (Cambridge, MA: Harvard University Press, 2014), 67–71.

14. And I should note that this view of things is not restricted to viewpoints from the left. For a quite similar view, see John Gray, *False Dawn: The Delusions of Global Capitalism* (New York: The New Press, 1998), 120ff.

15. Garry M. Leech, *Capitalism: A Structural Genocide* (London: Zed Books, 2012).

16. Two elaborations of this point are Marx on "estranged labor" and Adorno on "free time." Respectively, see Karl Marx, *The Economic and Philosophical Manuscripts of 1844 and the Communist Manifesto*, trans. Martin Milligan (New York: Prometheus Books, 1988); Theodor W. Adorno, "Free Time," *The Culture Industry: Selected Essays on Mass Culture*, ed. J. M. Bernstein (London: Routledge, 2001).

17. Cf. Tony Smith, "Technological Dynamism and the Normative Justification of Global Capitalism," in *Political Economy and Global Capitalism: The 21st Century, Present and Future*, ed. Robert Albritton, Bob Jessop, and Richard Vestra (London: Anthem Press, 2007). See also Max Weber, *The Protestant Ethic and the Spirit of Capitalism: And Other Writings*, trans. Peter Baehr and Gordon C. Wells (New York: Penguin, 2002), 1–203.

18. For this notion, see Charles W. Mills, *The Racial Contract* (Ithaca, NY: Cornell University Press, 1997); "Race and the Social Contract Tradition," *Social identities* 6, no. 4 (2000).

19. Charles W. Mills, "White Right: The Idea of a *Herrenvolk* Ethics," in *Blackness Visible: Essays on Philosophy and Race* (Ithaca, NY: Cornell University Press, 1998).

20. Carole Pateman and Charles W. Mills, *Contract and Domination* (London: Polity, 2007), 233.

21. Jean-Jacques Rousseau, "Discourse on the Origin of Inequality," in *Basic Political Writings*, ed. Donald A. Cress (Indianapolis, IN: Hackett, 1987), 37f.

22. On this point, see Mills, *The Racial Contract*, 68–69; "Race and the Social Contract Tradition," 443–45; Pateman and Mills, *Contract and Domination*, 232.

23. Mills, *The Racial Contract*, 126.

24. Ibid., 127. Cf. "The 'Racial Contract' as Methodology," in *From Class to Race: Essays in White Marxism and Black Radicalism* (Lanham: Rowman & Littlefield Publishers, 2003), 242f.

25. *The Racial Contract*, 126.

26. "Race and the Social Contract Tradition," 443–44. Mills is explicitly relying on Jean Hampton's suggestion that "social contract arguments provide plausible descriptions of political societies as conventionally-generated human creations." See Jean Hampton, "Contract and Consent," in *A Companion to Contemporary Political Philosophy*, ed. Robert E. Goodin and Philip Pettit (Cambridge: Blackwell, 1993), 383.

27. See Mills, *The Racial Contract*, 20–21. Note how the contract affects the way in which space (and time) is understood. Ibid., 41ff.

28. *The Racial Contract*, 18. See also "White Ignorance," in *Race and Epistemologies of Ignorance*, ed. Nancy Tuana and Shannon Sullivan (Buffalo, NY: State University Press of New York, 2007).

29. This raises a question about the exact nature of agency, epistemology, and thereby metaphysics Mills is committed to—on this point, see Matthew Congdon, "Epistemic Injustice in the Space of Reasons," *Episteme* 12, no. 1 (2015). In a different context, for a development of a view of agency that would countenance Mills views, see Martin Shuster, *Autonomy after Auschwitz: Adorno, German Idealism, and Modernity* (Chicago: University of Chicago Press, 2014).

30. Carole Pateman, *The Sexual Contract* (Palo Alto, CA: Stanford University Press, 1988), 2. Crucial here is also Teresa Brennan and Carole Pateman, " 'Mere Auxiliaries to the Commonwealth': Women and the Origins of Liberalism," *Political Studies* 27, no. 2 (1979).

31. Cf. Pateman, *The Sexual Contract*, 3ff.

32. Ibid., 59. See also how Pateman stresses that paternity is "invented" (35), that is, socially constructed and thereby normative in nature.

33. Pateman and Mills, *Contract and Domination*, 227–28. Furthermore, the role of such a contract is unavoidable in any proper account of genocide. See Elisa von Joeden-Forgey, "Gender and Genocide," in *The Oxford Handbook to Genocide Studies*, ed. Donald Bloxham and A. Dirk Moses (Oxford, UK: Oxford University Press, 2010).

34. Étienne Balibar, "The Nation Form: History and Ideology," in *Race, Nation Class: Ambiguous Identities*, ed. Étienne Balibar and Immanuel Wallerstein (London: Verso, 1991), 96ff.

35. Ibid., 96.

36. In this way, I am rejecting any idea of the "nation" as primordial, as in Harold Robert Isaacs, *Idols of the Tribe: Group Identity and Political Change* (Cambridge, MA: Harvard University Press, 1975).

37. Ernest Gellner, *Nations and Nationalism* (Ithaca, NY: Cornell University Press, 2008).

38. Benedict Anderson, *Imagined Communities: Reflections on the Origin and Spread of Nationalism* (London: Verso, 2006).

39. Jacqueline Stevens, *Reproducing the State* (Princeton, NJ: Princeton University Press, 1999).

40. Elie Kedourie, *Nationalism* (Oxford, UK: Blackwell,1993).

41. On this important point, see chapter 3 of Stevens, *Reproducing the State*. Stevens puts the larger point quite well in a later work when she writes that "nations that reproduce by securing membership through carefully codified kinship rules are not protecting discrete lines of genetic descent but the *myth* of this." See *States without Nations: Citizenship for Mortals* (New York: Columbia University Press, 2011), 76.

42. Balibar, "Racism and Nationalism," 53.

43. Ibid., 58.

44. "The Nation Form: History and Ideology," 102ff; Stevens, *Reproducing the State*.

45. See, for example, Gellner, *Nations and Nationalism*, 109ff. Cf. Anderson, *Imagined Communities: Reflections on the Origin and Spread of Nationalism*, 49.

46. For another take on the connection between nationalism, gender, and race, see the last chapter of Anne McClintock, *Imperial Leather: Race, Gender, and Sexuality in the Colonial Conquest* (London: Routledge, 2013).

47. On this point, see Fernand Braudel, *Civilization and Capitalism, Volume 3: 15th–18th Century: The Perspective of the World* (Los Angeles: University of California Press, 1982), 92–116; Immanuel Wallerstein, *The Modern World-System I: Capitalist Agriculture and the Origins of the European World-Economy in the Sixteenth Century* (Los Angeles: University of California Press, 2011), 164–300.

48. *TSMR*, 27–28, translation modified and emphasis mine.

49. Cf. Robert Brandom, *Making It Explicit: Reasoning, Representing, and Discursive Commitment* (Cambridge, MA: Harvard University Press, 1994), 19.

50. See Henri Bergson, *Creative Evolution*, trans. Arthur Mitchell (Mineola, NY: Dover, 1998). As Bergson puts it: "From this point of view obligation loses its specific character. *It ranks among the most general phenomena of life*" (*TSMR*, 20, emphasis mine). For Bergson, all human functions and faculties, including reason, and thereby normativity, originate from life, itself a complex concept, but one that is natural and indeterminable. On this point, see especially chapter 4 of Frédéric Worms, *Bergson Ou Les Deux Sens De La Vie* (Paris: Presses Universitaires de France, 2004). Cf. John Protevi and Keith Ansell-Pearson, "Naturalism in the Continental Tradition," in *The Blackwell Companion to Naturalism*, ed. Kelly James Clark (Malden, MA: Blackwell, 2016), 40.

51. *TSMR*, 28.

52. On this point, cf. Paola Marrati, "Mysticism and the Open Society: Foundations of Bersgonian Politics," in *Political Theologies: Public Religions in a Post-Secular World*, ed. Hent de Vries and Lawrence Sullivan (New York: Fordham University Press, 2006), 592–97.

53. With John McDowell, we might say habit is thereby a bit of "second nature." See John McDowell, *Mind and World* (Cambridge, MA: Harvard University Press, 1996).

54. *TSMR*, 76, emphasis added.

55. See especially Bergson's suggestion that even Robinson Crusoe exists fundamentally in society, "because his memory and his imagination live on what society has *implanted* in them" (*TSMR*, 7, emphasis mine).

56. *TSMR*, 94.

57. Michael O. Hardimon, *Hegel's Social Philosophy: The Project of Reconciliation* (Cambridge, MA: Cambridge University Press, 1994), 234. Cf. G. W. F. Hegel,

Elements of the Philosophy of Right (Cambridge, UK: Cambridge University Press, 1991), §324. This, however, is *not* to imply that Hegel's views of war somehow justify or promote totalitarianism or totalitarian projects. On this point, see Shlomo Avineri, "The Problem of War in Hegel's Thought," in *The Hegel Myths and Legends*, ed. Jon Stewart (Evanston, IL: Northwestern University Press, 1996).

58. *TSMR*, 31, emphasis added. For a concise and cogent discussion of the "problem" that war serves philosophically for Bergson, see the first chapter of Lefebvre, *Human Rights as a Way of Life: On Bergson's Political Philosophy*.

59. Frédéric Worms, "The Closed and the Open in *the Two Sources of Morality and Religion: A Distinction That Changes Everything*," in *Bergson, Politics, and Religion*, ed. Alexandre Lefebvre and Melanie White (Durham, NC: Duke University Press, 2012), 30, 31.

60. *TSMR*, 84–101.

61. Ibid., 38, emphasis added.

62. Bergson, *Creative Evolution*. The significance of this lack of determination has been explored in Marrati, "Mysticism and the Open Society: Foundations of Bersgonian Politics," 600ff.

63. *TSMR*, 32–33.

64. Lefebvre, *Human Rights as a Way of Life: On Bergson's Political Philosophy*, 23.

65. Steven Pinker, *The Better Angels of Our Nature: Why Violence Has Declined* (New York: Viking Press, 2011).

66. Pinker's definition of violence, as exactly excluding the forms of psychological violence diagnosed by critical theorists, is likely deficient.

67. For an example, see the discussion of how God could have created a world full of beings who *choose* the good in every situation (in other words, there is no logical impossibility in *choosing* the good every single time one's confronted with a choice between good/evil). See John L. Mackie, "Evil and Omnipotence," *Mind* 64 (1955): 209ff.

68. *TSMR*, 84, emphasis mine.

69. *TSMR*, 32, emphasis mine.

70. *TSMR*, 28, translation modified and emphasis added.

71. I have drawn an analogy between Bergson's and Cavell's views of language in another context. See Martin Shuster, "Humor as an Optics: Bergson and the Ethics of Humor," *Hypatia* 28, no. 3 (2013).

72. Stanley Cavell, *The Claim of Reason: Wittgenstein, Skepticism, Morality, and Tragedy* (Oxford, UK: Oxford University Press, 1979), 20. Emphasis mine. I have explored this point in more detail in Martin Shuster, "Nothing to Know: The Epistemology of Moral Perfectionism in Adorno and Cavell," *Idealistic Studies* 44, no. 1 (2015).

73. Cavell, *The Claim of Reason: Wittgenstein, Skepticism, Morality, and Tragedy*, 20. Emphasis mine.

74. Ibid.

75. For an exploration of this point, see Martin Shuster, "On the Ethical Basis of Language: Some Themes in Davidson, Cavell, and Levinas," *Journal for Cultural and Religious Theory* 14, no. 2 (2015).

76. See Martin Shuster, "Loneliness and Language: Arendt, Cavell, and Modernity," *International Journal of Philosophical Studies* 20, no. 4 (2012).

77. This raises a host of additional questions that are far beyond the scope of this chapter. For example, it just is a fact that there may exist political structures (say, totalitarianism, as Hannah Arendt and George Orwell each forcefully explore) that may in fact prohibit outright even the most basic operations; similarly, there may be economic and social structures (say, the culture industry) that equally warp the functions of language to the point of impossibility.

78. *TSMR*, 32.

79. Ibid., This is then to stress that if we are to speak of "human rights," it must only be in the "ethical" sense proposed in Lefebvre, *Human Rights as a Way of Life: On Bergson's Political Philosophy*, 133ff. It is exactly to oppose the sort of project outlined in Hannibal Travis, *Genocide, Ethnonationalism, and the United Nations: Exploring the Causes of Mass Killing since 1945* (London: Routledge, 2013).

80. At a high enough altitude, the problem of the "general will"—a fixture in political philosophy since the modern period is simply a version of this issue: any state must speak for its citizens, but such speech, in addition to being plagued by the (normative possibility of) disagreement inherent to any speech, is also complicated by the fact of human plurality and multiplicity in the political realm, an issue Hannah Arendt explicitly engaged in her work.

Chapter 3

The Politics of Sympathy in Bergson's *The Two Sources of Morality and Religion*

MELANIE WHITE

At first glance, the concept of sympathy does not appear to play a significant role in Henri Bergson's last great work *The Two Sources of Morality and Religion* (1932).[1] The word appears occasionally and when it does, it expresses a particular experience of social life, namely the feeling of mutual solidarity between members of a social group. Now, this notion of sympathy is common enough: it captures something of the emotional connection felt by those who share similar cultural experiences, traditions, and attitudes. Sympathy expresses the feeling of belonging to a particular group, and its absence is connected to feelings of not belonging. In short, sympathy operates on an affective register that simultaneously includes (those who share the same history, ethnicity, and/or sociopolitical views and values) and excludes (those who have a different heritage or cultural background, or those who do not share the sensibility of the prevailing social group). From this vantage, sympathy informs solidarity projects that run the gamut from what Sally Scholz terms "parasitical" solidarity (which involves a feeling of connection, and consequently, a high degree of sympathy for someone in difficult circumstances, but which ultimately lacks moral obligation) to "political" solidarity (which is based on moral relationships of care and hope for those who have a direct experience of suffering or who share something in common with distant others).[2]

The purpose of this chapter is to argue that Bergson's *The Two Sources*, despite its scant mention of sympathy, is a thoughtful reflection on the limitations and possibilities of sympathy to address systemic forms of racism and exclusion.[3] In this chapter, I develop two distinct notions of sympathy from *The Two Sources*: a *natural sympathy* and a *complete sympathy*. This distinction is inspired by the philosophical problem underlying *The Two Sources*, namely, the question of the origins of morality and religion. Bergson's answer to this question is "life," but as we go on to discover, life expresses itself as two fundamental tendencies: a "closed" tendency and an "open" tendency. The meaning of the closed tendency draws on its ordinary meaning as that which is bounded and exclusive. From the vantage of social life, the closed tendency reflects a basic attitude of social life toward self-preservation, reproduction, and stability. Bergson uses the "closed society" to express society's tendencies toward exclusion, group solidarity, and war. The open tendency, in contrast, is characterized by indeterminacy and inclusivity. When considered from the perspective of human societies, the open tendency reflects an attitude of continuous change *and* a spirit of generosity (of love and care) that reaches beyond the borders of the social group. Bergson characterizes this tendency as that of an "open society."

What I call natural sympathy is formed at the nexus of belonging and boundary-making, and occupies part of the affective register of Bergson's closed society. For just as sympathy unites and divides, so too does the closed society. Indeed, sympathy would seem to encompass affective tendencies associated with the closed society: the concept captures the natural feelings—of love, pain, sorrow, concern, care—that we have for members of our family, our city, and our country. In what follows, I develop this idea of a natural sympathy as consonant with Bergson's description of the closed society. Next, I identify another kind of sympathy at work in *The Two Sources*, one that goes beyond the characteristic *us-them* orientation of closed societies. Readers familiar with Bergson's argument in *The Two Sources* will correctly anticipate that it is found in Bergson's understanding of the open society. The open society designates the attitude of those rare individuals who have broken free from the pressures, constraints, and exclusions of the closed society; Bergson argues that they alone have the capacity to love without object, boundary, or division. He considers such people mystics. I want to argue that they foster another form of sympathy that designates the social relation that pulls or attracts others into the mystic embrace. I call this form of sympathy a "complete sympathy," to distinguish it from the natural sympathy of the closed society. Ultimately, I wish to argue that the idea of a complete sympathy helps us to understand the *sociality* of the open society (as necessarily distinct from, but also dependent on, the closed society).

The distinction between natural sympathy and complete sympathy contributes to recent scholarship on the social and political implications of Bergson's thought.[4] It encourages us to reflect on what is understood by calls for sympathy in advocating for a more inclusive society. In addition, it helps us to consider how Bergson's thinking might contribute practically to ameliorating what we might call the "general politics of exclusion" of our contemporary moment. These contributions are perhaps most apparent when we weigh Bergson's insights against more recent work that seeks to develop sympathy through "mutual recognition"[5] or by "creating capabilities"[6] to resolve problems of exclusion. Such work reflects a widely held view that exclusion and processes of othering through race, gender, sexuality, class, and otherwise can ultimately be eradicated.

Bergson's argument complicates this received wisdom. Although specific experiences of racism, sexism, homophobia, xenophobia, imperialism, and neocolonialism can be challenged, criticized, and argued against, he argues that the general tendency toward exclusion and othering is fundamental to social life. In other words, the organization of social life functions at the intersection of boundary and belonging: some are included while others are excluded. Bergson argues that this is a basic, seemingly *natural* tendency of all social relations. And yet, as we will see, what distinguishes the sociality of human beings from other social beings is that this tendency to exclude is, in principle at least, not altogether necessary.

Bergson's contribution therefore consists in reconfiguring the problem of exclusion. Once we acknowledge the presence of a natural tendency toward exclusion, it forces us to adjust our expectations as well as our practical efforts. It helps us to understand how sympathy sometimes reinforces exclusion and racism in our societies. It shifts our attention away from irresolvable problems (such as thinking that it is possible to eliminate all forms of social exclusion once and for all), toward other more manageable ones (such as identifying concrete instances of racism and xenophobia and challenging them, along with finding ways to move beyond our own personal desires to care for, or rather exhibit sympathy for, the world in general). To put Bergson's lesson in the terms presented by this chapter, we must accept the presence of natural sympathies that are ultimately ineradicable, and equally, we must resist them by seeking out opportunities to cultivate a more complete sympathy.

To make this argument, my discussion follows Bergson's in *The Two Sources* and proceeds in three parts. First, I draw out the idea of natural sympathy from Bergson's depiction of the closed society, and then I develop the idea of a complete sympathy in relation to the open society. I conclude with some reflections on the practical implications for what it means to cultivate a "lived sympathy."

Natural Sympathy

The word *sympathy* has a long history. The etymology of the French *sympathie* derives from the Ancient Greek, *sumpátheia* (*sún*: with together; *pathos*: suffering), as does the English version *sympathy*. If we consult the *Dictionnaire de l'Académie française*, current at the time Bergson published *The Two Sources*, *sympathie* is defined as both a "fellow-feeling" and a "natural or instinctive inclination that attracts people together."[7] Certainly Bergson would not be the first to see the potential for sympathy to capture something of the social and moral relations we have with others. One only need recall David Hume's commitment to the idea of "a tender sympathy with others" as the basis of moral life,[8] or Adam Smith's use of sympathy as the fellow-feeling that grounds social order.[9] But if we keep in mind Bergson's admission that he considered his last book a sociological book,[10] it is helpful to emphasize the sociological inflections of the word. With Auguste Comte—widely considered to have invented the neologism *sociology*—we find a robust commitment to sympathy as the basis of his positive philosophy.[11] Comte's particular brand of positivism consists in a primary commitment to concrete and established facts; it is this commitment that allows him to produce an objective synthesis of human feelings and actions. For Comte, social feeling—and sympathy in particular—is the central focus of this synthesis and, consequently, the basis of his positive morality.[12]

Now, much could be said about the conversation Bergson has with Comte in *The Two Sources*, but for the moment, we will simply emphasize their shared methodological commitment to the primacy of facts, especially those established by the laws of nature. While Comte uses facts as the basis for his utopian vision of the religion of humanity, Bergson exhibits what Vladimir Jankélévitch has termed a "superior positivism": he confines himself strictly to experience,[13] for "nothing can resist facts."[14] But what facts can we glean from experience that will guide us in understanding sympathy?

When we think about sympathy, in the first instance, Bergson observes that "we are fond of saying that the apprenticeship to civic virtue is served in the family, and that in the same way, from holding our country dear, we learn to love mankind [*sic*]. Our sympathies are supposed to broaden out in an unbroken progression, to expand while remaining identical, and to end by embracing all humanity."[15] Here, sympathy is associated with the commonsense idea that our feelings of attachment for our families and nation extend to the rest of humanity in a continuous, unbroken progression. Sympathy would seem to express the essence of fellow-feeling. As Bergson points out, however, this idea contains some common intellectual errors. First, the emphasis on a progressive evolution that proceeds by expanding our affection for larger and larger groups is not grounded in experience. It is an error of sheer intellectualism: "This is *a priori* reasoning, the result of a purely intellectualist conception of the soul. We observe that the three groups to which we can attach ourselves comprise an increasing number of people, and we conclude that a progressive expansion of feeling keeps pace with the increasing size of the object we love."[16] In truth, the reality is that the feelings we have for family and country are fundamentally different from those associated with the love of humanity. The former inspires a desire to protect and defend, whereas the latter requires an attitude capable of love without boundary or attachment.

Bergson seeks to understand the source of our tendency to protect and defend our social groups. He turns to experience and trains his attention on the experience of war. He observes that it is commonplace for society to say "that the duties it defines are indeed, in principle duties towards humanity, but that under exceptional circumstances, regrettably unavoidable, they are for the time being inapplicable."[17] Such is the power of war to legitimate killing and other forms of violence. Bergson argues that the tension between principle and practice cannot be resolved by appeal to a single moral principle, since they clearly point to fundamentally different moral ideals. Bergson says that the very presence of this tension implies that there must be another principle, another source of moral inspiration from which we can draw. But before we might consider this possibility, Bergson must concentrate on the facts at hand. War is a basic fact and one that must be explained: Why is it such a constant feature of our experience? Does the answer have anything to do with the fact that we are so often defensive, judgmental, and parochial?

Bergson offers an explanation that relies, in the first instance, on argument by analogy and, in the second, on the presence of an original human nature. I want to use these arguments as the basis for developing the idea of a "natural sympathy." Typically, sympathy consists in the feeling of being closely united; it symbolizes closeness, intimacy, and connection. It highlights a feeling of being in relation *together*. Examples range from growing up in a closely knit family, to ethnic enclaves in particular neighborhoods (such as Hasidic Jewish enclaves in Brooklyn), to the impassioned defense of *Laïcité* in France. The term *closeness* carries with it a certain ambiguity that is instructive. It implies intimacy and togetherness (as in the sense of a "close friendship"), but it also conveys the quality of confinement (as in the sense of shutting down, or of closing the door). To be united then, is at once to be both intimate and confined. It is this double meaning that helps us to graft the idea of sympathy onto Bergson's conception of the closed society. I want to suggest that if group members are closely united, they rely on a sympathetic feeling that also ensures a sense of closure between groups. In short, sympathy captures precisely the *feeling* of unity and defensiveness that Bergson ascribes to the closed society. Sympathy (along with the closure that it implies) conditions a virtual hostility toward others such that one must always "be prepared for attack or defence."[18]

Now, let us turn to Bergson's explanation for the persistence of war by considering his argument by analogy to deepen these initial reflections. He begins by noting the resemblance between laws of nature with their origin in biology and social laws with their origin in society. Biological laws condition societies such as those of bees and ants whereas social laws are the province of human societies. Yet, both kinds of society appear to be subject to necessity. There is a basic similarity, to be sure, but Bergson repeatedly cautions against taking the analogy too far. Why? He says that it is undeniable that necessity is a law of nature, but the command of society is structured by rules and laws that—although compelling—are not strictly necessary. This difference is absolutely crucial. For what distinguishes animal societies from human societies is that individuals in human societies can break rules, challenge laws, and breach conventions, whereas the members of animal societies cannot. Consequently, Bergson observes that "in a hive or an ant-hill the individual is riveted to his task by his structure, and the organization is relatively invariable, whereas the human community is variable in form, open to every kind of progress."[19]

Bergson finds our capacity to break free from the strictures of society a remarkable fact. And yet, equally remarkable is the fact that we rarely do so. The reason is simple—it is much easier to comply! We accept the discipline of society out of habit, and we fulfill our obligations without complaint or resistance. It is this fact that allows Bergson to establish a functional similarity between animal societies and human societies: "in the former each rule is laid down by nature, and is necessary: whereas in the latter only one thing is natural, the necessity of a rule."[20] In other words, we conform to social rules *as if* they were necessary. Bergson draws on this analogy to argue that instinctive societies are the counterpart of human societies. But to make the analogy work, we must distinguish between natural tendencies and the acquisitions of history. The former are natural: they are biological, relatively fixed, and therefore, incapable of change. The latter are products of invention and intelligence and function as the repositories of shared experience. They are susceptible to change, spurred on by the intelligence, and are open to every kind of transformation.[21] To explain why we conform to social rules, even when we are capable of change, Bergson argues that we must clear away the accretions of habit and custom to determine what "obligation *would have been* if human society had been instinctive instead of intelligent."[22] Only by doing so will we understand why we comply *as if* we were compelled by necessity.

Dispensing with acquired knowledge helps us to bring into relief a natural tendency that Bergson calls the habit to make habits. He defines habit as an activity that may start out as intelligent but progresses toward an imitation of instinct. He observes that "the most powerful habit, the habit that is made up of the accumulated force of all the elementary social habits is necessarily the one which best imitates instinct."[23] This habit of contracting habits is not only a condition for society, but exercises a force that is analogous to instinct in terms of intensity and regularity. It forms what Bergson calls the "totality of obligation" or "obligation in general,"[24] and exerts a pressure on each member of society that ultimately ensures each part maintains the shape of the whole.[25]

The idea of a natural sympathy begins to take shape at this point. In order to be successful, that is, in order to determine social behavior, the force of obligation must be felt. Generally, we come to accept the force of this pressure as an expression of what we feel our own desires to be. To help us appreciate the link between sympathy and obligation, it is interesting to consider the meaning of *obligation*: it involves a "binding together" that derives from the Latin root *lig* (to bind, tie, fasten). Here, we might also recall that sympathy also has its roots in "togetherness." If we place both words alongside one another, we see that even though the feeling of obligation is not precisely one of necessity, since it expresses the solidarity of a group being held together, the individual *feels* a compulsion *as if* it were necessity. Can we not see that the feeling of obligation is reinforced by the idea of a fellow-feeling? Admittedly, the feeling of sympathy is implicit. Yet, Bergson gestures to it again when he reflects on the pleasure of fulfilling our obligations to one another. Indeed, he seems to channel the spirit of his contemporary, Émile Durkheim, who observes that performing his duties as a brother, husband, and citizen hardly feels like coercion, since he seemingly conforms to them of his own free will.[26] For Durkheim, as for Bergson here, fulfilling these obligations is a source of satisfaction that is associated with well-being. To this end, Bergson remarks, "the consciousness of these pure obligations, assuming they were all fulfilled would be a state of individual and social well-being similar to that which accompanies the normal working of life. It would resemble pleasure rather than joy."[27] Here, the idea of sympathy expresses the pleasure of belonging and reinforces our general feelings of social satisfaction.

Now, of course, the very idea of belonging implies that some individuals are *in* and some are *out*. One recent attempt to explain the natural origins of our feeling of belonging is Joshua Greene's *Moral Tribes* (2013). Greene combines utilitarianism and evolutionary theory to argue that feelings of love and morality are biological mechanisms that ensure cooperation and reproduction of group members. In short, he argues that these biological mechanisms inscribe divisions between groups. As he puts it, "Insofar as morality is a biological adaptation, it evolved not only as a device for putting Us ahead of Me, but as a device for putting Us ahead of Them."[28] In many ways, Bergson seemingly anticipates this sort of argument. For Bergson, not only are natural societies *close* with one another, they are *closed* to others. In other words, they "include at any moment a certain number of individuals, and exclude others."[29] The idea of a natural sympathy can therefore help us to explain why we might feel hatred or prejudice toward others. First, natural sympathy reinforces our obligations to one another: we *feel* the satisfaction that comes from supporting those who are close to us, and we *feel* the desire to protect them. Put slightly differently, we feel sympathy for those that share similar customs, values, and experiences, and we feel the desire to defend them when we are threatened. Bergson's innovation, if we could put it that way, is to claim that this is a natural, ineradicable tendency. Second, the presence of a natural sympathy with its inclusions and exclusions helps to explain why it is not possible for our sympathies to broaden out in an unbroken progression from family to city to country to humanity. This is because the social groupings of the family and society are conditioned by nature; in other words, we depend on them in order to survive. But humanity as a social group is not natural in the same way: it is not a requirement of nature that our sociality be defined in terms of humanity. Rather, humanity has emerged as an ideal that has its roots in a particular worldview. The decision to cultivate humanity as a particular ideal requires us to forgo our natural sympathies and to resist some (but perhaps not all) of our social obligations. In short, it would demand a not insignificant effort to dispense with those general pleasures and satisfactions that are obtained through the particularlity of feeling that we belong. No wonder exclusion and racism persist!

Now let us consider Bergson's commitment to an original human nature as another explanation for the persistence of war, and also as a means of deepening our understanding of natural sympathy. So far, we have posited the idea of a natural sympathy as a fellow-feeling that binds individuals together. Insofar as a feeling of kinship persists, it fosters a defensive attitude toward others. To reach this idea, we cleared away the acquisitions of culture and knowledge to reach obligation in general. Bergson now takes this point in a new direction. He observes that when we offer up psychological explanations for human experience, we tend to focus on the cultivated or the acquired at the expense of the natural. Just as we tend to ignore, and even refuse, our natural tendencies toward closure in our social explanations of the persistence of war, our psychological explanations are similarly inadequate. To this end he remarks, "Does not the difficulty lie precisely in the fact that our psychology is not sufficiently concerned with subdivision of its subject in accordance with the lines laid down by nature?"[30] Accordingly, if we accept that the *social* ground of obligation is natural, then it stands to reason that a psychological explanation must consist in natural *individual* instincts that foster or encourage fellow-feeling. But again, these instincts must not be confused with the acquired habits forged through communal living. They are what human nature *would have been* before the overlay of acquired knowledge and tradition.[31]

There are two basic features of this instinct, which Bergson also calls our "original nature" or "natural tendency." The first is a psychical dimorphism that engenders in each of us the capacity to obey and the capacity to command. Given the foregoing, it is no wonder that Bergson observes that the tendency to obey predominates in most people.[32] The second is a predisposition to conflict that Bergson calls a "war-instinct." It is organized by discipline, protection, and hatred—all of which are expressions of closure (derived, by implication, from the fellow-feeling of sympathy). My discussion focuses on this second aspect of this natural instinct.

Bergson's commitment to the idea of a primordial human nature is based in part on an argument he makes in *Creative Evolution* (1907). There he observes the evolution of animal life on two main lines, namely, the arthropods and the vertebrates. Recall that the instinct of insects is found at the end of the former, and the intelligence of humans at the end of the latter. Instinct and intelligence are means by which insects and humans transform raw matter.[33] Instinct relies on tools that form part of the body that uses it, to which corresponds a knowledge of how to use it. In contrast, intelligence, at its origins, is the faculty of "manufacturing artificial objects, especially tools to make tools, and of indefinitely varying the manufacture."[34] The first are internal to the body, and are "supplied by nature and hence immutable"; the second are external to the body, and are "varied and unforeseen."[35]

Rehearsing this argument allows us to appreciate Bergson's explanation for the human tendency to war. Since we need tools in order to survive, and because they are by necessity external to us, the tools that we manufacture engender claims to ownership—a fact that in turn produces inevitable conflicts over who owns what. We now have Bergson's explanation for the origin of war: "No matter the thing taken, the motive adduced: the origin of war is ownership, individual or collective, and since humanity is predestined to ownership by its structure, war is natural. So strong, indeed, is the war instinct, that it is the first to appear when we scratch below the surface of civilization in search of nature."[36] Threats to ownership, to tools, to inventions and items of manufacture all contribute to the legitimation of the war instinct. This fact, combined with our mutual obligations to one another and the feeling of sympathy that reinforces them, generates the need to defend against contests over ownership (land, tools, and territory)[37] and to protect those whom we love (our families, our cities, and our countries).[38]

So far, I have sought to demonstrate that Bergson's argument by analogy and his defense of an original human nature is enhanced by the idea of a natural fellow-feeling that fosters "a cunningly woven veil of ignorance, preconceptions and prejudices."[39] This idea of sympathy reinforces Bergson's account of natural obligation in the closed society: "The closed society is that whose members hold together, caring nothing for the rest of humanity, on the alert for attack or defense, bound, in fact, to a perpetual readiness for battle."[40] Here we might recall the etymological roots of *pathos* (suffering) in sympathy, for is it not possible that the natural sympathy that binds us together is also what enables us to accept and legitimate the suffering of others in times of war?

This idea of a natural sympathy stands in sharp contrast to the common idea that sympathy can form the basis of a mutual recognition of the other.[41] One representative example of this latter conception of sympathy is found in Lynn Hunt's *Inventing Human Rights* (2007). Hunt argues that contemporary human rights discourse is directly related to the cultivation of a deep and robust sympathy that extends beyond the immediate confines of one's own group. She argues that sympathy emerged as a common solution to the privileging of individual rights in the eighteenth century. Accordingly, it was through the work of Scottish philosophers such as Francis Hutcheson that the idea of sympathy provided the spark of morality:

> For Francis Hutcheson, sympathy was a kind of sense, a moral faculty. More noble than sight or hearing, senses shared with animals, but less noble than conscience, sympathy or fellow feeling made social life possible. By the power of human nature, prior to any reasoning, sympathy acted like a kind of social gravitational force to bring people outside of themselves. Sympathy ensured that happiness could not be defined by self-satisfaction alone.[42]

For Hunt, it is this kind of community-building sensibility that generates the commitment to rights that transcend nation and circumstance. Indeed, much of her book attempts to provide evidence for the extension of universal rights as a series of ever-widening inclusions after the French Declaration of the Rights of Man and Citizen in 1789. In short, it is through a broadening of sympathy that human rights not only come into being, but increasingly have practical effect. Hunt's account is clearly at odds with Bergson's account of natural sympathy. For as Alexandre Lefebvre observes, Hunt's argument depends on a commitment to the idea that sympathy for other people can radiate out indefinitely—from family, to nation, to humanity writ large. The difficulty for Bergson, however, as Lefebvre puts it, is that closed morality "is not infinitely extendable. It has limits, biologically built-in limits, and to turn a blind eye to these is catastrophic for the theory and practice of human rights."[43]

For Lefebvre and for me, the very fact that human societies have acquired habits and sensibilities over time through knowledge and education warrants explanation. We are not now a society direct from nature. And certainly the presence of ideas about human rights, cosmopolitanism, and multiculturalism, their critiques aside, are evidence of our capacity to change. But to concentrate on these apparent successes at the expense of Bergson's natural sympathy risks misunderstanding the origins of racism and exclusion. The idea of natural sympathy helps us to see that the feeling of belonging is grounded in the exclusionary tendency of closed groups. It helps us to see that the fellow-feeling associated with a particular group cannot be extended to include the whole of humanity. In other words, we cannot expect the sympathy for our own particular groups or attachments to form the basis of a broader, inclusive more global attachment to others. This is one of Bergson's basic lessons for us. For just as war is an expression of sympathetic fellow-feeling, so too is racism. Both war and racism therefore share similar roots, insofar as they are both consequences of a robust and unquestioned natural sympathy.

Complete Sympathy

We might well ask if things are bound to follow their natural course.[44] If so, this paints a pretty grim portrait of human potential. Bergson himself asks whether we must we live in fear, or if we may live in hope?[45] Now, *The Two Sources* is not the only time that Bergson raises such far-reaching questions. Recall the high pitch of his fears about the debasement of morality in *The Meaning of the War* (1915), written during the height of the Great War.[46] The resonance between the questions posed in that text and those posed by *The Two Sources* is striking in retrospect. To them, we might add some of our own: Is there anything more to be said about sympathy? Must it always lead to exclusion? Is it always, by necessity, the source of racism and xenophobia? These questions are addressed through my claim that Bergson rests his hope in part on the possibility of something I call a "complete sympathy." Again, it is important to note that Bergson does not explicitly present the idea in *The Two Sources*, for just as natural sympathy was found latent in his conception of the closed society, so too, is complete sympathy buried in his idea of the open society. Recall that the open society reflects an attitude of continuous change *and* a spirit of generosity (of love and care) that reaches beyond the borders of the social group. It simultaneously complements and contrasts the tendency of the closed society toward exclusion and group solidarity. To uncover this "complete sympathy," my discussion proceeds in two parts. First, I will briefly consider the role of the mystic in forming what Bergson has called "open societies." My aim is to establish the presence of a social relation that differs in kind from the natural sociality of closed societies. Second, I will consider the idea of a complete sympathy as that which enables mystics to pull others in their wake. This will allow me to elaborate the idea of a "lived sympathy" in my conclusion. We begin, as we did in our first discussion, by considering the facts. In short, we return to experience.

Just as each of us has experienced the pleasure of belonging, many of us have had the experience of a remarkable individual who has inspired us (out of principle, deeply felt conviction, admiration, or otherwise) to resist social conventions, to speak out against oppression, and to challenge prevailing wisdom. Bergson calls these extraordinary individuals "heroes" or "mystics": they are individuals who have the capacity to overcome the limitations imposed on the species by its material nature.[47] In our contemporary moment, we only need to bring to mind the efforts of Liu Xiaobo, who took part in the student protests of Tiananmen Square in 1989 and spent much of his life fighting for a more open and democratic China; or alternatively, Kailash Satyarthi and Malala Yousafzai, who struggled in India and Pakistan, respectively, for the right of all children to an education. To Bergson, such extraordinary individuals do not derive their strength from reason or habit, still less from the defensive feelings that stem from natural sympathy. Their force comes from a deeper moral source, one that embraces all of humanity.[48] As we have seen, it is not possible to love humanity as an extension of the way that we love our families or other social groups. The love of humanity is acquired—it must be cultivated, developed, and ultimately, learned. This is what makes human beings unique for Bergson. We have the capacity to love without boundary or attachment, and it is this capacity that distinguishes human sociality from nonhuman social life. To put it bluntly: the ability to cultivate an open society is only available to humanity.

What sets mystics apart is that they are able to access the source of an emotion that is nothing less than the "vital impetus" of life, an impetus that Bergson describes variously as "joy of joy" or "love of love."[49] This impetus is not, therefore, a joy *in* friendship, or a love *for* family. For here, we must be mindful that the prepositions *in* and *for* designate particular objects, and insofar as they express a particular attachment, they inevitably return us to the source of our natural inclinations. Whether we use the "joy of joy" or the "love of love" to describe this impetus, Bergson's emphasis on the preposition *of* designates a grounding in the principle of the thing, in this case the feeling. Such a principle is broader and wider than the feeling itself. The idea allows Bergson to detect the vital impetus (as principle, as ground, as spirit) in the mystic capacity to detach from the particular (love for family) and attach to the general (love in the principle that conditions this love). Elsewhere, Bergson describes life as a striving, as an effort of creation, of the capacity to transform and make different.[50] In *The Two Sources*, Bergson associates this striving, this desire for action, with the mystic: "Its attachment to life would henceforth be its inseparability from this principle, joy in joy, love of that which is all love."[51] We might say then, that mystic experience is to be defined by its relation to the vital impetus, one that makes the shift from closed attachments to love without boundary possible.

What interests me in this discussion is less the experience of pure mysticism (for Bergson acknowledges that it is extremely rare), but rather how mysticism engenders a social relation that distinguishes itself from the natural fellow-feeling of the closed society. In what does this sociality consist? Bergson gives some clues in the sentences that immediately follow the passage cited above. He says that the mystic "would give itself to society, but to a society comprising all humanity, loved in the love of the principle underlying it."[52] The mystic, having discovered another source of moral feeling (in God or otherwise), finds in the love of love a force powerful enough to resist the impulsion of nature. This love is no longer *of* the closed society. But this does not mean that the mystic is no longer *of* society for two reasons. First, society conditions the possibility of the mystic; and second, the mystic may inspire others to adopt this attitude of openness. The society of the mystic is one that is in the process of transforming itself—it is therefore useful to distinguish between the society of humanity (open) and a society of humans (closed).[53] It is by means of an attitude that opens oneself to others that enables us to see beyond the strictures and exclusions of the closed society.

The idea of giving or of passing on the mystic experience gives us a glimpse, ever so faintly, of the possibility of a deeper source of sympathy, one that is complementary, but different in kind to the one found in nature. Bergson gestures to the idea when he observes "That a soul thus equipped for action would be more drawn to sympathize with other souls, and even with the whole of nature, might surprise us, if the relative immobility of the soul, revolving in a circle in an enclosed society, was not due precisely to the fact that nature has split humanity into a variety of individuals by the very act which constituted the human species."[54] There are two facets of Bergson's claim that are worth considering here. First, Bergson locates the origin of the mystic in the process by which nature simultaneously created the human species and, in so doing, split humanity into a variety of individuals. Mystics, like the rest of us, are conditioned by nature in that we are both living beings and social beings. (It is for this reason that Bergson says that the social underlies the vital.)[55] But because mystics can overcome the pressures of natural sociality, they are no longer held to any particular society. In effect, they replace their attachment to society in particular with an attachment to life in general. But this suggests the possibility of another sociality that allows the mystic to share, to give and to persist in giving without which a love of humanity would not be possible. Second, let us draw out on Bergson's observation that mystics would be *more drawn to sympathize* with other souls. For if only natural sympathy prevailed, wouldn't mystics be less drawn to sympathy? Put differently, if natural sympathy compels one to particular attachments, and by implication to the material comforts and pleasures of belonging to a group, the only way to account for the capacity of mystics to be more drawn to sympathize with others souls is if there is a deeper source of sympathy.

Let us call this deeper source of sympathy a "complete sympathy." How is it distinct from natural sympathy? We might use the language of closure to describe the centripetal force of natural sympathy as distinct from the centrifugal force of complete sympathy. We might also say that complete sympathy is a social relation that does not compel, oblige, or command as does natural fellow-feeling; nor does it close in on itself or seek to exclude. The best way to characterize the sociality of its relation is that it is a form of fellow-feeling that is *of* rather than *for*—that is, a feeling *of* humanity rather than a feeling *for* humanity. It expresses the quality of a pull or an attraction, the basis of which is a feeling *of* connection, rather than a feeling *for* a particular connection. Thus, we might say that complete sympathy is a form of sociality that consists in the sympathy of relation; it is this relation and the emotion that expresses the feeling *of* humanity that allows the mystic to "carry the rest of humanity with it."[56] The idea of complete sympathy helps us to better understand what Bergson means when he says that if mysticism is able to transform humanity, it can only do so "by passing on, from one man to another, slowly a part of itself."[57] Here, Bergson's language of "passing on" resonates with his earlier suggestion that the mystic "gives" to society—it captures the spirit of feeling that has been scrubbed of the constraint we might associate with natural sympathy. Both passing and giving imply the capacity to "receive," to smell the "perfume," to experience the "residue of emotion," and ultimately, to feel the "contagious influence" of the mystic.[58] These are undeniably social relations, albeit relations of sociality that differ profoundly from those experienced in the closed society. All these terms imply a social relation—of one to another. We might be tempted to call the sociality of the mystic a relation of call and response.[59] It expresses a sympathetic relation that pulls us away from the "already made" and, in the process of detaching, it attaches us to that which is being made.

Conclusion

How does this distinction between natural and complete sympathy help us practically? Just as the closed and open refer to tendencies that are not found in their pure form, so too does this observation extend to natural sympathy and complete sympathy. Our lived experience is composite, and consequently, so too is our experience of sympathy. We might say that we live with sympathy, even if we do not always live sympathetically. Thus, for Bergson, a lived sympathy is the confluence of feelings that draw us together and others that draw us out of ourselves.

The distinction between natural and complete sympathy helps us to see how Bergson reconfigures the problem of (the general tendency toward) exclusion, which manifests itself more specifically in, for example, racism, xenophobia, and imperialism. We see that the force of natural sympathy is such that it is not possible to eradicate exclusion once and for all. This is a fact of nature. We cannot simply extend our natural sympathy and expect to reach a love for humanity. As Bergson insists, "We cannot repeat too often that it is not by preaching the love of our neighbour that we can obtain it. It is not by expanding our narrower feelings that we can embrace humanity."[60] Once we accept this fact, and abide by it, then some problems disappear (such as thinking that we might be able to put an end to the possibility of exclusion or the persistence of war), and others emerge (such as finding ways to repress our exclusionary tendencies). Indeed, our natural tendencies cannot be eradicated; but in saying this, we do not need to give in to the feeling that war, racism, or other forms of hate are inevitable.

The first step is to face this truth. We may not be able to eradicate the natural tendencies that lead to war or racism once and for all, but equally, we must understand that neither war nor racism is inevitable. Both racism and war are functions of a sympathy derived from the natural solidarity associated with the feeling of belonging. Such sympathy is essentially a protective mechanism, which seek to enhance feelings of security and safety. But insofar as it constructs and reinforces boundaries between "us" and "them," natural sympathy is the source of both war and racism. Both are expressions of a defensive attitude toward an enemy, whether real or imagined. The second step is to acknowledge that the problem of sympathy is not just an intellectual or philosophical problem. It consists in a lived reality, one that stems from the experience of belonging and not belonging, of sympathy and suffering. Whatever problems we face, they must be posited in terms of experience, and in terms of experience, they are "progressively, and always partially solved."[61] Even though we are bound by our natural tendencies, we must commit to the truth that history is not necessity. We can change (some things) if we want to. Indeed, "There is no obstacle which cannot be broken down by wills sufficiently keyed up, if they deal with it in time."[62] We can learn by experience. We must try not to forget what we have learned; but, of course, we must always be mindful of the fact that it is not possible to overwrite our natural sympathy. Our experience can help us to be sensitive to those opportunities that can resist the press of our natural sympathies, and help us to respond to the call of the mystic. In short, we can try to find ways to detach from our natural sympathies now and then, and to try attach ourselves to a more complete sympathy. This is indeed where something resembling hope lies. As Bergson remarks, "Anyone who is thoroughly familiar with the language and literature of a people cannot be wholly its enemy."[63] For the experience of learning another language begins a process of breaking down the boundary fostered by that habitual tendency to love that which we already know. It forces us to encounter something different and, through the delight of learning something new, helps us to open ourselves up to something that reaches beyond our nature. For Bergson, I think, this is the starting point for a complete sympathy, one that offers the possibility for building solidarity between and across different groups.

Notes

1. Henri Bergson, *The Two Sources of Morality and Religion*, trans. R. Ashley Audra and Cloudesley Brereton (Notre Dame, IN: University of Notre Dame Press, 1977). Hereafter referred to as "*TSMR*."

2. Sally Scholz, *Political Solidarity* (University Park, PA: Pennsylvania State University Press, 2008), 47, 48, 79.

3. Bergson does however treat the idea of sympathy in *Creative Evolution* (1907), where he posits the idea of sympathy as a metaphysical explanation for

instinct. See Henri Bergson, *Creative Evolution*, trans. Arthur Mitchell (Mineola, NY: Dover, 1998), 176. For a discussion see David Lapoujade, "Intuition and Sympathy in Bergson," *Pli* 15 (2004): 1–17.

 4. See, for example, Alexandre Lefebvre, *Human Rights as a Way of Life: On Bergson's Political Philosophy* (Stanford, CA: Stanford University Press, 2013). See also Alexandre Lefebvre and Melanie White, *Bergson, Politics, and Religion* (Durham, NC: Duke University Press, 2012).

 5. Here are some classic examples of this tendency: Charles Taylor, "The Politics of Recognition," in *Multiculturalism: Examining the Politics of Recognition*, ed. Amy Gutmann (Princeton, NJ: Princeton University Press, 1992), 25–73; and Axel Honneth, *The Struggle for Recognition: The Moral Grammar of Social Conflicts* (Cambridge, MA: MIT Press, 1995). And more recently, see Nancy Fraser and Axel Honneth, *Redistribution or Recognition? A Political-Philosophical Exchange* (New York: Verso, 2003).

 6. See Martha C. Nussbaum, *Creating Capabilities: The Human Development Approach* (Cambridge, MA: Belknap Press, 2011).

 7. *Dictionnaire de l'Académie française*, 8th ed. (1932–35), accessed January 15, 2017, https://artfl-project.uchicago.edu/content/dictionnaires-dautrefois.

 8. David Hume, *An Enquiry Concerning the Principles of Morals* (Chicago: Open Court Publishing Co., 1912 [1751/1777]), 10.

 9. Adam Smith, *The Theory of Moral Sentiments*, 9th ed. (London: T. Cadell and W. Davies Publishers, 1801), 5. For a useful secondary discussion, see Fonna Forman-Barzilai, *Adam Smith and the Circles of Sympathy: Cosmopolitanism and Moral Theory* (Cambridge, MA: Cambridge University Press, 2010).

 10. Henri Bergson, "Bergson à P. Masson-Oursel, 8 septembre 1932," *Correspondances* (Paris: Presses Universitaires de France, 2002), 1387.

 11. And yet, as Jacques Guilhaumou has recently shown, the term *sociologie* was actually created by Emmanuel-Joseph Sieyès in 1780. Sieyès (1748–1836) was a member of the Catholic clergy and played a central role in the French Revolution of 1789 and the coup d'état that brought Napoleon Bonaparte to power in 1799. See Jacques Guilhaumou "Sieyès et le non-dit de la sociologie: du mot à la chose," *Revue d'histoire des sciences humaines, Naissance de la science sociale (1750–1850)* 15 (2006): 117–34.

 12. See Auguste Comte, *The Positive Philosophy of Auguste Comte*, vol. 1, trans. H. Martineau (London: John Chapman, 1853), 44–45; and Auguste Comte, *System of Positive Polity*, vol. 1 (London: Longmans, Green and Co., 1875 [1851]), 10, 11, 31, 74, and 76.

 13. *TSMR*, 112. See Vladimir Jankélévitch, *Henri Bergson*, trans. Nils F. Schott (Durham, NC: Duke University Press, 2015 [1959]), 157.

 14. Ibid., 109.

 15. Ibid., 32. This idea is exemplified by W. E. H. Lecky's statement that moral progress is an expansion of responsibility through the use of an ever-expanding

circle: "The question of morals must always be a question of proportion or degree. At one time the benevolent affections embrace merely the family, soon the circle expanding includes first a class, then a nation, then a coalition of nations, then all humanity, and finally its influence is felt in the dealings of man with the animal world. In each of these stages a standard is formed, different from that of the receding stage, but in each case the same tendency is recognized as a virtue." See W. E. H. Lecky, *History of European Morals: From Augustus to Charlemagne* (London: Longmans, Green and Co., 1913), 100–1.

16. *TSMR*, 32.
17. Ibid.
18. Ibid., 57.
19. Ibid., 27–28.
20. Ibid., 28.
21. Thus, Bergson acknowledges that our societies reflect the accumulation of an "enormous mass of knowledge and habits" that has been absorbed over the course of history. But of course such knowledge is not transmitted through the biological reproduction of our species. Indeed, there is no hereditary transmission of habit: "We have dwelt on the question of the transmissibility of acquired characteristics. It is highly improbable that a habit is ever transmitted; if this does occur it is owing to a combination of many favourable conditions so accidental that it will certainly not recur often enough to implant the habit in the species." *TSMR*, pp. 272 and 127.
22. *TSMR*, 28.
23. Ibid., 26.
24. Ibid., 27.
25. Ibid., 55.
26. See Émile Durkheim, *The Rules of Sociological Method* (New York: The Free Press, 1982 [1895]), 51.
27. *TSMR*, 51 and 58.
28. Joshua Greene, *Moral Tribes: Emotion, Reason, and the Gap between Us and Them* (London: Penguin, 2013), 24.
29. *TSMR*, 30.
30. Ibid., 107.
31. See Bergson's statement to this effect: "So, let us keep to ascertained facts and to the probabilities suggested by them: in our opinion, if you eliminated from the man of today what has been deposited in him by unceasing education, he would be found to be identical, or nearly so, with his remotest ancestor." *TSMR*, 273.
32. *TSMR*, 278.
33. *Creative Evolution*, 136; *TSMR*, 27.
34. *CE*, 139.
35. *TSMR*, 27.
36. Ibid., 284.
37. Ibid., 32.

38. Ibid., 33.
39. Ibid., 285.
40. Ibid., 266.
41. See, for instance, Martha C. Nussbaum, *Not for Profit: Why Democracy Needs the Humanities* (Princeton, NJ: Princeton University Press, 2010), 96; and Axel Honneth, *Reification: New Look at an Old Idea* (Oxford: Oxford University Press, 2008), 152.
42. Lynn Hunt, *Inventing Human Rights: A History* (New York: W. W. Norton, 2007), 65.
43. See Alexandre Lefebvre, "Human Rights and the Leap of Love," in *Journal of French and Francophone Philosophy* 24, no. 2 (2016): 21–40, 26; See also Alexandre Lefebvre, *Human Rights as a Way of Life: On Bergson's Political Philosophy* (Stanford: Stanford University Press, 2013).
44. *TSMR*, 287.
45. Ibid., 291.
46. Henri Bergson, *The Meaning of the War: Life and Matter in Conflict* (London: T. Fisher Unwin, 1915), 33.
47. *TSMR*, 220–21.
48. Ibid., 38.
49. Ibid., 212, 255.
50. See Henri Bergson. "Life and Consciousness" in *Mind-Energy: Lectures and Essays,* trans. H. Wilson Carr (Westport, CT: Greenwood, 1920), 35.
51. *TSMR*, 212.
52. Ibid.
53. Now, there is, of course, no such thing as a human society that is completely closed, nor one that is completely open—the closed and the open are pure tendencies of one and the same society.
54. *TSMR*, 52.
55. Ibid., 119.
56. Ibid., 52–53.
57. Ibid., 235.
58. Ibid., 50.
59. Ibid., 68.
60. Ibid., 53.
61. Ibid., 263.
62. Ibid., 293.
63. Ibid., 286.

Part II

Bergsonian Themes in the Négritude Movement

Chapter 4

Bergson, Senghor, and the Philosophical Foundations of Négritude

Intellect, Intuition, and Knowledge

Clevis Headley

This chapter focuses on Henri Bergson's major contribution to the development of Léopold Sédar Senghor's philosophy of Négritude. Being sensitive, however, to the charge of epistemological dependency, I am not arguing that Senghor merely mimicked Bergson's ideas. Nor am I claiming that Senghor supplied only experience while Bergson provided the theory, which enabled Senghor to impose form on his raw experience and, ultimately, articulate his conception of Négritude. It may seem that joining Bergson and Senghor is a paradigmatic instance of intellectual obfuscation because, after all, Bergson's philosophical interests include, among other things, mathematics, physics, and philosophy, and Senghor was a poet and politician, even if he flirted with philosophy. Early stages of befuddlement should evaporate when it becomes clear that Bergson's critical encounters with mathematics, physics, and philosophy took place within the French intellectual tradition, and more specifically, the French epistemological tradition. Senghor's formal intellectual training was within the French intellectual tradition; hence, he was indeed very familiar with Bergson's work. The surprise, if it is indeed one, is that Senghor was perceptive enough to have appreciated the intellectual value of Bergson's critique of some of the fundamental assumptions of Western thought. Senghor employed some of Bergson's insights to make the case for an African epistemology and ontology consistent with Bergson's advocacy for, among other things, intuition and duration. The generic strategy of the following chapter is as follows: I present a discussion of some of the core notions of Bergson's philosophy. After this presentation, I turn to discuss Senghor's conception of Négritude with the purpose of establishing the profound Bergsonian influence on his thinking.

Bergson in Context

As to be expected, there exists a conspicuous interpretative cluster of contested expositions of Bergson's philosophy. While some of these accounts of Bergson's philosophy are favorable, others are dismissive. These negative portrayals are ironically interesting not because of their accuracy, but because of the sheer absurdity of their caricatures of Bergson's thought. Bertrand Russell denounced Bergson's thinking as not informed by argument and as hopelessly nonresponsive to argumentation. He brazenly claimed that Bergson's "imaginative picture of the world, regarded as a poetic effort, is in the main not capable of either proof or disproof."[1] And Isaiah Berlin also found nothing of philosophical worth in Bergson's philosophy since, as he claims, it abandons "rigorous critical standards and [substituted] in their place [. . .] causal emotional responses."[2] The merit of mentioning these criticisms of Bergson will slowly emerge as we place Bergson in his correct philosophical context. Far from being a victim of irrationalism and illogical, poetic thinking, Bergson's thinking, as previously mentioned, engages core epistemological assumptions in the areas of mathematics, physics, biology, philosophy, and so on. As a matter of fact, as Suzanne Guerlac convincingly argues, "mathematics and the philosophy of physics significantly informed Bergson's thought."[3] Jean Millet also states that "[i]t is well-known that the philosophical thought of Bergson was shaped by his contact with scientific, specifically mathematical, thought. It is the concepts of the physicists and the mathematicians of his time which interested him, but even more, their manner of 'thinking through' problems, in short, their epistemology."[4] If traditional Western philosophy preaches the virtues of suppressing the corrosive effects of temporality, Bergson courageously embraced temporality, that is, time. Indeed, Guerlac credits Bergson for his "critique of Western metaphysics for its suppression of time, a suppression reinforced by discursive language."[5]

Of course, we need to be cautious in our characterization of Bergson and resist the urge to view him as initiating a simplistic inversion of traditional metaphysics. Bergson does not argue in support of suppressing permanence, stability, and absoluteness. Rather, Bergson seeks to twist free of the traditional philosophical practice by granting priority to time (duration). In so situating his thinking in duration or time, Bergson considers "space [as] the great unconscious presupposition of Western thought."[6] Again, Bergson's intention is not merely to dethrone space as a foundational presupposition of Western metaphysics. Bergson's point is as follows: the exaltation of space has created a situation in which spatial presuppositions and spatial root metaphors have infused Western thought. Because of this spatialization of thought, there has been an uncritical addiction to quantification. So ingrained is the preference for quantification that anything that is not amendable to quantification is denigrated and, in some cases, things that should not be quantified are quantified, awkwardly resulting in confusion, contradiction, and distortion. Ultimately, Bergson's thinking is not beholden to the project of reducing the complexity of reality to formal mathematical calculability.

We witness in Bergson's thinking the philosophical centering of a set of core concepts: duration, intuition, difference, and multiplicity. As a matter of fact, Bergson particularly emphasizes difference, viewing difference as affirmation, creation, invention, and continuity. Bergson directed much of his critical focus at the intellect (reason), viewing the intellect as complicit with styles of thinking incapable of thinking the flux and heterogeneous continuity of reality.

Bergson on Intellect

Bergson initiates his critical accounting of things by focusing on the intellect or the understanding. He claims that the primary task of the intellect is to think matter. And he also maintains that a main disposition of intellect or mind is to construct a mechanical or geometrical explanation of things. Since the intellect is preferentially skewed to engender mechanical or geometrical constructions of things, it favors stability, permanence, noncontinuity, and immobilization. Accordingly, the intellect facilitates the instrumental manipulation of experience. Intellect does not direct its focus to the real but, instead, on abstract substitutions of the real, to schematizations of the real. The intellect, on Bergson's view, facilitates a certain kind of knowledge, knowledge that is the product of quantification. According to Bergson, since the intellect is so deeply invested in quantification and abstract substitution, it predictably "dislikes what is fluid, and solidifies everything it touches. We do not *think* real time. But we *live* it, because life transcends intellect."[7] For intellect, then, to think is to think about solids.

The intellect also models concepts on solids, precisely because it utilizes a logic grounded on solids and immobile objects. Indeed, the preference for a logic of solids promotes a geometric and rigid conception of reality. So, intellect, to the extent that it understands things as beings like solids, cannot think its own source of being, namely, life. This is the case precisely because intellect can think only on the basis of an ontology of solids and life is not a solid, in the sense of being a substance. Let us turn to briefly review Bergson's take on science and, after this, examine his construal of the thinking associated with science as cinematography.

Bergson on Science

With regard to science, Bergson states that it views "nature as a succession of fixed moments, as opposed to our lived experience of continuous time."[8] Bergson, as to be expected, had reservations about mathematics, particularly with regard to its spatialization of time. He states, "It was my mathematical studies which stirred my interest in [duration], at a time when I had no pretensions to doing metaphysics. At first, this was no more than a kind of puzzlement at the value given to the letter t in the equations of mechanics."[9] Mathematics' complicity with spatiality renders it unable to handle time, for, according to Bergson, "every clear idea of number implies a visual image in space."[10] Accordingly, since mathematics cannot appropriately accommodate time, it deals with a "world that dies and is reborn at every instant, — the world which Descartes was thinking of when he spoke of a continued creation."[11] Again, to the extent that quantificational computation characterizes mathematical practice, and since mathematics represents things as solids and as immobile, it follows that it cannot accommodate phenomena that are primarily altered by time. Keith Ansell-Pearson writes in support of Bergson: "Change, transformation, and evolution are bound up with living and open systems, and the features of novelty that characterize such systems will always elude a mathematical treatment."[12] Bergson's strong interest with thinking in time led him to embrace infinitesimal calculus precisely because of its ability to deal with time and motion without having to treat them from within an exclusively spatial framework. Since infinitesimal calculus accommodates rates of change, hence, integrates temporality, Bergson describes it as "the most powerful of the methods of investigation known to the mind."[13] On Bergson's way of thinking, it is important to draw a distinction between two conceptions of mathematics: A mathematics capable of integrating the ontological significance of time as a process or becoming, and, on the other hand, a mathematics amenable to the spatialization of time, one which treats time as an inert magnitude. Bergson's comments on modern mathematics clearly reveals his strong interest in emphasizing reality as becoming, difference, and process: "Modern mathematics is precisely an effort to substitute for the ready-made what is in process of becoming, to follow the growth of magnitudes, to seize movement no longer from outside and in its tendency towards change, in short, to adopt of the mobile continuity of the pattern of things."[14] Bergson's critical remarks directed at science should not be construed as evidence in support of Bergson as an enemy of science. He opposes scientism, the rigid attempt to impose the quantitative methods of science on the study of all phenomena. Indeed, Bergson considers consciousness incapable of quantitative, scientific study. Any successful reduction of consciousness to physical laws would be dependent on mathematics. But mathematical forms are artificial constructions and are not faithful reflections of the flux of the real. Bergson, however, was a friend of modern physics, in particular quantum mechanics. The fact that knowing the position of an entity at the subatomic level precludes knowing its velocity and that knowing its velocity precludes knowing its position, proved amenable to Bergson's way of thinking. As Guerlac claims: "But when Bergson writes that his conception of duration [i.e., time] 'lay in the direction in which physics would tend sooner or later,' the tendency in which it was moving was the theory of quantum mechanics that entailed, at least for physicists like Max Born and Niels Bohr, a tendency toward indeterminism."[15] And Bergson, referring to the philosophy of physics, states that it "was for me something essential [. . .] closely related to my theory of duration [. . .] which lay in the *direction* in which physics would move sooner or later."[16]

Cinematographic Method

In another context, while supportive of quantum mechanics, Bergson complained about the freeze-frame view of the world supported by science. Bergson specifically denounces modern science's addiction to a "cinematographical method," meaning that science approaches reality not as a continuous flux but as a succession of instantaneous snapshots extracted from the flux of being. Indeed, as Bergson, proclaims, "the very mobility of being, escapes the hold of scientific knowledge."[17] Bergson uses the metaphor of cinema to describe scientific thinking and, more generally, the intellect precisely because this style of thinking breaks down reality into component parts. This move leads us to project things into space and then to quantify them, that is, to arrange the components of reality into a homogeneous space. This practice enables us to measure and count things. Our basic interactions with things becomes one not of caring engagement but, rather, abstract manipulation. After our artificial dismantling of reality, we artificially string the discrete frames of reality together in order to return them to the mode of heterogeneous time. When we indulge in this activity, we obtain the semblance of continuous motion analogous to the projection of images on a screen in order to produce the impression of motion and continuity. Bergson writes,

> Instead of attaching ourselves to the inner becoming of things, we place ourselves outside them in order to recompose their becoming artificially. We take snapshots, as it were, of the passing reality, and, as these are characteristic of the reality, we have only to string them on a becoming, abstract, uniform and invisible, situated at the back of the apparatus of knowledge, in order to imitate what there is that is characteristic of this becoming itself. Perception, intellection, language so proceed in general [. . .] *The mechanism of our ordinary knowledge is of a cinematographical kind.*[18]

It should be noted that even as Bergson explains the intellect and its proclivity to quantify things, to treat the real as an aggregate of objects, all subject to mathematical and geometrical manipulation and identification, he was also attuned to the limitations of the intellect. "The Intellect," Bergson declares, "is characterized by a natural inability to comprehend life."[19] An unshakable pillar of his thinking concerns the ineptitude of the intellect to fully capture the dynamism, power, agency, and the sheer differentiating tendencies of life. Bergson declares the construction of life provided by the intellect to be "artificial and symbolic, since it makes the total activity of life shrink to the form of certain human activity which is only a partial and local manifestation of life."[20] In order to understand life, according to Bergson, we must think in duration. Let us now turn to discuss his conception of duration.

Duration

The radicality of Bergson's conception of duration, particularly his engagement with the immediate stuff of experience, entails a comparable rethinking of epistemology. We cannot know duration if we conceive of duration as modeled on homogeneous time. Scientific time is measured time, time measured by instruments. Time, so construed, can be divided into discrete moments. The time of duration is a heterogeneous and continuous process. It is not a homogeneous and immobile time, an aggregate of "moments." Duration rhythmically flows. Duration is the lived unfolding of time that permeates our lives. In another context, Bergson identifies duration as "the continuous progress of the past which gnaws into the future and which swells as it advances."[21] Bergson's goal is to engage philosophically with the experience of duration while deflating the geometric (spatialized) modes of experience and thought provided by the intellect.

In rejecting traditional substance ontology with regard to characterizing duration, Bergson favors connotations associated with energy, motion, and the pulsations of positive and negative charges, to frame his conception of duration. Again, he suggests that in duration "there is, in reality, only a current of existence and the opposing current; thence proceeds the whole evolution of life."[22] So dynamic and potent is Bergson's conception of duration that he considers duration pregnant with ontological implications. Duration is not some mysterious force seeking to impose form on inert matter. Rather, according to Bergson, duration "means invention, creation of forms, continual elaboration of the absolutely new."[23] Indeed, duration is the real; it is being and not some transcendental being outside or underneath being. Bergson states that duration "is the foundation of our being and [. . .] the very substance of the world in which we live."[24]

Another aspect of Bergson's conception of duration is the fact that our subjectivity is not alienated from duration but, rather, is linked to it. According to Bergson, we need not view duration as a form of objectivity opposed to our subjective existence. Consequently, Bergson also refers to duration as pure consciousness, referring to our insertion in duration, as well as expressions of duration. As a matter of fact, unlike the traditional model of the philosopher as spectator who passively gazes on an external, alien world of things, Bergson's inclination is to establish a complicity between all things, meaning that there is symmetry among the respective durations or temporal records of all things. Similarly, "It is not necessary," as Merleau-Ponty claims, for the philosopher "to go outside himself in order to reach the things themselves; he is solicited or haunted by them from within."[25]

Finally, it bears noting that Bergson does not believe one can become immersed in duration without struggle and effort. To become attuned to duration, one must fight against rationalistic thinking that privileges the use of spatialization and quantification. As Guerlac maintains, "To make contact with immediate, or pre-reflexive, experience is a philosophical task that requires effort. It involves something like swimming upstream against a very strong current—the obsession with space that haunts Western thought, and the structure of language, which infuses space into concepts and immobilizes thought."[26] Bergson maintains that it is possible to avoid the contradictions produced by the intellect's efforts to think reality by turning to an alternative source of knowledge and an alternative kind of knowledge. Hence, Bergson insists that conceptual thought and its identitarian logic do not exhaust the possibilities of knowledge. He identifies intuition as another source of knowing.

Intuition

Intuition, Bergson intimates, is thought thinking through its own duration, as well as other durations. "To think intuitively," according to Bergson, "is to think in duration."[27] Put differently, to think in duration is to think in time, but not clock time. Similarly, the intuition that engages with duration is, unlike the intellect, not a conquering instrument seeking to aggressively conquer things. Indeed, intuition desires to fuse with things. Accordingly, intuition encourages knowing as the caressing of things or, rather, of being. Intuition, to the extent that it is not contaminated by the intellect, represents an immersion in the flow of duration, in the continuous heterogeneous flow of life and thought.

As we recall, science, on the one hand, deals with inert things, immobilized objects, precisely because its methods of inquiry are dedicated to gross quantification. On the other hand, intuition, according to Bergson, deals with living beings, processes, and dynamic states of consciousness.

The upshot of this distinction is the acknowledgment of two types of knowing: one focused on manipulating things in order to serve practical purposes, and the other type of knowing pursues communion with things, seeking continuity and movement. Whereas intellect and science depend on mathematics, logic, and formal concepts to produce knowledge, intuition is construed by Bergson as capable of leading to truth without the assistance of concepts or logical constructions. Let us now look in greater detail at Bergson's conception of intuition.

Bergson's conception of intuition should be understood as outside the structural logic of traditional rationalist philosophy, in which intuition is the opposite of reason and is commonly viewed as a vague, ineffable experience or feeling. Intuition is not a mysterious source of knowledge whereby one can predict the future, nor is it some kind of extrasensory form of perception whereby one can apprehend abstract truths and obtain objective knowledge.

Bergson intimates that intuition is the means by which we are able to discern the inner, qualitative differences, or the tendencies that facilitate the inventive and creative thrust of life. Put differently, intuition is the method of merging with the dynamic flow of being. In this view of intuition, the focus of intuition is a surrender to the inner cohesion of things. Elizabeth Grosz tells us,

> Intuition is not simply the discernment of natural differences, qualitative differences or differences in kind. It is the inner orientation to tendencies, to the differences between tendencies. It is the capacity to understand natural differences beyond a monistic or dualistic model, not as a relation of two terms, but as the convergence of two tendencies or dispositions, not connected through Hegelian negation but brought together through contraction/dilation.[28]

From a different perspective, intuition entails a double revelation. First, intuition requires a descent into the depths of immediate consciousness in order to escape the restrictions of practical utility. This descent enables us to "perceive our own inner continuity above and beyond action and definable results."[29] Second, intuition also requires a reversal of the revelation of the downward movement. Just as the downward movement reveals the inner durational flow beyond action, one also encounters "the durational flow that also characterizes the very surface of objects in their real relations with each other."[30]

Another important element of Bergson's conception of intuition is the idea of intuition as sympathy. Sympathy, in this context, connotes a displacing of the praxis of manipulation, a transcending of the seduction of practical utility. We recall that the intellect focuses on quantifying the predicates of objects that accommodate measurement. Of course, not everything can be measured or subjected to quantification without distortion, since this approach does not focus on the inner duration of things. So, unlike the intellect, "Intuition is a mode of 'sympathy' by which every characteristic of an object (process, quality, etc.) is brought together, none is left out, in a simple and immediate resonance of life's inner duration and the absolute specificity of its objects."[31] Intuition as sympathy should not connote a naive, juvenile infatuation with the external appearance of an object. Sympathy is not the act of being responsive to the glitter of things but, rather, is an attraction to the duration of things. Bergson writes, "We call intuition [. . .] *the* sympathy by which one is transposed into the interior of an object in order to coincide with what here is unique and consequently inexpressible in it."[32] In this sense, Bergsonian intuition might be framed as an ethics. Ansell-Pearson writes, "The 'ethical' character of this method of philosophy [i.e., intuition] resides [. . .] in the cultivation of a 'sympathetic communication' that it seeks to establish between the human and the rest of living matter."[33] Yet, all the while, intuition is a form of "intellectual sympathy," not a sensual fascination bordering on obsession. Intuition is the opposite of the intellect, precisely because, as Martin Jay puts it, "only intuition [. . .] can provide the sympathetic entry into the interiority of the object, which is blocked by intellectual analysis, linguistic symbolization, and visual representation."[34]

Perhaps the most intriguing feature of Bergson's conception of intuition concerns his assimilating of intuition as analogous to aesthetic experience. This brief discussion is important because of the subsequent discussion of African art forms and the notion of participation connected to Senghor's account of Négritude. Bergson refers to the artist as "placing himself back within the object by a kind of sympathy [. . .] by an effort of intuition."[35] One reason why Bergson decided to connect intuition with aesthetic experience is to displace the rigidity and artificial abstraction of the intellect and its facilitations of quantification, measurement, and causal determinism. Furthermore, within the context of science, sensations are explained in terms of being causally connected with an external stimulus. Bergson's objective is to argue that, unlike causal explanations found in science, in the realm of aesthetics there can be no appeal to cause and effect, there is no link between feelings of joy and objects of joy. The emotional states associated with aesthetic experiences are not sensations. Guerlac argues,

> Esthetic experience becomes the paradigm for inner feeling, then, because it is defined very broadly, as "any feeling that [. . .] has been *suggested* in us, not caused in us." This is why the relation between the dancer and joy we feel is quite different from the relation between the light and the feeling of brightness we experience. The light source causes the effect of brightness. The relation of cause and effect is a necessary one [. . .] Art, however, does not operate like a physical cause. It addresses us. It invites us into a relation of sympathy. We feel with the poet, dancer, or musician by entering into the rhythms of his or her art.[36]

It is crucial that we understand why modeling intuition on aesthetic experience segregates intuition from the nexus of causation. Just as the art object invites certain emotional reactions, in intuition, the object similarly invites sympathy. Guerlac continues,

> Art, then, suggests feelings to us; it does not cause them. What does Bergson mean by suggestion? Suggestion influences our attention, the way music does when it invites us into its rhythms, or the way hypnotic suggestion disarms us, so to speak, and opens us up to its influence. In a similar way, art places us in a kind of dream state. It elicits a sympathetic response on our part, a virtual participation in the feeling or idea, which is imprinted in us by the artistic manipulation of qualities through rhythm, tone, or color.[37]

If intuition, like an aesthetic understanding, is an immersion in the inner durational qualities of an object, we should note that an object, whether an art object or a natural object, is not reducible to its formal qualities. According to Grosz, "The observation and aesthetic appreciation of, say, a work of art is not the simplification of the work to its most recognizable features; it is an immersion in as much as the art object's qualities as one can achieve, not simply to learn something or do something but primarily to feel something, which may, but often does not, have a practical concern."[38] The objective of an intuitive engagement with an object is not for the purpose of controlling or exploiting the object. Rather, the objective is to be receptive to the call of the object, to respond to the invitation of the object, to enter the rapture of its rhythms.

What emerges from Bergson's thinking, among other things, is an ontology of being. This ontology can best be described as the rhythm of being. To understand being is to understand being as duration, and to understand duration is to feel the rhythm of being, the rhythm of the real. In other words, to truly experience the real is to feel it as a whole and not be seduced by the analytical disintegration of the intellect and its fascination with discontinuity and immobilization. As Bergson tells us, "We can thus conceive of succession without distinction, and think of it as a mutual penetration, an interconnexion and organization of elements, each one of which represents the whole, and cannot be distinguished or isolated from it except by abstract thought."[39] Our involvement with things, at least from the perspective of intuition, should be geared toward receptivity to the flow or the rhythm of their being instead of subjecting things to a violation of their qualitative and durational reality. We should not deny the rhythm of things. Bergson maintains that "the poet is he with whom feelings develop into images, and the images themselves into words, which translate them while obeying the laws of rhythm. In seeing these images pass before our eyes we in our own turn experience the feeling which was, so to speak, their emotional equivalent."[40] Finally the rhythms of objects resonate in us. For there seems to be an ontological compatibility between the rhythms of things as well as the rhythms we experience in our bodies. This ontological correspondence is evidence of the rhythmic profile of duration itself. Bergson concludes: "We should never realize these images so strongly without the regular movements of rhythm by which our soul is lulled into self-forgetfulness, and, as in a dream, thinks and sees the poet."[41]

We have reached a point where we must confront an obvious question: why all this extensive discussion? The simple answer is follows: without this background, Négritude runs the risk of appearing nonsensical, as so many of its critics have asserted. For to the extent that Négritude entertains a questioning of reason, many of its critics have automatically viewed it as courting irrationality, championing idiotic emotionalism, or promoting an equally unsavory ideological position. In order to correct these wild accusations, we must now plunge into an investigation of Senghor's position. However, prior to providing this discussion of Senghor's position, it is necessary to review the cluster of criticisms launched against his conception of Négritude.

Bergson, Senghor, and the Philosophical Foundations   91

Critiques of Négritude

Since my thesis is that Senghor modeled his conception of Négritude on certain core elements of Bergson's philosophy, specifically following Bergson's persistent critique of Western philosophy, I want to review some criticisms of Senghor to demonstrate the unmitigated failure of his critics. Of course, Senghor's critics consist of an impressive list of thinkers: Stanislas Adotevi, René Depestre, Frantz Fanon, Paulin Hountondji, Abiola Irele, Donna Jones, Es'kia Mphahlele, Jean-Paul Sartre, Tsenay Serequeberhan, Wole Soyinka, Cheikh Thiam, Marcien Towa, and Kwasi Wiredu. My contention is that these various critics fail to appreciate the distinctive philosophical thrust of Senghor's position, and his concern with the attitude of a people toward being—their sense of their basic way of being-in-the-world. Put differently, Senghor frames Négritude as a distinctive ontological orientation; it is a "certain affective attitude towards the world."[42] In misconstruing Senghor's philosophical project as, among other things, a crude ideological political agenda, a literary-inspired identity discourse, a vulgar biological essentialism, a defensive psychological stance infused with an inferiority complex, and so on, these critics dismally fail to acknowledge the philosophical impetus by Senghor to capture the basic ontological orientation of an African mode of existence.

Donna Jones's Critique of Biological Vitalism

Let us first critically scrutinize two recent texts on Négritude to determine the extent to which they have misidentified the thrust of Senghor's thinking in their critical appraisal of Négritude. Jones in *The Racial Discourses of Life Philosophy: Négritude, Vitalism, and Modernity* struggles to provide a sophisticated and nuanced interpretation of Négritude. However, even as Jones declares her intent to treat Négritude with more favorable hermeneutical sympathies she, nevertheless, finds it complicit in morally objectionable intellectual pursuits. Jones seemingly indicates that her target of attack is vitalism and, more specifically, vitalism's unfortunate influence on Négritude. Accordingly, Jones argues that, although scholars have been correct to acknowledge vitalism's role in Négritude discourse, scholars have not been sufficiently critical in investigating the negative consequences of this relationship. Of course, one bitter implication of Jones's thesis is that if vitalism is morally problematic, then, to the extent that vitalism serves as a transcendental condition of the possibility for models of Black emancipation, Black thought is also analytically and theoretically compromised. Jones states,

> I have therefore attempted to rethink vitalism—even apart from its racial implications—to explain its full cultural context. In the end, I argue that *Négritude's* grounding of black oppositional culture in vitalism needs to be handled much more critically than it has been by the scholars who have noted the connection. At the least, I hope to show that some of the dominant models of emancipation within black thought cannot be understood except through recourse to the vitalist tradition.[43]

Despite Jones's effort to deliver her nuanced reading of Négritude insofar as she amplifies Négritude's connection to vitalism, her laudatory goal ends in failure. Jones provides an explication of Bergson's thinking, stressing his efforts to think in duration, to infused thinking with time. However, Jones concludes this discussion by announcing that even if Bergson struggled to escape vitalism, he was unsuccessful. The message is clear: Bergson does not succeed in transcending vitalism; Bergson's thinking, then, is a vulgar vitalism.[44] The trouble with Négritude, in Jones's view, is its unfortunate involvement with vitalism by way of its theoretical fraternizing and intellectual dependence on Bergsonism. Négritude's bold association with vitalism led Négritude thinkers to ruinously embrace an equally unsavory essentialism.[45]

I consider Jones's reading of Bergson, as well as her reading of Négritude, to be flawed. These flawed readings naturally follow from her skewed reading of Bergson's thinking as reducible to biological vitalism. Seemingly refusing to acknowledge Bergson's efforts to repudiate vitalism, Jones casually reads a vulgar vitalism back into Bergson's text even as Bergson, himself, persistently struggled to expose the intellectual shortcomings of vitalism. Jones, unfortunately, considers Bergson a vitalist because she ignores his emphasis on the fact that, within consciousness, past, present, and future interpenetrate, a process consistent with the movement of heterogeneous multiplicities. Bergson's conception of things is not dependent on the foundational, metaphysical, or transcendental status of an abstract principle or ontologizing entity.

Cheikh Thiam's Afri-Centered Reading of Senghor

Another recent reading of Négritude, specifically Senghor's Négritude, is found in Thiam's *Return to the Kingdom of Childhood: Re-Envisioning the*

Legacy and Philosophical Relevance of Négritude. Thiam's concern centers on a new generation of scholars and their interpretation of Négritude. He states that these new scholars consider Négritude as a philosophy: an ontology, and an epistemology. Furthermore, Thiam claims that these scholars correctly attribute Senghor's ideas as emergent from his influence by French thinkers. Referring specifically to Souleymane Bachir Diagne and Donna Jones, he writes, "Using Bergson's *lebenphilosophie* [sic] as the foundation of Senghor's theory, they both attempt to unearth the frequently ignored epistemology and ontology that constitute the crux of the philosophy of Négritude."[46] Nevertheless, Thiam quickly qualifies his approval of these new interpreters of Senghor. He considers Diagne's and Jones's reading of Senghor as weak insofar as they render Senghor's thinking dependent on Western philosophical sources of influence.

The upshot of Thiam's position is that Senghor's thinking was influenced by Bergson, among other Western thinkers. However, he claims that Senghor developed a distinctive epistemology and ontology rooted in an Afri-centered perspective. Ultimately, Senghor's philosophy is an African philosophy, and efforts to ground his thinking in Western philosophy betray his authentic intellectual heritage.[47] Despite Thiam's effort to situate Senghor in an alternative Afri-centered paradigm, Thiam succeeds in undermining his thesis concerning Senghor's authentic Afri-centered context. It was Bergson who prior to Senghor stated that to think is to think in duration (time). Phrases such as *duration, time, movement,* and *becoming,* and ideas regarding the interpenetration of past, present, and future are all basic ingredients of Bergson's thought.

Accordingly, the problem with Thiam's position is that it is neither coherently stated nor critically defended. Thiam gives the reader the impression that he welcomes readings of Senghor that do not restrict Senghor to a colonialist context. Hence, he declares his support for scholars such as Diagne and Jones who have called attention to Bergson's influence on Senghor's thinking. Thiam then quickly warns that these scholars have been too quick to link Senghor to colonialist modes of thought. Consequently, Thiam argues that Senghor articulated a distinctive Afri-centered epistemology and ontology. Last, Thiam then proceeds to attribute views to Senghor that are clearly and distinctively views articulated and defended by Bergson. The fact that Senghor admits to his attraction to Bergson would seem to indicate that he was intimately familiar with Bergson's philosophy and directly endorsed and appropriated those aspects of Bergson's philosophy that enabled his philosophical conception of Négritude.

If Jones and Thiam sought to correct misconceptions of past critics, they seem not to have succeeded in their efforts. Their respective updated interpretations of Négritude are off target, for the fundamental philosophical orientation of Senghor's thinking is absent from their critical discourses. In any event, we need to critically review the barrage of criticisms of Négritude leveled by an earlier generation of critics.

The Condition of Antinégritude Discourse

It is not an exaggeration to claim that the transcendental condition of the possibility of anti-Négritude discourse is a rejection of essentialism: biological, racial, cultural, or psychological. Put differently, most, if not all criticisms of Négritude in one way or another chastise the movement for an alleged embrace of essentialism. Bennetta Jules-Rosette describes anti-Négritude writing as follows:

> Antinégritude negates the essentialist theses of négritude. Taking négritude as its point of departure, antinègritude acknowledges racism and oppression as the roots of a universal problem but denounces négritude as its solution. This antidiscourse contrasts with the complementary discourse of revolutionary writing and contradictory discourses of non-négritude.[48]

The general strategy is to implement a reductionist methodology such that Négritude is dissolved to a basic element (e.g., race, culture, personality) and then denounced as a crude essentialist mode of thought or as being one dimensional in scope.

Négritude as Antiracist Racism

As we recall, Sartre famously describes Négritude as a negation of a negation, or more specifically, as an antiracist racism.[49] Being a negation of negation, Négritude as a positivity signaled the phenomenon of the Black (the African) responding to the former European masters. Négritude signaled the active embrace of the negative stereotypes of Blacks. It injected into these prevailing images of Blacks positive attributes instead of negative and degrading ones. Unlike the decadent and life-denying features of Europeans, Africans embodied the dynamism of life itself, the energy and creative forces propelling the becoming of being, of life itself. But just as quickly as he called attention to the positive core of Négritude, to what he called the subjective and objective poles of Négritude, Sartre, in amazing dialectical sophistication, deflated the ontological and existential pretense of Négritude by delivering the message that Négritude is just another contingent stage of the universal unfolding of the history of class conflict. Négritude offered Blacks temporary relief from the existential hell of racial hatred and colonial dehumanization. However, Négritude, being a contingent stage in a universal dialectal process, would have to eventually yield the stage of world history to the universal class struggle. What began as a tribute to Négritude ended in predictions of its dialectical transcendence, if not its demise.

We also find in Fanon's critical response to Négritude the tendency to resort to a reductionist mode of reading.[50] This tendency is likewise accompanied by an immediate retreat to a psychological, explanatory scheme whereby Négritude is read as intended to provide a source of ethnic and racial pride to victims of European colonialism. Fanon famously denounced Négritude as engaged in the worship of ancient African history and as encouraging the folly of worshiping a mystical African past. Fanon considered this obsessive interest in ancient African history as politically, economically, and culturally misdirected, in that this concern was not grounded in the various political, economic, and cultural exigencies of the present. For it would seem that Fanon favored the formation of a national culture appropriately connected to the political struggles and the general existential situation of the working classes, namely, those persons constituting the largest portion of the populations of the African colonies. It is clear, however, that Fanon's reading of Négritude depended on the act of treating Négritude as a static doctrine in search of a mysterious or nonexistent entity.[51] So, as is the case with Sartre, we do not witness in Fanon an effort to treat Négritude as inspired by philosophical critiques of Western philosophy and the positive efforts to articulate an epistemology and ontology more adequately reflective of the African mode of being-in-the-world. Fanon's critical reaction to Négritude remains within the auspices of a reductive methodology.

Materialist and Nonessentialist Critiques of Négritude

Many critics of Négritude also denounce it because, according to them, Négritude is an irrationalism that erroneously encourages and irresponsibly promotes the unjustifiable denigration of reason. The incessant and clamorous championing of emotion is not a viable emancipatory strategy but, at best, the cunning and ruinous embrace of repugnant racialist stereotypes of Africans. Hence, Négritude is an impostor, a pernicious manifestation of a decaying consciousness. Irele has similarly identified the charge of Négritude courting irrationalism as its greatest sin. Commenting on Soyinka's criticism of Négritude, Irele states, "Perhaps the most important charge against Négritude is the one that underlies Soyinka's criticism, namely, its apparent acquiescence in the stereotype of the Black man as a non-rational creature."[52] Irele isolates a certain kind of criticism of Négritude. He describes these criticisms as follows: "They proceed from what one might call a *positivist* standpoint, involving a materialist view of society. In their concern with achieving an immediate sense of reality, they have little or no sympathy for any theory of African development that does not appear to bear a direct relation to an objective and practical scheme of historical action in the contemporary world."[53]

Let us quickly review a few of these materialist-inspired critiques of Négritude. Towa's[54] criticism of Négritude has centered on the claim that it is inconsistent with African progress and development, and that ultimately, as Jules-Rosette states, "It entails a type of fatalistic servitude leading to powerlessness."[55] Instead of offering constructive guidance whereby Africans can meaningfully and realistically pursue a future blessed with political stability and economic prosperity, Négritude offers next to nothing by way of constructive optimism. While emphasizing the importance of economic and technological development, Towa remains convinced that Senghor's reference to emotion and rhythm are not only politically and economically backward, but set the stage to render African peoples unfit to survive and prosper in the modern world. Towa is relentless in his contention that Senghor settles for a position of servitude for African peoples insofar as Senghor celebrates the rhythm of African peoples. If rhythm is the best that Africans can contribute to world civilization, then they are fated to be minor participants and not leaders.

Although Towa's main criticism of Négritude seems to have been inspired on the basis of a materialist understanding of society, Towa has also faulted Senghor for disastrously flirting with obnoxious biological and racial ideas. Here, Towa disavows Senghor's alleged essentialism. Again, in privileging the analytical veracity of a materialist paradigm, Towa identifies essentialism at the heart of Négritude. In so attributing a malicious metaphysical impulse in Négritude, Towa states, "[Négritude] presupposes a rigid essence of the Black race unaffected by time. To this permanent state is added a specific nature that neither sociological determinations nor historical variations nor geographical realities bear out. Négritude makes of Black people the same everywhere and through all time."[56] Not surprisingly, Towa attributes Senghor's unfortunate involvement with racial and biological thinking to the inevitable outcome of his influence by colonialist thinking. Hence, Senghor's anticolonialist language is ironically an extension of colonialist thinking. In Towa's view, as Jane Hiddleston points out, "Senghor's affirmation of emotion confuses culture with biology, and he draws direct links between colonial thinking and the rhetoric of Senghor's professed anti-colonialism."[57]

Adotevi is without doubt the most relentless critic of Négritude.[58] While brazenly adopting a Marxist framework, Adotevi variously denounces Négritude as politically ineffective and explanatorily retrograde. At times, Adotevi adopts a harsh apocalyptic tone—either castigating Négritude as stillborn, or accusing it of existing in a state of intellectual and political decay. Adotevi, in the gesture of a eulogy, states,

> There was a time when Négritude served a useful though limited purpose: it shook a few consciences and brought a few Negroes together, and this was a good thing [. . .] In consequence, we should consider it as a primitive period necessary to the African renaissance. But today it is no more than a "political mysticism" which impedes progress by perpetuating the myth of Negro irrationality and neglecting to provide practical solutions to Africa's most pressing problems. As an ideology it is "shallow, vague, inefficient" and dangerously misleading. Négritude was born dead; it was going to die and it died.[59]

In another context, Adotevi proclaims, "Négritude is dead [. . .] We need to free the Negro."[60] In keeping with his materialist castigation of Négritude, Adotevi insists that Négritude's praise of a distinctive African (Black) persona and its belief in the existence of a universal fraternity of all Blacks, are clearly indicative of false consciousness (essentialism). These notions of ahistorical Blackness are manifestations of an emotional mind-set and not representative of what Adotevi considers proper scientific (rational) thinking. He writes,

> First of all, Négritude in the fashion in which it is broadcast, rests on confused and nonexistent notions to the extent that it affirms, in an abstract manner, the fraternity of all blacks. Thus, because the underlying thesis is not only antiscientific, but also proceeds from fantasy, it presupposes the existence of a rigid black persona, which is unattainable. To this permanent persona is added a specificity that neither sociological determinations nor

historical variations, nor geographic realities confirm. It makes black people similar beings everywhere and at all times.[61]

Also consistent with his dialectical materialist style of thinking, Adotevi implements a materialist conception of culture. In other words, he views legitimate culture or cultural formations as transparent representations of material reality. In accordance with the Marxist conception of false consciousness as consciousness that distorts the truth about the existing material conditions of a society as determined by its mode of production, Adotevi considers Négritude to be a form of "political mystification."[62] It would seem that the main form of mystical falsification attributable to Négritude is the myth of Black homogeneity, that is, the idea of all Black people as sharing a common culture, a common psychology, or a common conception of existence (essentialism).

In light of Adotevi's forceful dismissal of Négritude as a pernicious mystification that is shamelessly predicated on the erroneous notion of Black unity and homogeneity (which Adotevi considers as nonentities), it would be fair to interpret Adotevi as treating Négritude as an instantiation of the religion of the oppressed. Négritude so interpreted as myth or as religion, in accordance with a typical Marxist analysis, functions as a drug, as an opiate of the oppressed. Indeed, this is exactly what Adotevi concludes. He states that "Négritude has to be the soporific of the Black. It's the opium, it's the drug that enables one, at the point of sharing out, to retain one's good Negroes."[63]

Soyinka is also widely known for his ridiculing of the concept of Négritude through his misleading and crude analogizing of Négritude to tigritude. He implies that the very idea of there being a need to affirm one's Négritude is as absurd as a tiger needing to shout its tigritude. But even more damning, Soyinka also advocates a derisive dismissal of the idea of Négritude as representing of a distinctive African style of thinking. In particular, Soyinka is especially opposed to the idea of European culture as an analytical culture and African culture being an intuitive or emotional culture. In a dramatic act of denunciation, Soyinka frames the position as follows:

> Analytical thought is a mark of high human development.
> The European employs analytical thought.
> Therefore the European is highly developed.[64]

He then formulates Négritude as follows:

Intuitive understanding is also a mark of high human development.
The African employs intuitive understanding.
Therefore the African is highly developed.[65]

Soyinka writes, "Suddenly we were exhorted to give a cheer for those who never invented anything, a cheer for those who never explored the oceans."[66] In accordance with Soyinka's take on things, reason or analytical thought is the opposite of intuitive understanding, meaning that analytical thought and intuitive understanding are incompatible. We recall Soyinka's claim that Senghor renders the Black man a nonrational creature. Clearly then, Négritude, from Soyinka's perspective, should be rejected because it naively glorifies emotion and intuition instead of recognizing and endorsing the superior style of thinking indicative of reason and analytic thought. Négritude is an unflattering irrationalism.

To quickly summarize, we witness in the proceeding discussions, among other things, charges of essentialism, mystification, emotionalism, and even a rejection of the realities of class struggle all lodged against Négritude. My basic point, however, remains: these criticisms do not directly address the core of Senghor's work, at least to the extent that his conception of Négritude is inspired by Bergson's thinking. Having now reviewed various criticisms of Négritude, we are well positioned to pursue a close reading of Senghor's position.

Senghor on Bergson and Developments in Modern European Epistemology

Senghor referred to Bergson's *Time and Free Will: An Essay on the Immediate Data of Consciousness* as "the revolution of 1889."[67] The revolution to which Senghor refers, the revolution that captivated his imagination, is the epistemological critique of scientific reason instigated by Bergson. Senghor interprets Bergson as maintaining that "facts and matter, which are the objects of discursive reason [the intellect], were only the outer surface that had to be transcended by intuition in order to achieve a vision in-depth of reality."[68] Senghor's close relationship to Bergson is significant precisely because it provides a context to better understand why so many critics have mistakenly considered his position, like Bergson's before his, an irresponsible, unwise, and unwarranted dismissal of reason, and a naive and ill-conceived praise of emotion. The fate of any literalistic interpretation of his strategic use of language is to inescapably reduce his view to self-evident absurdity.

Let us quickly review some of the specific charges leveled against Négritude. Its critics have variously denounced it as essentialist, as being ideologically counterproductive, and even as racist. Those critics with a political ax to grind have portrayed it as "a 'mystification' that aims to distract people from the real struggle and the real stakes."[69] Even the astute Ousmane Sembène describes Négritude as "an intellectual intoxicant used by the [ruling classes]."[70] And the criticism of ethnophilosophy as "an imaginary, intoxicating interpretation" similarly implicates Négritude.[71] These various criticisms misidentify Senghor's philosophical focus as political advocacy.

Strong evidence supports Senghor's concerns with epistemology, ontology, and with his understanding of Négritude as, among other things, a critique of colonial and scientific reason as well as the imperialistic designs of modern scientific rationality. Senghor, keenly being aware of the revolutionary developments in modern epistemology, states,

> The new discoveries of science—quanta, relativity, wave mechanics, the uncertainty principle, electron spin—had upset the nineteenth-century notion of determinism, which denied man's free will, along with the concepts of matter and energy. The French physicist Broglie revealed to us the duality of matter and energy, or the wave-particle principle that underlies things; the German physicist Heisenberg showed us that objectivity was an illusion and that we could not observe facts without modifying them; others showed that, on the scale of the infinitely small as on that of the immensely great, particles act on one another. Since then, the physico-chemical laws, like matter itself, could no longer appear unchangeable. Even in the field and on the scale where they were valid, they were only rough approximations, no more than probabilities.[72]

In another context, Senghor made comments that also established his intimate familiarity with epistemological issues. He writes,

> European [. . .] artists, philosophers, even scientists [are] going to the school of participant reason. We are witnessing a true revolution in European epistemology, which has been taking place since the turn of the century.

Bergson, Senghor, and the Philosophical Foundations 101

> The new method, and hence the new theory, of knowledge arose out of the latest scientific discoveries: relativity, wave mechanics, quantum mechanics, non-Euclidean geometries. And also out of new philosophical theories: phenomenology, existentialism [. . .] It was a response to the need to outgrow the scientific positivism of the nineteenth century [. . .] Nowadays, whether we look at science, philosophy or art, we find discontinuity and indeterminism at the bottom of everything, of the mind as well as the real, where they reveal themselves after the most detailed and at the same time the most passionate investigations.[73]

Clearly, Senghor, because of his critical awareness of the crises in modern science and epistemology, strategically used this crisis to advance a counter-epistemology. Hence, it is important to get the details of his epistemology correct.

Epistemology and Négritude

As previously stated, the abiding contention of this study is that the immediate influence on Négritude as epistemology comes from Bergson. Senghor, in developing his conception of Négritude, directly capitalized on Bergson's critique of the intellect:

> Since the Renaissance, the values of European civilization had rested essentially on discursive reason and facts, on logic and matter—as well as the other critiques of reason within the contexts of mathematics and physics. Bergson, with an eminently dialectical subtlety, answered the expectation of a public weary of scientism and naturalism. He showed that facts and matter, which are the objects of discursive reason, were only the outer surface that had to be transcended by *intuition* in order to achieve a *vision in depth of reality*.[74]

In another context, Messay Kebede directly linked Négritude with critiques of reason and not primarily with a nationalist, anticolonialist agenda. He maintains that "the best way to connect Négritude with Western philosophical positions is via the debate opposing the defenders of reason and those who rebelled against its dominance."⁷⁵ Irele also underscored the intimate connection between Négritude and Bergson's epistemology, arguing that Bergson's epistemology served as the theoretical foundation for Senghor's development of Négritude. According to Irele,

> To Bergson, Senghor owes the concept of intuition on which revolves his explication of the African mind and consciousness. Bergson abolished with this concept of positivist dichotomy of subject-object, and proposed a new conception of authentic knowledge as immediacy of experience, the organic involvement of the subject with the object of his experience. It is largely the epistemology of Bergson that Senghor has adopted in his formulation of Négritude.⁷⁶

Hinting at the possible epistemological origins of Négritude is not enough to conclusively establish its epistemological signature. However, Senghor did not pursue epistemology in the Cartesian sense of treating epistemology as first philosophy. His task was not to develop the a priori criteria of knowledge, provide an answer to skepticism, or articulate a theory of normative justification. Senghor took a radically different avenue to epistemology. Indeed, while conceding Bergson's heavy influence on his thought, Senghor applied some of Bergson's insights to African art. Senghor first broached African art and then transitioned to epistemology. The preliminary focus on African art forms is justified due to the intimate relation between aesthetic experience and intuition, a relationship underscored first by Bergson and later by Senghor.

African Art as Philosophy

Senghor grafts Bergson's thinking to a conception of African art forms. Accordingly, it is fair to conclude that Négritude is, as Diagne states, a "theory of African knowing because it is a theory of African creating, art being itself knowledge of reality."⁷⁷ We recall that, as consistent with Bergson's position, aesthetic experience is a model of intuition, and intuition is knowledge of durations—knowledge of the internal qualities of an object that intellect cannot access. Senghor, similarly, conceives of African art forms as sources of knowledge. Indeed, one of Senghor's main tasks was to establish that "the African art forms [. . .] considered as 'aesthetic' [can also be interpreted] as philosophic observations about the nature of the world."⁷⁸ The goal of the artist in African art is not the passive reproduction of reality or an attempt to represent things in terms of resemblances. Additionally, the task of the African artist is not to produce art to elicit pleasure from the beautiful, or works of art that are said to represent ideals of beauty and symmetry. Rather, the focus is to merge with the object, to feel the qualitative flavor of the object as emergent from the relations composed by its qualities. Diagne comments,

> We find here [. . .] the register of the *power* of effects born of excess and the absence of proportions in the name of another logic internal to the work, a logic which does not aim at the pleasure of a "beautiful reality" consonant with our normal faculty of desire for what is "flesh and blood" but at the shock caused by the "free play of impulsive feeling," which is itself the image of the figure "*dissociated into its parts.*"[79]

If African art is the product of the African artist's participation in the object, then the goal of African artists, once again, is not a mechanical reproduction of the object. Rather, the goal of the African artist is an effort to capture the duration of the object, to capture the impulsive forces internal to the object as well as forces characteristic of life itself. Paul Guillaumet and Thomas Munro, in their interpretation of African sculpture, write,

> It is apt to be unmeaning or even disagreeable [. . .] But in shapes and designs of line, plane and mass, it has achieved a variety of striking effects that few if any other types of sculpture have equaled. These effects would be impossible in a representation of the human figure if natural proportions were strictly adhered to. They would be impossible in an ideal figure conceived, like the Greek ones mentioned, on a basis of what would be humanly desirable in flesh and blood.[80]

Note that the African artist does not segregate him- or herself from the object. The artist is not a spectator surveying a world of objects. Rather, the focus is participation, merging with the object or, put metaphorically, the attempt to establish intimate communion with the object. In this context, analysis, separation, alienation, and discontinuity are all deflated. Accordingly, the transition from art to epistemology requires a radically different approach to knowledge, an approach consistent with Bergsonian intuition. Diagne writes, "Transferred from the domain of art to that of knowledge, 'participation' becomes, for Senghor, the non-Aristotelian logic called for by the new developments in contemporary science which thus testify that the approach that does not separate is a true path of knowledge."[81]

Senghor on Négritude as Epistemology

Senghor claims that "it is the attitude towards the *object*—towards the external world, the *Other*—which characterizes a people, and thereby their culture."[82] Contrary to his hostile critics and their reductionist claims, we witness here Senghor's indisputable philosophical concerns. Translated into a Bergsonian framework, the contrast is between an approach to the world that is exploitative, utilitarian, and manipulative and an approach that is one of disinterested engagement with the object characterized by a caring focus on the object without any practical harassment. At the risk of trying the reader's patience, Bergson is worth quoting in full:

> Intelligence, by means of science, which is its work, will deliver up to us more and more completely the secret of physical operations; of life it brings us, moreover only claims to bring us, a translation in terms of inertia. It goes all around life, taking from outside the greatest possible number of views of it, drawing it into itself instead of entering into it. But it is the very inwardness of life that *intuition* leads us—by intuition I mean instinct that has become disinterested, self-conscious, capable of reflecting upon its object and of enlarging it indefinitely.[83]

Senghor repudiates the metaphysical dualism that grounds modern Cartesian epistemology. Modern epistemology, crippled by the scourge of dualism, alienates the knowing subject from the object of knowledge. Indeed, the knowing subject, standing apart from the object, the thing known, is a spectator of sorts, bearing no affective relation to the object of knowledge. Viewing the object as an alien being, the subject is freed to conquer the object, to instrumentally subjugate the object to his/her interests. The violation of the object renders the object, as it were, voiceless and vulnerable in the midst of its complete domination by the concepts and instruments of the knower. According to Senghor,

> [The European] distinguishes himself from the object. He keeps it at a distance, immobilizes it outside time and in some sense

outside space, fixes it and slays it. Armed with precision instruments, he dissects it mercilessly so as to arrive at a factual analysis. Learned, but moved by practical considerations, the European [. . .] uses the Other, after slaying it, for practical ends: He treats it as a *means*. And he *assimilates* it in a centripetal motion; destroys it by feeding on it.[84]

Senghor, then, immediately describes the African approach to the object, to the Other. The contrast is vividly striking if not jolting. He writes,

[The African] does not distinguish himself, to begin with, from the object: from tree or pebble, man or animal, fact of nature or society. He does not keep the object at a distance, does not analyze it. After receiving its impression, he takes the object, all alive, into his hands—like a blind man, anxious not to fix it or to kill it. He turns it over and over in his supple hands, touches it, *feels* it [. . .] It is in his subjectivity and at the end of his antennae, like those of an insect, that he discovers the *Other*. And at this point, he is *e-moved* [. . .] and carried [. . .] from subject to object on the waves which the Other emits.[85]

Senghor not only explains the differences between the African subject and the European subject in terms of an epistemological distinction, but also acknowledges significant conceptual variation with regard to their respective conceptions of reason. The European tradition models reason on the basis of mechanical and atomistic thinking. Reason, according to this view, functions as a tool of manipulation, hence, predisposed to dissect the object in order to expose its hidden essence. The African tradition models reason on the basis of an organic relation; here the focus is on cultivating and sustaining an affective relation with the object such that there is a reciprocal exchange of energy and influence. Furthermore, there exists no barrier between subject and object, for as Senghor claims, the African "keeps his senses open, ready to receive any impulse, and even the very waves of nature, without screen [. . .] between subject and object."[86] Senghor prefers words such as "embrace," "contact," "participation," and "communion" to describe the African encounter with the object.[87] Instead of the subject seeking to manipulate the object, the goal is to intermingle with the object. Here, the abiding hope is that the object discloses its being, relative to the temporal unfolding of the subject's encounter with it. Senghor states that for the African "reason is not discursive but synthetic; it is not antagonistic, but sympathetic [. . .] European reasoning is analytical, discursive by utilization; Negro-African reasoning is intuitive by participation."[88] Clearly, Senghor's take on reason escapes the critical focus of his critics.

We should note here that Senghor's intention is to deflate the epistemological pretensions of scientific thinking, meaning that he is not convinced that the only source of knowledge is scientific inquiry. He is not denouncing the restricted legitimacy of scientific reason. However, like Bergson, he claims that there is another significant source of knowledge. Accordingly, he writes that knowledge

> is a matter of *participating* in the object in the act of knowledge; of going beyond concepts and categories, appearances and preconceptions shaped by [reason], to plunge into the primordial chaos, not shaped as yet by discursive reason [. . .] Knowledge is then no artificial product of discursive reason made to cover up reality, but discovery through emotion, and not so much discovery as *re-discovery*. Knowledge coincides [. . .] with the being of the object in its originating and original reality, in its discontinuity and indeterminacy: in its life.[89]

For Bergson, scientific thinking ought to be criticized for its inability to think reality in duration. It is incapable of thinking reality as anything other than aggregates of immobile solids. This being the case, the scientific style of thinking, according to Bergson, could not think reality as a heterogeneous continuity. Senghor also uses a similar structural distinction in his characterization of reason as discursive and as intuitive. "Discursive reason," according to him, "merely stops at the surface of things; it does not penetrate their hidden resorts, which escape the lucid consciousness. Intuitive reason is alone capable of an understanding that goes beyond appearances, of taking in total reality."[90] Here, we witness not a passive repetition of Bergson but, rather, an historical example of people not only actually thinking in duration but also existing within duration.

As mentioned earlier in this chapter, the various epistemological differences Senghor attributes to the African style of thinking and the European style of thinking also entail certain ontological implications with regard to conceptions of the world. Not surprisingly, Senghor maintains that the European style of thinking projects a world that is immobile, one consisting of an aggregate of meaningless objects; whereas the world as conceived by Africans is, for the most part, viewed as consistent with the flow of being itself and as receptive to difference and otherness. Senghor writes that the

European conception of the world is "*static, objective*, and *dichotomic*; it is in fact, dualistic, in that it makes an absolute distinction between body and soul, matter and spirit. It is founded on separation and opposition: on analysis and conflict. The African, on the other hand, conceives the world, beyond the diversity of its forms, as a fundamentally mobile, yet unique, reality that seeks synthesis."[91] He elaborates on this ontological contrast, stating that "as far as African ontology is concerned, [. . .] there is no such thing as dead matter: every being, every thing—be it only a grain of sand—radiates a life force, a sort of wave-particle; [. . .] and artists all use it to help bring the universe to its fulfillment."[92]

As to be expected, although Senghor was influenced by European thinkers, he also integrates root metaphors of African culture into his conception of African epistemology. These metaphors are consistent with a distinctive conception of knowledge. However, let us quickly review root metaphors of knowledge in Western philosophy. Traditional Western epistemology utilizes the metaphor of sight and vision to frame knowledge. Indeed, common conceptions of knowledge are highly dependent on visual metaphors, which in turn suggest perception as the natural way of interacting with world. Hence, common expressions such as "the mind's eye," "the light of reason," "the inner eye," "truth as correspondence or picturing of reality," and finally, the notion of "grasping something with the mind," meaning to see something clearly, are all intended as epistemological grids. The visual conception of knowledge, according to Senghor, is not dominant in the African context.[93] However, Senghor, using Bergson's conception of intuition as the source of knowledge of the inner realities of things, unapologetically resorts to music and dance (fundamental aesthetic phenomena) as the root metaphors grounding the African approach to knowledge. Sight presupposes separation from the object, but music and dance, according to Senghor, do not require the extensive use of only one sense or part of the body but, rather, the entire body. And to the extent that the entire body becomes implicated in the knowledge process, Senghor claims that the whole body becomes responsive to the rhythms of being, the object, or the Other. Senghor's point is not the celebration of sensual pleasure; rather, it concerns a different approach to knowledge. He writes,

> Let us pause for a moment to illustrate this proposition about the rhythm of a movement in music and dance. When I see a team in action, at a soccer game for example, I take part in the game with my entire body. When I listen to a jazz tune or an African [. . .] song, I have to make every effort not to break into song or dance [. . .] The reason for all this is that team

play reproduces the gestures natural to man, and that African [. . .] music and dance [. . .] reproduce the movements of the human body, which are in turn attuned to the movements of the brain and of the world [. . .] all the rhythms of the universe.[94]

Senghor also celebrated the rhythm of being that Bergson prior to him attributed to the creative and inventive forces of life. Since the notion of rhythm plays a prominent role in his thinking, a brief review of his account of rhythm is in order.

The Ontology of Rhythms

There is no exaggeration in claiming that every epistemology presupposes an ontology. At this time, we need to briefly review a crucial element of the ontology of being that sustains Senghor's epistemology. Again, like Bergson, his ontology is an ontology of rhythms. Diagne states that, following Bergson, Senghor "joyfully brought to light an ontology in which being is rhythm, an ontology which is at the foundation of [. . .] African religions."[95] Reference to rhythm, particularly in the context of Négritude, requires prudent clarification in order to distance our discussion from vulgar notions of rhythms that associate rhythm with pejorative conceptions of emotion, the absence of reason, and the lack of self-control. In the context of this chapter, the use of rhythm should conjure up the notion of style—but style that is not mechanical, style that is not the aggregate of discrete actions. Here we refer to style in the sense of being-in-groove such that the there is a durational profile to both action and the qualities of things.

Senghor identifies the existence of an African style an asymmetrical parallelism.[96] And he tells us that the "ordinary force that constitutes [African] style is rhythm."[97] This ontology of rhythm is not restricted to any particular kind of artistic activity but infuses a fundamental mode of existence.

Rhythm is not disorder nor is rhythm uncontrollable emotive acting out. Rhythm as style is also structure, form, and pattern. Rhythm also should connote the entanglements and the effects of powerful impulses and intense elements. As Diagne states, "Creation [in African arts] consists [. . .] in the composition of rhythms, in building a rhythm from units, which are themselves rhythms, by repeating them without repeating them exactly and by making them respond to each other through contrast and inversion."[98] If we were to abandon the passive focus on a fixed object and, instead, focus on the dynamic interaction of spaces and colors, Senghor, sounding very much like Bergson, claims, "A world of life forces that have to be *tamed* is substituted for a closed world of permanent and continuous substances that have to be *reproduced*."[99] Clearly, for Senghor, the appropriate response to the object is to view it as a composition and unity of rhythms, "a unity of rhythmic series that respond to one another."[100] The indisputable thrust of Senghor's conception of rhythm is its gesture toward continuity and communion with being. Though the common view is that rhythm is primarily a bodily phenomenon, Senghor, no enemy of the body, prefers to frame rhythm primarily as the dance of being. Being speaks through the sensual and material expression of rhythm. He writes,

> *What is rhythm?* It is the architecture of being, the internal dynamism that gives it form, the system of waves it gives off toward *Others*, the pure expression of vital force. Rhythm is the vibrating shock, the power which, through the senses, seizes us at the roots of our *Being*. It expresses itself through the most material and sensual means: lines, surfaces, colors, and volumes in architecture, sculpture and painting; accents in poetry and music; movements in dance. But, in doing this, it organizes all this concreteness toward the light of the *Spirit*. For the Negro African, it is insofar as it is incarnate in sensuality that rhythm illuminates the Spirit.[101]

Reason and Emotion in Négritude Epistemology

There are two other issues that warrant critical attention. The first concerns the normative status of reason in African epistemology. Some exasperated critics have maintained that Senghor in his unguarded moments advocated or hinted at ideas consistent with the view that Africans are incapable of rational thinking. Senghor, sensitive to these criticisms, denied that he attributed irrationality to Africans. Indeed, Senghor acknowledges the universality of reason in the sense that all human beings make use of reason. Senghor states that "reason is one, in the sense that it is made for the apprehension of the Other, that is, of objective reality. Its nature is governed by its own laws, but its modes of knowledge, its 'forms of thought,' are diverse and tied to the psychological and physiological makeup of each race."[102] Reason is instrumental but its instrumental orientation is not expressed uniformly among all cultures. Senghor's pluralistic view of reason is consistent with the existence of alternative systems of logic. He also extends this plurality from logic to the possibility of alternative cognitive and psychological structures. He quotes Gaëtan Picon approvingly: "There are several geometries, several possible kinds of logic, mentality and irreducible psychological structures."[103] Then, Senghor adds, "The mind, as well as the real, manifests itself through varied and conflicting images."[104] The core of Senghor's position is an endorsement of pluralism, specifically acknowledging different styles of thinking. Senghor, using the basic Bergsonian distinction between intellect and intuition, and the two different kinds of knowing associated with intellect and intuition, describes European thinking as thinking that is dominated by the features of the intellect, while African thinking is dominated by the features of intuition. He describes the difference in style of thinking as follows:

> Until the twentieth century, the European always separated himself from the object in order to know it. He kept it at a distance. I add that he always killed it, and fixed it in his analysis to be able to use it in practice [. . .] However paradoxical it may seem, the vital force of the Negro African, his surrender to the object, is animated by reason. Let us understand each other clearly; it is not the *reasoning-eye* of Europe, it is the *reason of touch* [i.e., of sympathy], better still, the reasoning embrace, more closely related to the Greek *logos* than to the Latin *ratio*. For *logos*, before Aristotle, meant both reason and the word. At any rate, Negro-African speech does not mold the object into rigid categories and concepts without touching it; it polishes things and restores their original color, with their texture, sound, and perfume [. . .] European reasoning is analytical, discursive by utilization; Negro-African reasoning is intuitive by participation.[105]

As previously noted, failure to appropriately contextualize Senghor's position, that is, a failure to situate his view about the difference between European analytical thinking and African reasoning as intuitive by participation within a Bergsonian context will result in rendering his position a shameful absurdity. Nevertheless, to the extent that Senghor capitalizes on Bergson's critique of the intellect, Senghor does not dogmatically set up an untenable metaphysical difference or biological difference between the African and the European; what he does with a degree of theoretical sophistication

Bergson, Senghor, and the Philosophical Foundations 111

and poetic ingenuity is to underscore a difference in approach to, in the words of Bergson, the stuff of "immediate experience." For if there exists a specific type of nondiscursive knowledge that is accessible only by intuition, knowledge emergent from fusion and harmony with things, then Senghor claims that this tradition of knowing is indisputably compatible with an African way of knowing or style of thinking. Acknowledging this style of thinking does not entail the claim that Africans are biologically incapable of rational thinking. Africans certainly are capable of rational and analytical thinking, but Senghor, like Bergson, concludes that this type of formal thinking is incapable of capturing the continuous, heterogeneous flow of duration, which is "the foundation of our being."[106]

A second critical concern is the ontological status of emotion in Senghor's conception of African epistemology. Senghor's critics suggest that he celebrates the vulgar racist view that African peoples are primarily emotional. The thrust of this stinging criticism is a reaction to Senghor's famous declaration: "Emotion is Negro as reason is Greek." As has been the tendency of his critics, the literal reading of this statement is that there are two racial groups: African and Europeans. Africans are by nature emotional and Europeans are by nature rational.

Ngũgĩ wa Thiong'o considers Senghor's statement as "mellifluous metaphysical nonsense."[107] Senghor has acknowledged the intensity of his critics, stating that, "Young people have criticized me for reducing Negro-African knowledge to pure emotion for denying that there is an African 'reason' or African techniques."[108] Senghor, sensitive to these criticisms, insists that his mentioning of vital force, African intuition, "does not contradict the present scientific ideas."[109] Again, it is important to note that if Senghor's take on reason is removed from the context of Bergson's distinction between intellect and intuition, and also his claim that intuition is the means by which we obtain knowledge of duration, Senghor's idea appears absurd and contradictory. For example, we recall Bergson's contention that the intellect uses the rigid categories and concepts of mathematics and logic to construct conceptions of reality. Bergson, however, variously claims that life, duration, consciousness, and vital force were not amenable to being regimented by mathematics and logic, but are agreeable to being captured by intuition. Senghor, actively embracing this Bergsonian take on things, claims that "Negro-African" reason is not deductive and does not subscribe to the traditional principles of logic that presupposes an ontology of permanence and stability. He radically concludes that African thought transcends the principles of identity, noncontradiction, and the excluded middle. Again, this is not to suggest that Africans never employ these logical principles. The more intriguing philosophical point is that, if classical logic is a logic of solids, a logic of dead matter, then it is inadequate when applied to the inventive and creative thrust of life. Senghor sets the appropriate context of intelligibility:

> The vital force of the African negro, that is, his surrender to the Other, is thus inspired by reason. But reason is not in this case, the *visualising* reason of the European White, but a kind of *embracing* reason which has more in common with *logos* than with *ratio*. *Ratio* is compass, T-square and sextant; it is measure and weight. *Logos* on the other hand was living word before Aristotle forged it into a diamond. Before the most typical human expression of a neural and sensory expression, *Logos* does not mold the object (without touching it) into rigid logical categories. The *word* of the African negro, which becomes flesh [. . .] restores objects to their primordial color, and brings their true grain and veins, their names and odors.[110]

Senghor, in another context, while further underscoring a basic Bergsonian orientation, unapologetically and in captivating poetic form, writes, "The Negro-African sympathizes, abandons his personality to become identified with the other, dies to be reborn in the other. He does not assimilate: he is assimilated. He lives a common life with the other; he lives in a symbiosis."[111]

Let us return to Senghor's statement, "Emotion is Negro as reason is Greek;" for there are other reasons that explain Senghor's statement, interpretations that preclude the need to impose a biological or an exclusively epistemological gloss on it. Senghor apparently first uttered the statement in the context of referring to African art and not as a declarative statement about the cognitive abilities of African peoples. Diagne offers the following analysis of Senghor's statement: "In my view it is at first and essentially in the aesthetic reflections of Senghor that what is primarily and above all an *analogy* found its meaning before it was transferred, with less fortune certainly, to the field of epistemology."[112] If Senghor's controversial statement is not exclusively about epistemology or about the cognitive abilities of Africans, then what is the focus of Senghor's statement? Diagne correctly establishes that Senghor is discussing African art, specifically African sculpture. Furthermore, Diagne claims that the context of intelligibility of the sentence is the fact that it "makes reference to the contrast between Greek statuary and African plastic art on which the authors of *Primitive Negro Sculpture* based their analysis of difference in aesthetic pleasures."[113] Yet, from another perspective, Senghor made his statement in the context of describing what he considers Africa's major contribution to the global culture of the twentieth century. As consistent with his pluralism and humanism, as well as his weariness about one-dimensional technological culture, Senghor claims that African art is a major contribution to the twentieth-century world of culture.[114] Third, after making his statement, Senghor, acting with the highest degree of intellectual responsibility, immediately construes emotion in terms of "rhythmic attitude" in anticipation of his discussion of African art. Hence, according to Diagne, the statement can be understood as follows: "Emotion is to African works of art what reason is to Hellenic statuary [. . .] It is in Senghor's aesthetic reflections that what is primarily and above all an *analogy* found its meaning before it was transferred [. . .] to the field of epistemology."[115] Here, the context of declaration is important. We must connect Senghor's contentious statement to his understanding of African art, as well as his utilization of Bergson's epistemological distinctions and resist the complacent urge to impose mind-boggling interpretations on his thought.

As with rhythm, Senghor also raised the question: what is an emotion? He rejects the view that an emotion is a mechanical muscular reaction or that an emotion is an unthinking immediate reaction. In seeking to distance emotions from being construed as arbitrary and immediate, Senghor endorses Sartre's conception of an emotion as "a sudden fall of consciousness into magic."[116] He further appropriates from Sartre the claim that "in emotion, consciousness is degraded and abruptly transforms the determined world in which we live in into a magical world."[117] Emotion, in this context, represents the transformation of consciousness, as a perspective in the world of determinism, the world governed by deterministic scientific laws and static logical rules and laws, to another mode of consciousness that is the accomplishment of forces behind the world of material objects. Similarly, Senghor also refers to the fact of one being moved to joy or tears as indicative of emotions, which, he states, are responses to the deep realities of things and are not merely uncontrolled reactions or instincts. After working through inadequate views of emotion, he writes,

> To be still more precise, an emotion is the seizure of one's entire being—both of consciousness and body—by the world of indeterminism; it is the irruption of the world of the mystical—or of magic—into the world of determinism. What emoves [i.e.,

what causes one to feel emotion] an African [. . .] is not so much the external aspect of an object as its profound reality: its *sub-reality*, and not so much the *sign as its sense* [. . .] To the extent that the sensible aspect, with its individual characteristics, is clearly perceived through the sense organs and nerves, it is only the sign of the sense of the object. Body and consciousness, sign and sense, constitute the same ambivalent reality. But the emphasis lies on the sense.

This means that an emotion, under its initial aspect as a fall of consciousness, is on the contrary *the rise of consciousness to a higher state of knowledge*. It is consciousness of the world," "a certain way of apprehending the world." It is an integrated consciousness, for "the 'emoved' subject and the 'emoving' object are united in an indissoluble synthesis" [. . .] [E]motion is a higher form of knowledge.[118]

Clearly, a careful reading of Senghor's text precludes misleading interpretations and caricatures of his thinking. Senghor was no mad ideologue; he was a serious thinker.

Conclusion

In concluding, it is hoped that this brief study has contributed to a rethinking of Négritude, as well as cultivated greater appreciation of the role of Bergson's thinking in its articulation. Accordingly, Négritude is not another nationalist, ideological fad. Nor is it another naive essentialist position, touting the virtues of a myopic identity. Rather, if we are serious about truly understanding Négritude, we must realize that Senghor strategically exploited resources from the French tradition of epistemology pertaining to logic, physics, mathematics, the critique of Western metaphysics, and so on to translate an African style of thinking in a language palatable to the world beyond Africa. If it is indeed true, as Leonard Lawlor claims in his recent study of Bergson, *The Challenge of Bergsonism*,[119] that Bergsonism fundamentally challenged phenomenology, ontology, and ethics, Senghor also employed Bergsonism to pose a fundamental challenge to colonialism, imperialism, and the violence of metaphysics. However, his major challenge was to directly confront the imperialistic epistemological orientation of scientific reason.

Notes

1. Bertrand Russell, *History of Western Philosophy* (London, Routledge, 2004), 722; cited in Daniel Alipaz, "Bergson and Derrida: A Question of Writing Time as Philosophy's Other," *Journal of French and Francophone Philosophy* 29, no. 2 (2011): 106.

2. Isaiah Berlin, "Impressionist Philosophy," *London Mercury* 32, no. 191 (1935): 489–90; cited in Daniel Alipaz, "Bergson and Derrida: A Question of Writing Time as Philosophy's Other," *Journal of French and Francophone Philosophy* 29, no. 2 (2011), 106.

3. Suzanne Guerlac, *Thinking in Time: An Introduction to Henri Bergson* (Ithaca, NY: Cornell University Press, 2006), 2.

4. Jean Millet, "Bergsonian Epistemology and Its Origins in mathematical Thought," in (eds.) Andrew Papanicolaou and Pete Gunter, *Bergson and Modern Thought: Towards a Unified Science* (New York: Harwood Academic Publishers, 1987), p. 29.

5. Guerlac, *Thinking in Time*, 185.

6. Guerlac, *Thinking in Time*, 65.

7. Henri Bergson, *Creative Evolution*, trans. Arthur Mitchell (Mineola, NY: Dover, 1998), 46.

8. Gary Gutting, *French Philosophy in the Twentieth Century* (Cambridge, UK: Cambridge University Press, 2001), 52.

9. Quoted in F. C. T. Moore, *Bergson: Thinking Backwards* (Cambridge, UK: Cambridge University Press, 1996), 59.

10. Henri Bergson, *Time and Free Will: An Essay on the Immediate Data of Consciousness*, trans. F. L. Pogson (Mineola, NY: Dover, 2001), 79.

11. Bergson, *Creative Evolution*, 22.

12. Keith Ansell-Pearson, "Bergson's Encounter with Biology," *Angelaki: Journal of the Theoretical Humanities* 10, no. 2 (August 2005): 59.

13. Henri Bergson, *The Creative Mind: An Introduction to Metaphysics*, trans. Mabelle Andison (Mineola, NY: Dover, 2007), 161.

14. Bergson, *The Creative Mind*, 161.

15. Guerlac, *Thinking in Time*, 40.

16. Milič Čapek, *Bergson and Modern Physics: A Reinterpretation and Reevaluation* (Dordrecht, Holland: D. Reidell Publishing Company, 1971), xi.

17. Bergson, *Creative Evolution*, 337.

18. Ibid., 306.

19. Ibid., 65.

20. Ibid., xii.

21. Ibid., 4.

22. Ibid., 185.

23. Ibid., 11.

24. Ibid., 39.

25. Maurice Merleau-Ponty, *In Praise of Philosophy and Other Essays*, trans. John Wild (Evanston, IL: Northwestern University Press, 1988), 14–15.

26. Guerlac, *Thinking in Time*, 71.

27. Bergson, *The Creative Mind*, 22.

28. Elizabeth Grosz, *Becoming Undone: Darwinian Reflections on Life, Politics, and Art* (Durham, NC: Duke University Press, 2011), 50.

29. Grosz, "Bergson and the Becoming of Unbecoming," *Parallax* 11, no. 2 (2005): 8.

30. Ibid.

31. Ibid.

32. Bergson, *The Creative Mind*, 136.

33. Keith Ansell-Pearson, *Germinal Life: The Difference and Repetition of Deleuze* (New York: Routledge, 1999), 33.

34. Martin Jay, *Downcast Eyes: The Denigration of Vision in Twentieth Century French Thought* (Berkeley: University of California Press, 1993), 202.

35. Bergson, *Creative Evolution*, 177.

36. Guerlac, *Thinking in Time*, 51–52.

37. Ibid., 52.

38. Elizabeth Grosz, *The Nick of Time: Politics, Evolution and the Untimely* (Durham, NC: Duke University Press, 2004), 234.

39. Bergson, *Time and Free Will*, 101.

40. Ibid., 15.

41. Ibid.

42. Léopold Sédar Senghor, *Liberté I, Négritude et Humanisme* (Paris: Seuil, 1964), 316–17. Quoted in Jacques Louis Hymans, *Léopold Sédar Senghor: An Intellectual Biography: An Intellectual Biography* (Edinburgh: Edinburgh University Press, 1971), 73.

43. Donna V. Jones, *The Racial Discourses of Life Philosophy: Négritude, Vitalism, and Modernity* (New York: Columbia University Press, 2012), 6.

44. Ibid., 131.

45. Ibid., 148.

46. Cheikh Thiam, *Return to the Kingdom of Childhood: Re-Envisioning the Legacy and Philosophical Relevance of Negritude* (Columbus: Ohio State University Press, 2014), 6.

47. Ibid., 6.

48. Bennetta Jules-Rosette, *Black Paris: The African Writers' Landscape* (Urbana: University of Illinois Press, 1998), 244.

49. Jean-Paul Sartre, "Black Orpheus," in *"What Is Literature?" and Other Essays* (Cambridge, MA: Harvard University Press, 1988), 291–330. Originally published as "Orphée Noir" in *Situations* III (Editions Gallimard, 1949).

50. Frantz Fanon, "On National Culture," in *The Wretched of the Earth*, trans. Constance Farrington (New York: Grove Press, 1968), 206–48.

51. Pramod Nayar formulates Fanon's critique of Négritude into the following six theses:
"a rejection of negritude's idea of a single, homogenous black culture;"
"a rejection of negritude's theme of the purity of precolonial black culture, self-identical and complete;"
"a rejection of negritude's search for continuities with a precolonial era (negritude's concern with the past cultures of Africa);"
"a concern that negritude—with its overemphasis on culture—does not really alter the daily life of the black man in any significant way;"
"a refusal to see one's identity as formed *exclusively* by one's shin colour and culture (as Négritude seems to suggest);"
"an impatience with Négritude for privileging race over class in all cases."
Pramod Nayar, *Frantz Fanon* (New York: Routledge, 2013), 110–11.

52. Abiola Irele, *The Négritude Moment: Explorations in Francophone African and Caribbean Literature and Thought* (Trenton, NJ: African World Press, 2011), 112.

53. Ibid., 117.

54. For Towa's analogizing of Négritude with servitude see his, Marcien Towa, *Léopold Sédar Senghor: Négritude ou Servitude* (Yaoundé: Éditions CLE, 1971).

55. Jules-Rosette, *Black Paris: The African Writers' Landscape*, 245.

56. Quoted in Irele, *The Négritude Moment: Explorations in Francophone African and Caribbean Literature and Thought*, 115.

57. Jane Hiddleston, *Decolonizing The Intellectual: Politics, Culture, and Humanism at the End of the French Empire* (Liverpool, UK: Liverpool University Press, 2014), 44.

58. See Stanislas Adotevi, *Négritude et Négrologues* (Paris: Éditions Le Castor Astral, 1972).

59. Stanislas Adotevi, "Négritude is Dead: The Burial," *Journal of the New African Literature and the Arts* 7/8 (1969–70): 74–75. Quoted in Thiam, *Return to the Kingdom of Childhood: Re-Envisioning the Legacy and Philosophical Relevance of Negritude*, 117. Editorial Note: There are differences between the Adotevi 1969–1970 version of this text and the version quoted in Thiam 2014.

60. Adotevi, *Négritude et Négrologues* (Paris: Éditions Le Castor Astral, 1972), 216. Quoted in Thiam, *Return to the Kingdom of Childhood: Re-Envisioning the Legacy and Philosophical Relevance of Negritude*, 22.

61. Quoted in Jules-Rosette, *Black Paris: The African Writers' Landscape*, 92–93. Adotévi, *Négritude et Négrologues*, 45.

62. Quoted in Jules-Rosette, *Black Paris: The African Writers' Landscape*, 245.

63. Adotévi, *Négritude et Négrologues*, 45. Quoted in Irele, *The Négritude Moment: Explorations in Francophone African and Caribbean Literature and Thought*, 115.

64. Wole Soyinka, "Myth, Literature, and the African World," in *I Am Because We Are: Readings in Black Philosophy*, eds. Fred Lee Hord and Jonathan Scott Lee (Amherst: University of Massachusetts Press, 1995), 85.

65. Ibid.

66. Ibid., 86.
67. Léopold Senghor, "Négritude: A Humanism of the Twentieth Century," in *The African Reader*, eds. Wilford Cartey and Martin Kilson (New York: Vintage Books, 1970), 181.
68. Ibid.
69. Quoted in Souleymane Bachir Diagne, *African Art as Philosophy: Senghor, Bergson and the Idea of Négritude*, trans. Chike Jeffers (New York: Seagull Books, 2011), 19.
70. Ousmane Sembène, "Novelist-Critic of Africa," *West Africa* (September 1962): 1041. Quoted in Elizabeth Harvey, *In Senghor's Shadow: Art, Politics, and the Avant-Garde in Senegal, 1960–1995* (Durham, NC: Duke University Press, 2004), 45.
71. V. Y. Mudimbe, *The Invention of Africa: Gnosis, Philosophy, and the Order of Knowledge* (Bloomington: Indiana University Press, 1988), 159.
72. Senghor, "Négritude: A Humanism of the Twentieth Century," 182.
73. Léopold Senghor and H. Kaal, "On Negrohood: Psychology of the African Negro," *Diogenes* 10, no. 1 (1968): 8.
74. Senghor, "Négritude: A Humanism of the Twentieth Century," 181.
75. Messay Kebede, "Négritude and Bergsonism," *Journal on African Philosophy* 3 (2003).
76. Abiola Irele, *The African Experience in Literature and Ideology* (London: Heinemann, 1981), 80.
77. Diagne, *African Art as Philosophy*, 122–23.
78. Quoted in Diagne, *African Art as Philosophy*, 54.
79. Ibid., 66.
80. Paul Guillaume and Thomas Munro, *Primitive African Sculpture* (New York: Harcourt, Brace and Company, 1926), 32. Quoted in Diagne, *African Art as Philosophy*, 66.
81. Ibid., 129.
82. Senghor and Kaal, "On Negrohood: Psychology of the Negro African," 2.
83. Bergson, *Creative Evolution*, 176.
84. Senghor and Kaal, "On Negrohood: Psychology of the Negro African," 2–3.
85. Ibid., 3.
86. Ibid., 1.
87. Ibid., 9.
88. Léopold Senghor, *On African Socialism* (London: Pall Mall Press, 1964), 73–74.
89. Senghor and Kaal, "On Negrohood: Psychology of the Negro African," 10.
90. Senghor, *On African Socialism*, 75.
91. Senghor, "Négritude: A Humanism of the Twentieth Century," 184.
92. Ibid., 185.
93. For an explanation of nonvisual conceptions of knowledge in African contexts, see, Oyèrónké Oyěwùmí, "Visualizing the Body: Western Theories and

African Subjects," in *African Gender Studies: A Reader* (New York: Palgrave Macmillan, 2005): 3–21.

94. Senghor and Kaal, "On Negrohood: Psychology of the Negro African," 4–5.

95. Diagne, *African Art as Philosophy*, 10.

96. See Diagne, *African Art as Philosophy*, 45–96.

97. Léopold Sédar Senghor, "What the Black Man Contributes," in Bernasconi (ed.), *Race and Racism in Continental Philosophy* (Bloomington: Indiana University Press, 2003), 289.

98. Diagne, *African Art as Philosophy*, 68.

99. Senghor, "Négritude: A Humanism of the Twentieth Century," 188.

100. Diagne, *African Art as Philosophy*, 81.

101. Léopold Sédar Senghor, "Lesthétique négro-africaine," 211–12. Quoted in Diagne, *African Art as Philosophy*, 77–78.

102. Senghor and Kaal, "On Negrohood: Psychology of the Negro African," 7.

103. Ibid., 8.

104. Ibid.

105. Léopold Sédar Senghor, *Nationhood and the African Road to Socialism*, trans. Mercer Cook (Paris: Presence Africaine, 1962), 70–74. Quoted in Jones, *The Racial Discourses of Life Philosophy*, 144.

106. Bergson, *Creative Evolution*, 39.

107. Quoted in Devin Zane Shaw, "The Vitalist Senghor," *Comparative and Continental Philosophy* 5, no. 1 (2013): 93.

108. Senghor, *On African Socialism*, 74.

109. Léopold Sédar Senghor, "Constructive Elements of a Civilization of African Negro Inspiration," *Presence Africaine* 24–25 (February–May 1959), 274. Quoted in Messay Kebede, "Négritude and Bergsonism," *Journal on African Philosophy* 3 (2003).

110. Senghor and Kaal, "On Negrohood: Psychology of the African Negro," 7.

111. Senghor, *On African Socialism*, 72.

112. Souleymane Bachir Dagne, "Rhythms: L. S. Senghor's Négritude as a Philosophy of African Art," *Critical Interventions: Journal of African Art History and Visual Culture* 1, no. 1 (2007): 57.

113. Diagne, *African Art as Philosophy*, 70.

114. See, Diagne, *African Art as Philosophy*, 70.

115. Diagne, *African Art as Philosophy*, 71.

116. Jean-Paul Sartre, *Basic Writings*, ed. Stephen Priest (New York: Routledge 2001), 105.

117. Jean-Paul Sartre, *The Emotions: Outline of A Theory*, trans. Bernard Frechtman (New York: The Wisdom Library, 1948), 83.

118. Senghor, "On Negrohood: Psychology of the African Negro," 14–15.

119. Leonard Lawlor, *The Challenge of Bergsonism* (London: Continuum, 2003).

Chapter 5

The Spectacle of Belonging

Henri Bergson's Comic Negro and the (Im)possibility of Place in the Colonial Metropolis

ANNETTE K. JOSEPH-GABRIEL

In its December 1931 issue, the Paris-based journal *La Revue du monde noir* invited its readers to weigh in on the question "How Should Negroes Living in Europe Dress?" Henri Bergson's *Le Rire: Essai sur la signification du comique* was the point of departure for this conversation. That black intellectuals in France dialogued with Bergson's work comes as no surprise given the French philosopher's influence on writers such as Léopold Sédar Senghor, cofounder of the Négritude movement that sought to valorize blackness through literary and cultural production in the twentieth century.[1] *La Revue du monde noir* was one such avenue for these conversations on black identity in the African diaspora, with its stated aim to "donner à l'élite intellectuelle de la Race noire et aux amis des Noirs un organe où publier leurs œuvres artistiques, littéraires et scientifiques" ("To give the intelligentsia of the black race and their partisans an official organ in which to publish their artistic, literary and scientific works").[2] The editors, Martinican journalist and writer Paulette Nardal and Haitian doctor Leo Sajous, published essays, short stories, and poetry by a variety of contributors, including the Harlem Renaissance writer Claude McKay, Guyanese colonial administrators René Maran and Félix Éboué, and Martinican writer and cultural theorist Jane Nardal (writing under the pseudonym Yadhé).[3]

In the six issues that appeared between 1931 and 1932, the open question to readers on the racial implications of Bergson's study is the only "Question Corner" segment published in *La Revue du monde noir*. Of all the newsworthy events in the French empire at the time, including the 1931 colonial exposition in Paris, why would Bergson's study on laughter and dress become the rallying point for a direct and sustained conversation between the editors, contributors, and readers of the bilingual journal? The editors' direct address to readers, soliciting their opinions on how black people in France should dress, highlights the importance of Bergson's ideas on laughter for the journal's larger conversations on race, power, and place in the metropole. In reading contributions by writers such as Paulette Nardal, Marie-Magdaleine Carbet, and Louis-Thomas Achille through the lens of Bergson's study on the comic, I argue that black intellectuals in Paris in the early twentieth century critically interrogated questions of authenticity and belonging in Europe's urban centers. Their focus on dress as an outward manifestation of culture allowed them to navigate both their hypervisibility and invisibility in the metropolitan space. In their engagement with Bergson's theory on disguise as a source of laughter, black intellectuals explored what it meant to lay claim to the Parisian space, and to assert their presence as legitimate and authentic, rather than as interlopers in need of the disguise of French assimilation in order to belong.

Laughter and the Black Body[4]

Henri Bergson's *Le Rire: Essai sur la signification du comique* first appeared in three installments in 1900 in the journal *La Revue de Paris*. Later compiled into a single volume, this philosophical examination of laughter sought to identify and categorize the elements that constitute the comedic. Bergson's initial title *Le Rire* (*ou plutôt sur le rire spécialement provoqué par le comique/ Laughter or Rather on Laughter Particularly Provoked by the Comic*), used in his prefaces to both the 1900 and 1924 editions, is telling of his larger project. He focuses less on laughter itself and more on what provokes it. His observations, as he states, "portent moins sur le comique lui-même que sur la place où il faut le chercher" ("focus less on the comic itself and more on where it can be found").[5] Bergson identifies the human body as a key site of comedy. He argues that physical deformities provoke laughter in the viewer who imagines the deformity to be fabricated. For example, "le bossu fait l'effet d'un homme qui se tient mal" ("the hunchback suggests the appearance of a person who holds himself badly").⁶ The deformed person becomes the object of laughter because her or his deformity has been crystallized into reality through force of habit. This rigidity of the body gives rise to ironic laughter because it highlights the automation of the individual.⁷ Bergson also gives the example of the customs official who, upon rescuing the victims of a shipwreck, asked the boat's passengers if they had anything to declare. Thus, beyond bodily manifestations of rigidity, intractable social attitudes are also a source of laughter.⁸

The black body, too, Bergson argues, is a source of comedy that provokes laughter from white viewers because it appears to be a white body in disguise. Bergson asks, "Pourquoi rit-on du nègre?" ("And why does one laugh at a negro?").⁹ He goes on to respond,

> Je ne sais pourtant si elle [la question] n'a pas été résolue un jour devant moi, dans la rue, par un simple cocher, qui traitait de "mal lavé" le client nègre assis dans sa voiture. Mal lavé! Un visage noir serait donc pour notre imagination un visage barbouillé d'encre ou de suie [. . .] Voici donc que le déguisement a passé quelque chose de sa vertu comique à des cas où l'on ne se déguise plus, mais où l'on aurait pu se déguiser [. . .] Maintenant, la coloration noire ou rouge a beau être inhérente à la peau: nous la tenons pour plaquée artificiellement, parce qu'elle nous surprend.¹⁰

> And yet I rather fancy the correct answer was suggested to me one day in the street by an ordinary cabby, who applied the expression "unwashed" to the negro fare he was driving. Unwashed! Does not this mean that a black face, in our imagination, is one daubed over with ink or soot? [. . .] And so we see that the notion of disguise has passed on something of its comic quality to instances in which there is actually no disguise, though there might be [. . .] In the latter, although the black or red colour is indeed inherent in the skin, we look upon it as artificially laid on, because it surprises us.¹¹

Bergson argues that the white coach driver perceives his black passenger as a white man in costume, an image that immediately calls to mind the practice of blackface in theater and later in cinema, usually intended for comic purposes. Black skin here is perceived as comic because like a clown's red nose it can potentially be shed and represents therefore the desire to present oneself, in an exaggerated fashion, as something other than one's true identity. It is important to note Bergson's use of the verb *barbouiller*, indicative of blackness as whiteness that is smeared or dirtied by ink or soot. Similar to the case of the viewer who laughs at the hunchback because she or he sees first an able-bodied man who then twists himself into a deformed shape; here too we find whiteness to be the point of departure, the normative state of being which is then deformed by the costume of black skin.

Bergson further argues that it is the element of surprise, the fact of being unaccustomed to seeing black skin that provokes derisive laughter from white viewers. We might imagine that at the time of Bergson's writing at the turn of the twentieth century, white viewers would find the black passenger surprising and by Bergson's logic comical specifically because he was operating outside the spaces of servitude and abject misery that he would be expected to inhabit. To be *mal lavé*, then, is to be unfit to circulate freely in spaces marked as white through an action as mundane as being a paying client of a coach driver. In this instance, the white viewer both misrecognizes blackness as deformed whiteness and displaces it from the space of everyday life in the city.

For Frantz Fanon and Aimé Césaire, public transportation, symbolic both as a site of public interaction and as a means of mobility through contested space, functions as the site of this racial misrecognition and displacement. In *Peau noir, masques blancs*, Fanon describes the feeling of alienation brought on by the empty seats next to him on the train. The white passengers' refusal to sit next to him, coupled with the exclamation "regarde le nègre!" fixes his identity to his skin color and marks him as other, as out of place.[12] For Césaire, this alienation quickly becomes internalized. In *Cahier d'un retour au pays natal*, we no longer find the black passenger to be the object of a white viewer's mockery. Rather, it is a black viewer who adopts the role and position of the white viewer and engages in mocking laughter. Thus, Césaire's narrator describes with "un grand sourire complice" / "a wide smile of connivance," "un nègre comique et laid et des femmes derrière moi ricanaient en le regardant" / "a nigger who was comical and ugly, and behind me women were looking at him and giggling."[13] Here we see the supposedly comical black passenger from the concerted perspective of the narrator and the women behind him. In each of these cases, black people are denied recognition of their humanity and refused the possibility of being. Bergson's black coach passenger is therefore "thingified," to borrow

Aimé Césaire's formulation.[14] The dual process of rendering his personhood invisible while rendering his body hypervisible undergirds the possibility of racial laughter.[15]

This thingification, or the reduction of the human to an object, is central to the Bergsonian notion of laughter wielded as a tool of ridicule. As Michael Billig argues in *Laughter and Ridicule: Towards a Social Critique of Laughter*, Bergson's theory of the social function of laughter rests on three observations: that the object of laughter is always human or made by human hands, that laughter is accompanied by an absence of empathy, and that laughter is associated with collective identification.[16] The first two observations are particularly pertinent to the coach driver and his black passenger, for while the coach driver's derisive laughter is aimed at a fellow human being, that humanity is stripped away by the view of the passenger as but an imitation of a white man. As Billig notes, "Normal social life involves us taking the attitude of the other, continually imagining how others feel [. . .] With laughter we free ourselves from the customary restrictions of social empathy, as the target of our mirth momentarily becomes an object, and not a fellow human being."[17] Blackness, read as a sullying layer of ink or soot, stands in the coach driver's perception as that obstacle to empathy that precludes the possibility of identification across color lines.

As evidenced by the examples of the hunchback and the black coach passenger, laughter is provoked not only by the external—that is the sight of the body deemed comic—but also by internal assumptions in the mind of the viewer that determine how the supposedly comic body is perceived. What then is the function of this laughter? What does it tell us, not just about the person on the receiving end of derisive laughter but also about the person who laughs? Bergson argues that laughter is above all an act of complicity, an act by which the individual creates a form of identification with a larger group. Thus, if laughter as mockery suggests an inability to identify with a person or group deemed as other, it can also serve as a form of identification with those deemed similar to the person who laughs. In short, laughter has a dual function of othering and establishing affinity. As Bergson argues,

> Le rire cache une arrière-pensée d'entente, je dirais presque de complicité, avec d'autres rieurs, réels ou imaginaires. Combien de fois n'a-t-on pas dit que le rire du spectateur, au théâtre, est d'autant plus large que la salle est plus pleine; Combien de fois n'a-t-on pas fait remarquer, d'autre part, que beaucoup d'effets

comiques sont intraduisibles d'une langue dans une autre, relatifs par conséquent aux mœurs et aux idées d'une société particulière.[18]

However spontaneous it seems, laughter always implies a kind of complicity with other laughers, real or imaginary. How often has it been said that the fuller the theatre, the more uncontrolled the laughter of the audience! On the other hand, how often has the remark been made that many comic effects are incapable of translation from one language to another, because they refer to the customs and ideas of a particular social group![19]

Laughter therefore fulfills the social function of inclusion, of determining who belongs to a group defined by shared language and social codes. Despite the appealing image of social bonding through laughter, the process of inclusion suggests also an attendant process of exclusion for those defined as outsiders, those unable or unwilling to partake in complicit laughter.

Indeed, Bergson goes on to show that this process of inclusion is anything but benign, particularly for the newcomer. He gives the example of hazing, a process in which laughter serves a so-called corrective function, seeking to humiliate the object of laughter so that she or he may conform to the group's values. He notes, "S'il est permis de comparer aux petites choses les grandes, nous rappellerons ici ce qui se passe à l'entrée de nos Écoles. Quand le candidat a franchi les redoutables épreuves de l'examen, il lui reste à en affronter d'autres, celles que ses camarades plus anciens lui préparent pour le former à la société nouvelle où il pénètre et, comme ils disent, pour lui assouplir le caractère" ("If it is permissible to compare important things with trivial ones, we would call to mind what happens when a youth enters one of our military academies. After getting through the dreaded ordeal of the examination, he finds that he has other ordeals to face, which his seniors have arranged with the object of fitting him for the new life he is entering upon, or, as they say, of 'breaking him into harness' ").[20] The military academy here functions as a microcosm of a larger society and reveals the role of laughter in demarcating the newcomer as an outsider in need of molding to fit an acceptable new image. I use the word *mold* here deliberately. Recall the example of the hunchback whose supposedly comic deformity is viewed as the result of the long-term rigid pose in which he has held himself, or the customs official whose rigidity causes him to respond like an automaton even in an exceptional situation. For Bergson, laughter is provoked by rigidity, a lack of grace and flexibility that would allow one to adapt: "Si donc on voulait définir ici le comique en le rapprochant de son contraire, il faudrait l'opposer à la grâce plus encore qu'à la beauté. Il est plutôt raideur que laideur" ("If, then, at this point we wished to define the comic by comparing it with its contrary, we should have to contrast it with gracefulness even more than with beauty. It partakes rather of the unsprightly than of the unsightly, of RIGIDNESS rather than of UGLINESS").[21] Bergson reinforces his argument that it is one's inability or unwillingness to change, to adapt, to be flexible, that provokes laughter from others.

Laughter therefore has a social function. It "serves as a corrective that frees us of obsessions, rigidity, automatism and inelasticity and allows us to become full-fledged members of the community."[22] Yet Bergson's language ultimately reveals that this process of defining community and the attendant impulses of inclusion and exclusion enact a measure of violence. Thus, it is telling that in the example of the student's hazing, Bergson uses the verb *assouplir*, best translated as "to make supple or flexible," to describe the corrective function of laughter in this context. If not cruel enough to break the object of laughter, it is at least powerful enough to bend her or him toward the goal of conforming. As John Parkin so cogently argues in *Laughter and Power*, "What laughter does, for Bergson, is symbolise and embody society's punishment of the eccentric outsider who has in some way sold life and nature short by rendering them in whatever form mechanical, be it in his behaviour, words or appearance."[23] Mockery through laughter is ultimately a tool that allows the laugher to wield power over those who are ridiculed for their perceived difference and deviance from an accepted norm.

Reclaiming Authenticity in *La Revue du monde noir*

It is therefore not surprising that Bergon's *Le Rire* struck a chord with the editors of the Paris-based journal *La Revue du monde noir*. Many of the journal's black contributors and readers were or had once been students who had passed the first test that Bergson states in his hazing example, namely, that of gaining admission into France's most competitive and elite schools.[24] Now they were seemingly faced with the second test, that of conforming, of being molded, or—in French colonial parlance—assimilating. In using Bergson as the point of departure to ask how black people in France should dress, they were engaged in a conversation that went beyond sartorial choices. The journal's editors and contributors were interested in exploring, in political and philosophical terms, the power dynamics at work when white viewers misrecognize and displace Europe's black inhabitants from spaces coded as white through laughter as punitive action.

La Revue du monde noir took up the Bergsonian idea of comedy as part of a transatlantic conversation on race and belonging in the French empire. The specific framing of the question is strikingly similar to the phrasing of an essay topic assigned by a white teacher at the Lycée Schœlcher in Martinique. *La Revue du monde noir*'s December 1931 issue asked, " 'Pourquoi la vue d'un noir habillé à l'européenne provoque-t-elle le rire du Blanc?' s'est demandé Bergson dans son étude sur le rire. 'Parce que le Blanc a l'impression que le Noir est déguisé' " (" 'Why does the sight of a Negro dressed in European fashion provoke the laugh of the white man?' is the question which Bergson asked himself in his study on laughter. 'Because the white man thinks the Negro is disguised' is his answer").[25] The January 22, 1932 edition of the Martinican newspaper *L'Action Nouvelle* reported a similar question used as an essay prompt that sparked a protest in Fort-de-France: "Why does the Negro make Whites laugh when he dresses like a European?"[26] Their nearly identical misquoting of Bergson suggests that these two sources were in conversation both with each other and with the French philosopher who in his study on laughter asks simply: "Pourquoi rit-on du nègre?" ("And why does one laugh at a negro?").[27] Bergson's response on disguise, " 'Un nez rouge est un nez peint,' 'un nègre est un blanc déguisé' " (" 'A red nose is a painted nose,' 'a negro is a white man in disguise' "),[28] suggests that in the matter of perceiving race, the viewer experiences a desire to peel back the layers, even when there are none to peel, in order to uncover a fundamental identity beyond that which is outwardly portrayed. The impact of *La Revue du monde noir*'s open question to readers, then, seems to have been twofold. First, it situated this conversation on race and belonging in both metropolitan and overseas France. Second, the Bergsonian desire to look beyond outward appearance in order to uncover some inner, perhaps hidden identity allowed the journal's contributors to examine the possibilities of belonging in white spaces both through and beyond blackness.

The editors' focus on dress in their question to readers garnered responses that focused on the fashion choices of Europe's black inhabitants, thus departing somewhat from Bergson's formulation of blackness as whiteness in disguise. *La Revue du monde noir*'s framing refocuses attention away from the imagined white subject's approximating blackness as articulated in Bergson's study and toward the black subject's motives for imitating or adapting (the distinction between the two was a main point of contention for the respondents) European cultural norms and values. Consequently, *La Revue du monde noir* shifts the focus away from a dehumanized black body that is the object of laughter in Bergson's text, to black writers and intellectuals as speaking subjects. The journal's contributors are no longer the voiceless recipients of the epithet *mal lavé*, but rather speak for themselves in examining power, place, and representation in the metropole. In repurposing Bergson's image of bodies in disguise, the journal foregrounds the questions of power and belonging that remain implicit in the French philosopher's examination of laughter.

This reframing shaped the tenor of the responses received. As T. Denean Sharpley-Whiting notes, "The respondents took up the issues of identity, nationalism, colonialism, authenticity, and Europe as a universal culture."[29] All of these issues are central to the response provided by the Martinican novelist, poet, and essayist Marie-Magdaleine Carbet, writing under the pseudonym Magd Raney.[30] Carbet, like the other respondents—Louis-Thomas Achille and Clara Shepard—argues that black people in Europe should undoubtedly adopt European dress. Carbet chronicles her conversations with a white French tailor, famous for clothing all of the Quartier Latin, and a milliner whose clientele included "exotic Creole beauties."[31] Each of these experts gives advice on how to valorize skin tone and body build, all the while adhering to the latest Parisian fashion. Despite—or perhaps within—Carbet's focus on the glitz and glamour of French couture, two things are striking. First, her essay opens on a surprising note by arguing for the adoption of both European dress and weapons: "Il faut bien que sous les ciels froids de l'Europe civilisée le pardessus et le revolver remplacent le pagne, l'arc et les flèches en usage dans la jungle africaine" ("Of course, under the cold grey skies of civilized Europe, the overcoat and the revolver must replace the loincloth and the bow and arrows in use in the African jungle").[32] Carbet's parallel structure juxtaposes civilized Europe and the jungles of Africa and suggests that both spaces function similarly with cosmetic differences, a radical idea in the early twentieth century. In pairing the overcoat with the revolver, Carbet also underscores the violence present in this process of assimilation. This double juxtaposition of Europe and Africa, clothing and weapons, sets the tone for the rest of her examination of perceptions of blackness in public spaces in Paris.

Even more striking is Carbet's representation of the white viewer in Bergson's narrative. Having delivered her categorical answer on the need to adopt European dress in her opening lines she asks, "Alors? L'enquête de la revue n'a pas de raison d'être? Non, si l'on omet ceci que 'la vue d'un Noir habillé à l'européenne provoque le rire du Blanc.' Il faut compter avec le Blanc? Comptons avec lui. J'en ai questionné quelques-uns. Voici des réponses" ("Well, in that case, the inquiry of the Review is pointless. Not in the least; for we must keep in mind that 'the sight of a Negro dressed in European fashion always provokes the laughter of the white man.' Then we must reckon with the white man? Very well. I have questioned several, and here are their replies").[33] Carbet articulates the unequal power relation between white viewer and black object of laughter and challenges the white viewer's power to define. She responds to her own question with the firm resolve to "reckon with" and reverse the white viewer's objectification of blackness. She questions white acquaintances on their reactions to seeing black people on the streets of Paris and thus turns these white viewers into the ones to be studied and represented. This reversal mirrors the tenor of Bergson's study, which also invites readers to play the role of external observer to those who laugh, rather than to participate in laughter themselves. "To understand laughter" from the Bergsonian point of view, "we must observe others, not draw inwards on ourselves."[34] Carbet's reversal makes a similar claim by shifting the focus from *La Revue du monde noir*'s question on the physical appearance and self-presentation of black people in France, to white viewers' assumptions about race and belonging that make the journal's question a necessary line of inquiry in the first place.

The tongue-in-cheek nature of the responses of the white commentators that Carbet polls, however, suggest that they are the fictionalized products of her own attempts to inhabit the mind of an imagined white Parisian. The responses she garners are worth quoting here in their entirety because, while they focus on the exoticization of blackness, they reveal far more about the white viewers—whether real or imagined—than about those on the receiving end of their laughter:

>—Le noir? Mais il peut aller tout nu s'il lui plaît, on se retournera toujours sur son passage.
>
>—Qu'il veuille ou non, il attire l'attention. Qu'il tâche de la soutenir honorablement.
>
>[. . .]—Le pagne? Oui, sans doute, ce serait bien . . . La fringale d'exotisme du public s'en trouverait bien. Mais alors il nous faudrait un rudiment de cadre. Nous commanderions des paillotes et un bout de forêt vierge au décorateur de la scène

du Châtelet, un soleil aussi africain que possible à l'électricien qui embrase la Tour Eiffel au compte de Citroën et le tour serait joué.[35]

"The Negro? But he could go stark naked if he liked. People will always turn round to look at him."
"Whether he wants it or not, he will always attract attention. It is his duty to live up to it."
[. . .] "The loin-cloth? Yes, undoubtedly that would be very good especially since the recent fad for everything colonial. But then we would need at least a shade of background. We would order up some some [sic] thatched huts and a bit of virgin forest from the scenery director of the Châtelet and a sun as African as possible from the electrician who illuminates the Eiffel Tower and the trick would be turned."[36]

In these responses, the white viewer's fascination with blackness replicates the Bergsonian emphasis on the corporeal. The colonial rhetoric that objectifies blackness as spectacle is intertwined here with the language of desire, as evidenced by the assertion that a black person attracts the same kind of attention whether clothed or naked. The underlying sexual nature of this desire is articulated also through a focus on consumption. Carbet's white informants reveal the ongoing desire to consume an imagined and fabricated other, whose performance of alterity in the streets of Paris takes on a theatrical quality. That those responsible for providing electricity to the Eiffel Tower would also produce "a sun as African as possible" to serve as a backdrop for this performance of otherness further inscribes this desire in the long history of French constructions of so-called primitive cultures to serve as both proof of French modernization and progress and also as occasional escape from that very modernization.

Where Carbet explores the psyche of the laughing white viewer, Louis-Thomas Achille and Clara Shepard read Bergson through an afrodiasporic lens in order to address questions of adaptation and authenticity. Their responses connect the experiences of black Parisians to those of black Americans, furthering the internationalist project of *La Revue du monde noir*. Achille and Shepard both argue for a joint process of adoption and adaptation of European culture, manifested through dress. As Achille puts it, "Sous peine de vivre dans l'incommodité, de se faire constamment remarquer, en détonant dans une civilisation qui a son harmonie propre, les Noirs, vivant en Europe, doivent, semble-t-il, user des modes européennes. Mais comment? à la manière des Blancs, sans égard pour leur couleur? Oui, s'ils veulent s'exposer aux rires des Blancs" ("In my opinion, Negroes should follow European fashions when they live in Europe, if they do not want to feel uneasy or to introduce a false note in the harmony of the civilisation in which they come to dwell. But must they behave like white persons? Yes, if they wish to be laughed at").[37] Rejecting the overdetermination of blackness present in the French desire for an "authentic other" that Carbet exposes in her writing, Achille argues here for the conscious construction of a hybridized identity that draws on European influences in order to valorize black cultures.[38] While neither Shepard nor Achille explicitly refer to Bergson's argument on the comic nature of rigidity, they nonetheless implicitly engage with this idea through their emphasis on cultural adaptation. They articulate the possibility of shaping their cultural expressions through dress, rather than rigidly performing an imagined authentic black culture that would ultimately lead to the caricature of blackness that Carbet describes in her piece.

Reading assimilation through Bergson reveals that the comic in this case lies not in the unsuccessful mimicry of European culture but rather in the rigidity and unwillingness to adapt to a new culture and climate. Yet in this joint process of adoption and adaptation that Achille advocates lies ultimately the power to claim this adapted culture as one's own. Thus, Achille argues that European culture, a term that remains undefined in his essay, is a universal one, not by virtue of its superiority but rather due to the history of colonial erasure that makes claims to a pure and distinctly non-European culture impossible for some of France's colonized subjects.[39] For the contributors to *La Revue du monde noir*, the line between insider and outsider was to be constantly and carefully negotiated, particularly by France's colonized subjects who were engaged in the act of defining and representing themselves both on the streets of Paris and in the pages of bilingual journals.

Putting on Identities in the Metropole

The multiple dualities that underlie the debate in *La Revue du monde noir* resurface in another journal, *L'Étudiant noir*, published in Paris in 1935 by the Association of Martinican Students. Notably in her short narrative

"Guignol Ouolof," which appeared in the journal's first edition, Paulette Nardal addresses explicitly the dual consciousness of "une Noire antillaise trop occidentalisée" ("an overly Westernized Antillean Negro woman") confronted with the sight of a black man viewed as a comic spectacle.[40] Both *La Revue du monde noir* and *L'Étudiant noir* have been cited as early articulations of Négritude *avant la lettre*. Nardal's narrative in particular has been read at the intersection of feminism and race consciousness.[41] In this story that blurs generic boundaries between autobiography and fiction, Nardal tells the story of an Antillean woman catching a "quick lunch" in a Parisian café before attending a theater performance.[42] The approach of a comically dressed black peanut vendor causes the narrator to reflect on her own complex self-positioning as a relatively privileged black woman, and the (im)possibility of racial solidarity in the metropole. In *The Practice of Diaspora: Literature, Translation and the Rise of Black Internationalism*, Brent Edwards undertakes a nuanced reading of the subtle shifts in subject position that occur within the narrator as she nervously contemplates the peanut vendor's approach and her heightened awareness of the white café patrons' scrutiny. I will not replicate Edwards' astute reading here.[43] Rather I will show that "Guignol Ouolof" is also an extension of Nardal's engagement with Bergson's study on the comic. Read in this light, the story explores not just the articulation of racial solidarity, but also examines the terms on which black people may lay claim to European spaces.

Movement is key in parsing out Nardal's writing, as is indicated by the descriptions that bookend the narrative:

> Tout à coup, entre la lumière et moi s'interpose la silhouette d'un Noir immense. Costume de général d'opérette. Drap noir sur lequel éclatent des brandebourgs imposants, épaulettes, casquette plate d'officier allemande, galonnée d'or et de rouge, et détail encore plus inattendu, monocle à cordonnet noir, encastré dans l'arcade courtilière gauche. Ce détail incongru, dans ce costume absurde n'arrive pas à donner au long visage ouolof, l'effet de grotesque recherché. Pris en lui-même, il me rappelle curieusement certain visage blanc, au sourire grave et à l'air infiniment noble.
>
> Mais l'ensemble est indéniablement comique, et quand passé à coté de notre chasseur noir, vendeur de cacahouètes, son collègue métropolitain, éphèbe blond à la sobre livrée marron, et qui vend, lui, des cigarettes, le contraste est simplement révoltant.

[. . .] Poussée par la curiosité professionnelle, je n'hésite pas à lui poser une question dénuée de tact: 'Ne trouve-t-il pas pénible de porter ce costume ridicule, et de faire rire les gens?' La voix éraillée et un peu assourdie, il me répond avec beaucoup de bon sens: 'Pas plus qu'un acteur comique au théâtre. J'ai d'ailleurs été acteur. J'aime autant faire ce métier ridicule que d'être chômeur ou de vivre des femmes [. . .]' Et puis, avec un sourire d'une inimitable finesse: 'Les Blancs veulent qu'on les fasse rire; moi, je veux bien [. . .] au moins, je peux manger.'[44]

Suddenly, the silhouette of an immense Negro is interposed between me and the lights. A general's costume from the operetta. Black cape on which imposing brandenburgs glitter, epaulettes, the flat cap of a German officer, trimmed with braid of gold and red, and an even more unexpected detail, a monocle attached to a black cord, set in courtly arch to the left. This incongruous detail in the absurd costume does not succeed in giving the long Wolof face the desired grotesque effect. Taken by himself, he reminds me curiously of certain white faces, with grave smiles and an infinitely noble air.

But the ensemble is undeniably comic, and when next to our black bellhop, the peanut vendor, there passes his metropolitan colleague, a blond ephebe in a sober brown livery, selling cigarettes, the contrast is simply revolting.

[. . .] Pushed by professional curiosity, I do not hesitate to ask him a question devoid of tact: "Does he find it hard to wear that ridiculous costume, and to make people laugh?" His voice hoarse and slightly lowered, he replies with a great deal of sense: "Not more than a comic actor in the theater. Besides, I used to be an actor. I like doing this ridiculous job as much as being unemployed, or living off women [. . .]" And then, with a smile of inimitable finesse: "The Whites want us to make them laugh; me, I really want [. . .] at least I can eat."[45]

For Edwards, the concluding paragraph in particular is key to understanding the narrator's negotiation of "imperial fraternity [and] the ways it is predicated on certain gendered and racial exclusions."[46] He argues that there is no other way to read Nardal's direct quote at the end of the story than as an address to the black vendor, but referring to his white colleague.

She pointedly does not say "you," but asks about the cigarette seller. (The reader's resistance to this grammatical positioning—the reaction that she *must* mean the African vendor with the pronoun "he," that it *must* be a "slip," that it *must* be a faulty use of quotes indicating direct address—might best be considered a "symptom" of the reader's own implication in this narrative staging of the colonial spectacle).[47]

Resituating Nardal's use of the comic in the context of her larger body of work, however, suggests an alternative reading of this moment in her narrative.

Nardal's opening description of the African vendor's clothing is in fact a direct engagement with Bergson's ideas on racialized laughter. Note that unlike his white counterpart, the cigarette seller, who is dressed according to the norms of his occupation in a uniform, the peanut vendor is doubly disguised in Bergsonian terms, first by virtue of his skin color and second by virtue of his extraordinary ensemble, which Nardal describes as a costume. Recall also that for Bergson, it is the element of surprise, the unexpected sight of a black person that provokes the white viewer's laughter. Nardal underscores this notion of surprise in her description of the unexpected ("inattendu") and incongruous ("incongru") details of the peanut vendor's dress. Read through a Bergsonian lens, it is not the white vendor's uniform that is ridiculous but rather that of the African vendor who provokes laughter through the double disguise of his skin and costume. Nardal clearly associates the words "absurd" ("absurde") and "comic" ("comique") with the African vendor's costume in order to interrogate the source of laughter directed at him in the markedly white space of the Parisian café.

Nardal, however, makes this association as a step in her larger project of dissociating the costume from its wearer, notably in her insistence that "the absurd costume does not succeed in giving the long Wolof face the desired grotesque effect."[48] Instead, beneath the comic, she finds the "grave and noble air" of a black face that reminds her of a white one. The scholarship on "Guignol Ouolof" largely elides this moment, for what are we to do with the narrator's sighting of whiteness underneath a Wolof face, in a story about "the need for racial unity"?[49] Read through a Bergsonian lens, Nardal's narrative peels back the layers of costume and skin to catch a glimpse of what lies beneath the supposed disguise. She refuses the subject position of the white viewer who misrecognizes the black vendor in costume as an unsuccessful mimicry of whiteness and displaces him from the Parisian space. For Nardal, the peanut vendor is neither a white man in disguise nor a black man poorly imitating cultures to which he has no claim. Rather, like the white face whose nobility and gravity mirrors his own, the long Wolof face is not out of place in the space of Parisian everyday life. It too belongs in the Parisian café.

In his halting speech "I really want . . . at least I can eat . . . ,"[50] the black vendor writes himself out of the language of desire—in his inability, or more likely refusal to articulate what he really wants—that characterized Carbet's ventriloquizing of white viewers' desires in *La Revue du monde noir*. While the vendor echoes the language of consumption, he casts it in quotidian terms, in the context of everyday sustenance. His is a desire to exist in a space marked as white, a desire that remains suspended, held in the ellipses.

Indeed it is significant that the black peanut vendor was once an actor, not only because he brings the performative nature of identity from the stage into the context of everyday life, as scholars have noted, but also because disguise is central to his craft. Thus, in emphasizing the gravity, nobility, and finesse beneath the comic, Nardal rejects the making into spectacle of her interlocutor and his claims to the space. Césaire articulates the profound dehumanization of this making into spectacle in his long poem *Cahier d'un retour au pays natal* when he admonishes: " 'Et surtout mon corps aussi bien que mon âme, gardez-vous de vous croiser les bras dans l'attitude stérile du spectateur, car la vie n'est pas un spectacle, car une mer de douleurs n'est pas un proscenium, car un homme qui crie n'est pas un ours qui danse . . . ' " (" 'And above all beware, my body and my soul too, beware of crossing your arms in the sterile attitude of the spectator, because life is not a spectacle, because a sea of sorrows is not a proscenium, because a man who screams is not a dancing bear' ").[51] Césaire's evocation of the proscenium, the part of the theater stage in front of the curtain where the action takes place, is particularly pertinent here. Laughter as mockery, in Bergsonian terms, arises from the conflation of the vendor with his costume, the misrecognition of a man as a dancing bear and of pain as theatrical performance. Laughter refuses the peanut vendor's humanity, the human right to exist in the space. Thus, Nardal peels away the spectacular, laughter-inducing costume as the reader moves through the text in order to get to the vendor's most fundamental, intimate, and ultimately mundane desire to eat, that is, to sustain himself in this space. This encounter between a former actor and a theatergoer functions as an opening act, bringing the stage onto the streets as Carbet does when she critiques her white informants' desires for black Parisians performing their otherness in a landscape decorated by the Châtelet theater's stage director. Nardal's short story is therefore not only about the possibility for racial unification. It is also about the possibility of recognition and identification across a difference that seeks to dehumanize through laughter. At the heart of this narrative that stages an encounter between two black interlocutors is an exploration of what it means to lay claim to a space and culture from which black people have been excluded.[52]

Placing Nardal's narrative in the continuity of her engagement with Bergson demands that we read the question she poses at the end of her narrative, demarcated by quotation marks in the text, as a direct address both to the reader and to the peanut vendor. Nardal is not speaking to the black vendor of his white colleague. Instead, the moment in which she asks, "Does he find it hard to wear that ridiculous costume, and to make people laugh?"[51] represents a dual address to the reader and the African vendor as her interlocutors. Nardal pauses in her narrative to report directly to the reader, the implied "you," the specific question she posed both to and about the peanut seller, referred to here in the third person "he." Rather than signal a deviation from the descriptive mode of her storytelling up until this point, it is a rhetorical strategy that takes the reader back to the moment in *La Revue du monde noir* when Nardal pauses the journal's business as usual to open up a more direct conversation with readers in asking explicitly, "Why does the sight of a Negro dressed in European fashion provoke the laugh of the white man?" "Guignol Ouolof" is Nardal's extended response to the question she posed four years earlier in the pages of *La Revue du monde noir*. It is a continued conversation on race, authenticity, and place for France's colonial subjects in the metropole. For the black intellectuals who engaged Bergson in the pages of Parisian journals in the interwar years, laughter was anything but frivolous. Their repurposing of Bergson's study on the comic to focus on its racial implications represents also a philosophical engagement with the possibility of carving spaces of being in the colonial metropolis.

Notes

1. See Souleymane Bachir Diagne, *African Art as Philosophy: Senghor, Bergson and the Idea of Negritude* (New York: Seagull Books, 2011).

2. *La Revue du monde noir: The Review of the Black World, 1931–1932: Collection Complete*, 1 à 6 (Paris: Jean-Michael Place, 1992). All English translations in this essay are from published English versions unless otherwise indicated.

3. Jane Nardal is best known for her use of the term "Afro-Latin" to articulate ideas of cultural mixing as a way for black intellectuals to resist the

cultural erasure that the French colonial project of assimilation sought to enact. Nardal, like her compatriot Aimé Césaire and many of the writers in the pages of *La Revue du monde noir*, would advocate assimilating on one's own terms rather than to be assimilated. See T. Denean Sharpley-Whiting, "Femme Négritude: Jane Nardal, La Dépêche Africaine, and the Francophone New Negro," *Souls: A Critical Journal of Black Politics, Culture, and Society* 2, no. 4 (2000): 8–17. T. Denean Sharpley-Whiting, "Femme Négritude: Jane Nardal, La Dépêche Africaine, and the Francophone New Negro," *Souls: A Critical Journal of Black Politics, Culture, and Society* 2, no. 4 (2000): 8–17.

 4. Robin D. G. Kelley analyzes the frequent use of the term "black bodies" in contemporary scholarship and its increasing tendency to "stand in for actual people with names, experiences, dreams, and desires." I employ this term in the first part of this essay in order to analyze Bergson's specific emphasis on corporeal imagery in his attempts to situate bodies as sites of laughter. In the subsequent sections of this essay, the term is absent as I take up black intellectuals' efforts to counter dehumanizing colonial representations by shifting the emphasis from anonymous black bodies to culture and agency. See Robin D. G. Kelley, "Black Study, Black Struggle," *Boston Review: A Political and Literary Forum* (March 2016).

 5. Henri Bergson, *Le Rire: Essai sur la signification du comique* (Paris France: Alcan, 1900). 6; Henri Bergson, *Laughter: An Essay on the Meaning of the Comic* (New York: Macmillan, 1911), 3.

 6. Ibid., 18/23.

 7. Ibid., 26–27/23–24.

 8. For an analysis of the Darwinian roots of Bergson's theorizing of rigidity, as well as the impact of this theorizing on contemporary philosophers, see Donna V. Jones, *The Racial Discourses of Life Philosophy: Négritude, Vitalism, and Modernity* (New York: Columbia University Press, 2010), 52–54.

 9. Ibid., 24/40.

 10. Bergson, *Le Rire*, 24.

 11. Bergson, *Laughter*, 41.

 12. See Frantz Fanon, *Oeuvres* (Paris: Découverte, 2011), 153–76.

 13. Aimé Césaire, *Cahier d'un retour au pays natal* (Newcastle-upon-Tyne, UK: Bloodaxe Books, 1995), 108/109.

 14. Aimé Césaire, *Discourse on Colonialism* (New York: Monthly Review Press, 2000), 42.

 15. I am grateful to Mark William Westmoreland for his keen eye in parsing out the interplay between visibility and hypervisibility in Bergson's discussion of racial laughter.

 16. Michael Billig, *Laugher and Ridicule: Towards a Social Critique of Humor* (London: Sage, 2012), 119–21.

 17. Ibid. 120.

 18. Bergson, *Le Rire*, 11.

19. Bergson, *Laughter*, 6–7.
20. Bergson, *Le Rire* 60; Bergson, *Laughter*, 134.
21. Ibid., 19/29, emphasis in original.
22. Michael Roemer, *Shocked but Connected: Notes on Laughter* (Lanham: Rowman & Littlefield, 2012), 99.
23. Parkin, "The Power of Laughter," 122.
24. Contributors to the journal, including Paulette Nardal, Jean Price Mars, and Louis-Thomas Achille were among the generation of Antilleans who studied at the Sorbonne in the early twentieth century.
25. *La Revue du monde noir*, 129.
26. See Brian Weinstein, *Éboué* (New York: Oxford University Press, 1972), 134.
27. Bergson, *Le Rire*, 24; Bergson, *Laughter*, 26.
28. Ibid., 24–25/27.
29. Sharpley-Whiting, *Negritude Women* (Minneapolis, MN: University of Minnesota Press, 2002), 57.
30. Marie-Agnes Sourieau, "La Revue du Monde Noir," *Concise Encyclopedia of Latin American Literature* (London: Fitzroy Dearborn Publishers, 2000), 331.
31. *La revue du monde noir*, 183–84.
32. Ibid., 182.
33. Ibid.
34. Billig, *Laughter and Ridicule*, 121.
35. *La revue du monde noir*, 182–83.
36. Ibid. Linguistically, two things are striking in *La Revue du monde noir*'s English translation of Carbet's text. First, the idiomatic expression "le tour sera joué" is rendered word for word, resulting in an awkward nonexpression in English. Second, the translation omits Carbet's mention of Citroën as the financers of the Eiffel Tower's illumination, and therefore misses an opportunity to render for its English readers Carbet's biting critique of the Eiffel Tower as not just a Parisian landmark but also a site at which capitalism and cultural production intertwine.
37. Ibid., 185.
38. Ibid., 185–86.
39. Achille states in his essay, "Des Noirs, même dans leurs lointains pays extra-européens, ne connaissent d'autre costume national que ce même costume européen qui fait rire" ("Many Negroes have no national dress other than the European ones") (*La Revue du monde noir*, 184–85).
40. Brent Hayes Edwards, *The Practice of Diaspora: Literature, Translation, and the Rise of Black Internationalism* (Cambridge, MA: Harvard University Press, 2003), 182/183.
41. See Boittin, Jennifer Anne Boittin, *Colonial Metropolis the Urban Grounds of Anti-Imperialism and Feminism in Interwar Paris* (Lincoln: University of Nebraska Press, 2010); Edwards, *The Practice of Diaspora*; and T. Denean Sharpley-Whiting, *Negritude Women*.

42. *La Revue du monde noir*, 181.

43. Edwards concludes that the speaker and the black vendor work across the discomfort of the class difference that separates them, to articulate a sense of racial solidarity, speaking it into being as they try to locate themselves vis-à-vis the white cigarette seller and the white patrons of the café. See Edwards, *The Practice of Diaspora*, 186.

44. Edwards, *The Practice of Diaspora*, 181–82, Nardal quoted in Edwards.

45. Ibid., 183–84.

46. Ibid., 185.

47. Ibid., 186, emphasis in original.

48. Ibid., 186.

49. Boittin, *Colonial Metropolis*, 161.

50. Edwards, *The Practice of Diaspora*, 184.

51. Césaire, *Cahier d'un retour au pays natal*, 88/89.

52. While the speaker does not initially attract the same kind of negative attention from the other café patrons, she is aware of the tenuous nature of her assimilation and the possibility of what Fanon describes as regressing by association.

53. Edwards, *The Practice of Diaspora*, 183.

Part III

Race, Revolution, and Bergsonism in Latin America

Chapter 6

Racial Becomings

Evolution, Materialism, and Bergson in Spanish America

ADRIANA NOVOA

In *Becoming Undone*, Elizabeth Grosz explores "the conditions under which material and living things overcome themselves and become something other than what they were."[1] Her interest in the difference that constitutes subjects and how the relations between things are structured implies a concern with the same philosophical ideas that were relevant at the beginning of the twentieth century, exactly one hundred years before her writings on Charles Darwin and Henri Bergson. Historically, in fact, the similarities are striking: while Darwinian evolutionism led a revolution in philosophical conceptions about nature and humanity, materiality and spirituality, unity and diversity, and the emergence of a new humanism, the same happened at the end of the twentieth century with the revolution originated by genetics and the relationship between nature, human agency, and design.

Grosz's interest in Darwinism and the relationship between Darwin and Bergson is not a historical novelty. The same debate about materialism and humanism was at the core of the philosophical renewal that was fundamental in the Americas in the early 1900s. In this chapter, I analyze how Grosz's interpretation of Darwin and Bergson connects with this previous philosophical framework using works published mostly from the 1890s to the 1920s. Obviously there are important differences between these two periods. For instance, while Grosz focuses mostly on the understanding of feminist politics, those who wrote in the Americas used Bergson to address racial concerns. But my intention in comparing contemporary materialisms with the ones that existed before is to locate this philosophical approach historically, and to demonstrate how these authors were, and are, the source of a philosophical recontextualization of materialism at a time in which evolutionary science had transformed ideas about the relationship between nature and human difference. Like Diana Coole and Samantha Frost, I believe that theorists need to "rediscover older materialist traditions while pushing them in novel, and sometimes experimental, directions or toward fresh applications."[2] In using this comparison, I hope to make a contribution in this direction.

Darwinism and the Latin Race after 1870

The intellectual currents behind the independence movements in Spanish America had a conflictive understanding of nature and matter.[3] On one side, there was a view that implied the inferiority of the rule of nature as it was connected to the particularities of place and not the universal ideas of the Enlightenment; on the other, there was a Romantic perspective that anthropomorphized nature and emphasized its importance as a representation.[4] The latter also connected metaphysical ideas with aesthetics in the realm of politics, something that would continue into the next century. According to Carl Mitcham, for romanticism "the metaphysical reality of both nature and artifice is best denoted not by stable or well-ordered form but by process of change, especially as apprehended by the new aesthetic category of the sublime or the overwhelming and what Byron refers as 'pleasing fear.' "[5] This idea of representation had both political power and artistic connotations. Politically, this meant that those groups considered inferior could not be representable. According to the Argentine Carlos Calvo (1824–1906), this had happened in Mexico early in the process of independence when those in power declared that "*the Indians were a beastly race, full of vices and ignorance, automatons that were not dignified enough to represent the nation or be represented.*"[6] Artistically, this implied the determination of those who could be visible and included. These conflictive views on what was representable, either politically or artistically, were the product of an awareness that racial divisions were an important element of civilized societies.

The work of Manuel Carrasco Albano (1834–73), an important Chilean intellectual and politician, is an example of this perspective. In a speech delivered in 1855, he observed that the Latin race should not "succumb in

America." This population had a higher destiny ahead and did not need to "commit suicide out of discouragement."[7] By contrast with the "decrepit" Italy, "the old mother" Spain, and France, a nation extinguished by its "sterile strength," only the Latins who inhabited America could represent this "generous" race in the future. But in order to fulfill this mission, Latin Americans needed to pay attention to the actions of the United States in Texas and California. They showed that the Spanish race would perish in America if the ex-Spanish colonies did not work together against the "increased vigor and growth of the Anglo-Saxon."[8] He ended his speech emphatically affirming that "the Latin race should not, cannot, does not want to perish in the American continent!"[9]

Carrasco Albano's warning is an interesting case in the evolution of the use of the terms *Anglo-Saxon* and *Latin*. Over the first half of the nineteenth century, they were mostly used to describe the historical and linguistic consequences of the Germanic invasion in England, but in this text there is also an association with the power and might of the United States.[10] This anticipated the racialized use of these terms by the end of the nineteenth century, when *Latin* and *Saxon* became the expression of evolutionary races destined to compete with each other. It is for this reason that by the 1890s the Latin race, or those populations that were the result of the Roman occupation of Europe that had originated in the Mediterranean civilization, would be criticized as degenerate and prone to extinction. The sudden transformation of the meaning of civilization from a representational force to one that only operated through biological change, which decided who/what was represented in nature, began to emerge after 1870. The publication of Darwin's *Descent of Man* in 1871 coincided with France's recovery after its defeat at the hands of Prussia the previous year.[11] While this book attempted to explain the evolution of humans mostly through sexual selection, it did not succeed in answering the questions about how heredity worked.[12]

The discussions of Darwinian evolution in both Europe and America connected human diversity with race and, in doing so, the views that emerged not only explained variation in nature, but also the inferior or superior evolutionary outcomes of those differences. Ignorance of the mechanisms that operate in heredity made it easier to accommodate past racism into the new narratives that had begun to emerge. History became the study of peoples as they evolved over time, and this explains why the fall of France at the hands of Prussia was understood by those deemed as "Latin" as an expression of Anglo-Saxon evolutionary superiority in the face of Latin degeneracy. The Argentine Carlos O. Bunge (1875–1918) defined it clearly in 1903 when he wrote that modern civilization had been the result of the actions of two groups: first, the "*Latin or Latinized*" peoples (Italians, French, and Iberian Americans); and second, the *Saxon* and *Germans* (those from Belgium, Germany, Holland, Denmark, Scotland, Ireland, Sweden, Norway, and the United States).[13]

In the case of France, the emergence of an idea of modern racialized nation coincided with the ascendancy of an imperial culture immediately after the victory of Prussia. France's development of a colonial ideology that began during the Third Republic (1870–1940) was instrumental in developing a new representation of the country that contradicted the accounts of its decline. Originally part of an elitist and minority position, it "progressively became a coherent political doctrine strongly linked to a universalist discourse, and was partially reliant upon new bodies of knowledge impacting all domains of thought and experience."[14] One of the important aspects of this ideology was how it addressed Anglo-Saxon superiority and racial difference.

Philosophically, the work of Jean-Marie Guyau (1854–1888) and his stepfather, the neo-Kantian Alfred Fouillée (1838–1912), provided new ideas about difference, continuity, and human design. Their work became well known in Spanish America because their educational writings challenged the determinism and materialism of science that was being developed by in the 1880s. These philosophers associated the teaching and promoting of the humanities with the responsibility of the Latins to respond to the scientific teachings that were more connected with the Anglo-Saxons. According to Fouillée, France needed to promote an education that praised its national characteristics, which required that Frenchmen be "literary scientific and artistic if they are to maintain their influence and glory as a nation. If France chooses to become 'Americanized,' she will perhaps cease to be France, but she will certainly never become an America."[15] The Anglo-Saxon race was associated with the elite population of the United States, and this group was considered part of the new evolutionary lineage that was destined to replace the Mediterranean civilization originated by the Greeks and the Romans.

Guyau's *Education and Heredity* was also helpful in restoring the importance of education to the development of civilization, which was in defiance of biological determinism.[16] Like most French authors of the time, Guyau emphasized the importance of the environment in evolution, and the role that human will and design had in the process of controlling and modifying it. According to him, the "only hope for the vitality of a race" lay in a "change of environment, which corrects the evil influence by influences in a contrary direction."¹⁷ It is for this reason that education and culture had an important role in the transformation of matter. In this same context, Fouillée built a notion of Latin civilization that was universal and negated the racial theorists of the time who believed in determinism. This could happen because spiritual forces operated to produce a selection that would ultimately eliminate differences among humans. He wrote about Rome as the original point of Western culture because of its historical role in assimilating diverse populations. Fouillée writes,

> After all, where was the first sign of unity in the human race? Rome, the Eternal City, was not merely the Pantheon of the gods of conquered races, it was "a microcosm of the intellect of all nations." We may look forward, with M. Fornelli, in the more or less distant future, to a wider, more organic, and more spiritual unity, in which the whole of humanity will be concentrated and represented. There are many embryonic organs in the life of each modern nation which point to this organization in the future, to the distant fusion of the soul of every nation into a single soul.¹⁸

The formation of modern nations was for Fouillée a biological process organized around a spiritual and vital force. Philosophically, the main contribution of Fouillée to Spanish American thought was his restoration of representation. According to Laurent Dobuzinskis's translation of *La psychologie des idées forces*, Fouillée suggests that "all our representations of objects, all our sentiments, all our actions, the whole of our philosophy and our science are to some extent *symbolic*, for we do not know anything in an absolute and complete manner."¹⁹ But what can be considered an "inferiority of the representation in comparison to the real also creates a superiority: it makes possible the world of ideas, which is not a pure *copy* of the real world, but an extension of reality into thought, and where reality shifts in another direction: the world of ideas is thus, in all respects, a world of forces."²⁰ These forces are what he called *idée forces*, a concept that was incorporated into the philosophical language of the 1890s all over Spanish America. Confused about what was responsible for the dynamic origin of difference, Fouillée restored the importance of representation in opposition to the conception of the deterministic materialism that dominated post-Darwinian literature.

On the other side, Guyau's contribution was to legitimize the interest in idealism that Spanish American philosophers had acquired. Guyau's translator in England was the feminist realist Gertrude Kapteyn (1855–1920), who explained in 1898 that Guyau did not deny the evolutionism of Darwin and Spencer, but he was capable of recognizing "their golden grains of truth, [with] a mind open to accept some of their fundamental verities, but also a mind aware of their shortcomings."[21] According to Kapteyn, the lack of morality implied in Spencer's and Darwin's work was resolved in Guyau. In her interpretation, Guyau had made his contribution adding "to the sound and healthy naturalism of his day an idealism without which moral evolution lacks its vital spring and fullest meaning."[22] This way to understand Guyau's contribution explains exactly why his work was so influential among those who wanted to curtail the domination of biological materialism. Kapteyn captured that in introducing idealism and morality into the existent views on nature, Guyau was expanding the understanding of life itself, which had a direct connection to racial ideas. According to Kapteyn,

> This new faith, freed from the bonds and chains which but too often doom lower conceptions of morality or religion to sterility, opened up the prospect of a future in which it should become possible to realize the ideal of a sane, healthy, and strong race directing its powers and capacities to their highest use. Instead of the external authority of a God, or the equally external authority of categorical imperatives imposed upon our freedom (as even the great Immanuel Kant still more or less conceived morality), Guyau constructed a kind of natural determinism of impulses and sentiments, which, disciplined through reflection and experience, are a law unto themselves.[23]

Three important works on morality had appeared not long before Guyau's writings on ethics: Spencer's *The Data of Ethics* (1879), Hartmann's *The Phenomenology of the Moral Consciousness* (1879), and Fouillée's *The Criticism of Contemporary Moral Systems* (1883). Guyau published *Esquisse d'une morale sans obligation ni sanction* in 1885, and the book was "something of a sensation in its day, bringing him a reputation and a measure of notoriety as a sort of French Nietzsche."[24] In Spanish America its popularity was due to the very reasons that Kapteyn used to defend this work. Guyau agreed with some aspects of the work of Spencer and Fouillée, but he recognized that the problem with natural and positivist schools was that they furnished "no unchangeable principles, either in the way of obligation or in the way of sanction."[25] Guyau's moral theory addressed one aspect of philosophy that had been shaken by evolutionism, namely, "can a positive science of morals speak of obligation in strictly natural-biological connection?"[26] According to Geoffrey Fidler, Guyau started with proposing "an interior, non-mechanistic, and spontaneous vital principle." Life was for him one with thought: "Life is at one with the thought produced by the mind or conscience reflecting in itself—the object and subject of the immediate experience."[27]

This restitution of experience is another aspect that was important among Spanish American thinkers, together with a moral ideal related to harmony and reconciliation, which did not mean selfishness and crudeness, as in one common understanding of "natural law," but an extension of life itself. More importantly, Guyau's aim was "to find out what a moral philosophy would be without any absolute obligation, and without any absolute sanction," in order to answer a crucial question: "how far positive science can go in this direction, and where does the sphere of metaphysical speculations begin?"[28] His answer pointed to a new form to understand consciousness and reason.

Life for Guyau had a double character that was reflected on the two parts of the human: "unconscious and conscious life." While most moralists saw "only the sphere of conscious life," it was "the uncontious or subconscious life," which was "the true source of activity." But conscious life might in the long run "react upon and gradually destroy, by the acuteness of its analysis, that which the obscure synthesis of heredity has accumulated among humans or nations."[29] There needed to be awareness of the fact that consciousness had "a dissolving force, which the utilitarian and even the evolutionist school has not taken sufficiently into account." He thus called for "re-establishing the harmony between the reflection of consciousness and the spontaneity of the unconscious instinct. A principle of action must be found which shall be common to the two spheres," and this principle was connected to a notion of life that in "becoming conscious of itself, of its intensity and its extension, does not tend to its own destruction; it but increases its own force."[30] This view aimed at the reconciliation of reason with a realm not controlled by it, formed by a collective experience that could not be only expressed through words in a narrative. Moreover, a new conception of consciousness as related to an extended notion of life, prepared the way not only for Bergson, but also for a reconciliation of local experience at the level of the individual and the nation. In the context of the relationship between Guyau and Bergson, the latter would further develop a similar conception of life. In one case there was the "expansion of life," while on the other there was the *élan vital*. Both negated a goal for life and morality that was beyond the continuation of its own activity.

In 1878, a debate that took place at a gathering in Havana among those involved in the publication of *Revista de Cuba* shows the existence of some of the problems mentioned regarding philosophical systems and the problems with materialism. One of the speeches delivered during the evening was by Rafael Montoro (1852–1933), who was responsible for the introduction of neo-Kantian thinkers in Cuba, and was interested in the role of morality in nature.[31] He explained that the philosophy of his time was confusing two very different things. First, there was the transformation of philosophy due to the introduction of evolutionary ideas that made impossible the continuation of old schools; and second, there was the assumed end of speculative philosophy due to the emphasis on materialism. Montoro expressed his interest in metaphysics and the use of Kant's work, but he was criticized on this issue by José R. Montalvo (1843–1901), who affirmed that metaphysics "was dead" and in its place only remained the philosophy of science, which was providing more general laws that were being used to create a system that was sustained only by experience.[32]

This philosophical uncertainty continued in the years to come. In 1888, *Revista de Cuba* published an article by Manuel Sanguily (1848–1925) criticizing the Colombian Rafael Merchan (1844–1905), who had written in a journal published in his country that the "predominant" school of thought in Cuba was the positivist approach that resulted from the work of Herbert Spencer (1820–1903). According to Sanguily this claim was wrong, since the "predominant school in Cuba, if any, [was] still the spiritualist" rooted in work of the French philosophers Pierre Royer-Collard (1763–1845) and Victor Cousin (1792–1867). But there were also "Hegelians like Montoro, many Krausistas; Darwinists, like La Torre and maybe José Rafael Montalvo, positivists like Joaquín García Lebredo and José F. Arango, evolutionists like E. José Varona."[33] It is important to note that the spiritualist sources mentioned are the same ones that linked the French philosophical tradition with Bergson.

This correction about the main sources of Cuban thought is very illustrative of the 1880s. At this time Spanish American intellectuals were synthesizing different European philosophers in the middle of the chaos that was postevolutionary science and politics. This is the decade in which the problems with materialism began to be discussed, mainly in the context of restoring some sense of spiritualism that was more politically compatible with the needs of creating a nation. The work of Guyau and Fouillée was discussed in the 1890s in the context of this debate, and many times the reading of Guyau and Bergson took place simultaneously. The development of pragmatism and, for instance, the psychology of Bunge, exemplify this type of inquiry in the Americas.[34] I am not suggesting that this is a top-down case of reception, but that similar questions were posed in the robust intellectual exchanges of the second half of the nineteenth century. Bunge's *Principes de psychologie individuelle et sociale*, the translation of his doctoral thesis to French and published by the prestigious publishing house Alcan in Paris in 1903, continued with Guyau's separation of the conscious and unconscious life, developing a section on dreams that resembles Freud's work.[35]

Bergson became relevant by the beginning of the twentieth century in Spanish America because he addressed concerns that had already been established, and he provided an answer to philosophical questions that had been relevant since the 1870s. In other words, the emergence of Bergson as the main philosopher of the youth by the beginning of the twentieth century took place in an environment that was already moving in this direction, particularly with regard to the continued racialization in deterministic ways of those who populated Latin America.

Bergsonism and Racial Difference

The confusion brought about by Darwin's philosophical views in relation to moral and ethical principles became even more difficult to resolve by the 1890s, when materialist views of evolution based on the supremacy of natural selection erased any possibility of metaphysics, or of interpretations at odds with hard materialism, among those interested in science. As had been the case in the 1870s, this also happened at the same time in which the balance of power among nations was changing. In 1898 the Spanish-American War ended with the defeat of another Latin nation, Spain, which lost the last remains of its empire. As in France, this event was perceived as proof of the ascendancy of Anglo-Saxonism, this time in the Americas. The United States now belonged to the Nordic peoples who were described as evolutionary more advanced, particularly over the mixture of Latin peoples and those of indigenous and African origin.

During the 1890s the evolutionary camp had begun to be divided into schools called neo-Lamarckism, represented by Herbert Spencer

(1820–1903); and neo-Darwinism, whose leader was the German scientist August Weismann (1834–1914). The victory of the latter in 1893, after a series of articles in which both camps tried to prove their cases, was understood as the ascendancy of hard materialism, determinism, and the replacement of philosophy at the hands of biological sciences. This was accompanied by the acceleration of competition among nations based on a misguided conception that national selection was in a way analogous to natural law. It was for this reason that the biological survival of a nation was related to racial evolution and competition.

The intensification of materialist conceptions, and the implication that only the few favored by natural selection would constitute a future humanity, triggered a widespread pessimism in both Europe and the Americas. In order to change this situation, there was a growing interest in the works of thinkers who had proposed innovative views to understand materialism. As we saw, Kapteyn translated *Esquisse d'une morale sans obligation ni sanction*, originally published in 1884, in 1898. By this time Guyau's philosophy was connected with the need for a new humanism based on morality in order to infuse design and purpose into matter. It is for this reason that Kapteyn said that Guyau's morality's great merit was to bring "the conviction that to our time belongs the task of creating a new mental and moral guidance, which shall enable the individual and the race to steer a happier course."[36]

The Uruguayan José Rodó (1871–1917) published *Ariel* in 1900 to articulate this view in the context of Spanish American reality.[37] According to him philosophy and science had been working against the interest of civilization through their devotion to materialism, leaving the supposedly inferior Latins as not representable in the context of biological evolution. But the beginning of the new century announced the renewal of philosophy through the return of a vitalist perspective and ideas about life introduced mainly by Guyau and Nietzsche. Rodó clearly noted that the important split that was underway should not be understood in terms of racial differentiation, but rather in the emergence of a new way to understand civilization as embodied difference. In his view, the origins of civilization were in the process that favored human assimilation. In this way, the transformation that had made Europe did not operate to produce difference, but to erase it in order to achieve universality. The materialism of the post-Darwinian era, on the contrary, operated to favor the continuous production of differentiation through the introduction of variations that did not respond to higher design or purpose, but to the need of survival.

This shift on the notion of assimilation had generated a culture of death and pessimism in the late nineteenth century similar to the one described by Kapteyn. Rodó called for a philosophical renewal that implied a war on materialism and its political expression—U.S. imperialism—using a new form of idealism that restored the notion of sameness and universality. As had been the case with Guyau, for Rodó the world of the sensible explained evolutionary paths. According to both, the "higher pleasures" were the arts, reasoning, and learning. These nonmaterial practices helped the development of morality and the creation of sameness in the face of differentiation.

After the publication of *Ariel*, many scientists and intellectuals followed him in trying to renew philosophy to fight the pessimism and negativity with which the previous century had ended. In 1904 the lectures of the Puerto Rican Eugenio M. Hostos (1839-1903) were published. His *Tratado de Sociología* attempted to approach sociology through a project that balanced materialism through his use of the "conscience of the species" [*conciencia de la especie*] based on sympathy and sociability, very much influenced by Guyau.[38] The following year, the Cuban scientist Enrique Llauría (1863-1929) published a book in defense of materialism and evolutionary science that provided an extremely optimistic view of the future in contrast to the pessimism of the time.[39] One of the leading Spanish American intellectuals, the Dominican Pedro Henríquez Ureña (1884-1946), reviewed these two works analyzing the philosophy of the late nineteenth century in no uncertain terms:

> The last years of the nineteenth century were consumed by an acute pessimism that was influenced mainly by Schopenhauer and Hartmann, decadent poetry, Russian novels, the Scandinavian drama with its painful scenes, and D'Annunzio's *triumph of death*. Philosophically, the stronger influence came from Nietzsche's work that was also depressive.[40]

In 1908 the Peruvian Francisco García Calderón (1834-1905), a student of the spiritualist philosopher Alejandro Deustua (1849-1941), another follower of Bergson's, wrote an article in a French philosophical journal explaining how the thought among Latin Americans was by then impregnated with different strains of idealism. In psychology the new emphasis was on the supremacy of the will, and the originality of the psychological evolution; in metaphysics, the main concern was the condemnation of a mechanistic approach; while in ethics, the autonomy of the moral subject and the value of the ideal were the most common interests. According to him, there was a new generation that was moving philosophy away from positivism and into new ideas coming from France, particularly from Bergson.[41]

Bergsonian philosophy began to have an impact in Spanish America by 1907.[42] Henríquez Ureña recalled that by this year there were already several philosophical approaches against positivism in Mexico; some read Schopenhauer, others Vico, and he and Antonio Caso (1883–1946) started the reading of Bergson, William James (1842–1910), and Emile Boutroux (1845–1921), an important French philosopher at war with materialism and determinism, and a promoter of spiritualism in the form of morality and religion. Also in this year, García Calderón published his article on Bergson and Boutroux in the newspaper *El Comercio*.[43] In Argentina, Carlos Malagarriga (1860–1936), a Spaniard who had moved to Buenos Aires at the end of the nineteenth century, published in 1912 a translation into Spanish of *L'évolution créatice*.[44] One of his students was the writer Macedonio Fernández, who became follower of Bergson and James.[45] The philosopher Francisco Romero would say years later that Bergson might have been, in fact, the most studied thinker in Spanish America.[46]

Argentina's intellectuals had an old interest in experimental psychology, and through this connection the works of both Bergson and James were known.[47] In 1915, Bunge analyzed James's *Pragmatism*, describing this approach as a defense of the principle that "all useful creation is true," which for Bunge meant that "it attempted to fulfill two needs of the human spirit: the need to have positive knowledge and the need to have religious beliefs."[48] Pragmatism, in this way, seemed to defend a less materialist position. This philosophy was not like the utilitarianism of Locke, Berkeley, and Hume because it allowed the existence of religious idealism. It also differed from positivism since it accepted, besides religious idealism, the negation of the whole conception of uniform and stable causality.[49] More importantly, pragmatism held "the objective, phenomenological, and contingent world to the world of representations and subjective interests."[50] According to Bunge, this path led to a radical relativism that was extremely dangerous. He also understood Bergson's *L'évolution créatice*, published in 1907, as a rejection of an understanding of life in mechanist terms. In Bunge's analysis, Bergson's notion of being was "organic and evolved if not according to a creative thought, at least as creator of its own finalities; among them, scientific, philosophical, and ethical concepts."[51]

In 1916 two influential books were published to discuss Bergson's philosophy.[52] The Chilean Enrique Molina (1871–1964) wrote *The Philoso-*

phy of Bergson and the Peruvian philosopher Mariano Ibérico (1892–1974) published *La Filosofía de Enrique Bergson*, both very influential books in Spanish America. The preface of the latter was written by the prominent intellectual Víctor A. Belaúnde (1883–1966) who synthesized the importance of Bergson in relationship with the problems affecting society at the time. He criticized positivism "for its fatal connections with intellectualism, materialism and determinism," which had placed "an exhausting weight to carry in the human spirit" during the second half of the nineteenth century.[53] In response, Bergson had initiated a reaction that confronted "analytic intelligence" with "the value of intuition and the sympathy of those who put us in direct contact with life." Facing a "desolated determinism" the French thinker had "revealed freedom" through "infallible feeling."[54] In the same way, the "rigid transformations of matter" had been challenged by the "creating *élan*" that "revived the spirit." This approach resolved the problems brought by "the opposite worlds of matter and the spirit, of phenomena and being."[55]

Belaúnde concluded his comments by asking what were the benefits of this "new philosophy." In response, he returned to the problems of representing the nation, and using the work of Edouard Le Roy, a politically conservative follower of Bergson, Belaúnde criticized positivism for its static views, and insisted that Bergson's philosophy dealt with teaching how to feel and live the immediate [*lo inmediato*]. According to him, the "immediate" of the Peruvians was in the nature that "had not inspired" the local poets; "the sinister and colorful past" that was not shown in the work of historians; "the strange variety of life that brought together so many races," but that had not impressed "the fantasy" of the country's novelists; and, finally, in "the secret desire" to have their own ideal, a need that could not be satisfied by science and "the hollow wording" of Peruvian thinkers of the past.[56] Bergsonian philosophy was introducing the youth to feeling and intuition, and through this experience they were acquiring new eyes to see what had been invisible so they might "listen to the voice of the race."[57] In brief, through both philosophy and art, Bergson was providing a new way to deal with the problems brought by representation in the context of materialism.

In Mexico, the *Ateneo de la Juventud*, an association of writers and philosophers, led the exploration of new philosophical ideas by 1909, shortly before the Mexican revolution started.[58] Antonio Caso, Alfonso Reyes (1889–1959), Carlos González Peña (1885–1965), José Vasconcelos (1882–1959), and Henríquez Ureña, among others, were part of this movement, and they became leading voices among those interested in philosophy in Spanish America. Reyes explained how this generation regarded Mexican positivism as a philosophy that has turned into "a pedagogic routine" no longer applicable to the concerns of his generation.[59] In order to find new sources, these intellectuals begin to read all the philosophers that had been criticized by the positivists, from Plato, who, according to Henríquez Ureña, was their "most important teacher," to the recent works of "Bergson, Boutroux, James, and Croce," and they also began to read Spanish authors. The old intellectual separation with Spain disappeared and the philosophical exchanges created an Iberian American community.[60]

In a speech given in 1910 by Henríquez Ureña at the *Ateneo*, Rodó's *Los Motivos de Proteo*, published the previous year, is praised for articulating an ethic of the renovation that was in harmony with the *Creative Evolution* of Bergson.[61] In fact, Rodó had read Bergson and had taken notes on his ideas in the notebooks he wrote in preparing his own book. His use of this book was, though, not derivative, but rather in support of his interest in developing a new way to do philosophy in response to the racial ideas of the time. It is for this reason that the speech praises the "great originality of Rodó," who had linked "the cosmological principles of the creative evolution" to an ideal norm of action to guide life. Since, according to Henríquez Ureña, life was constant transformation that could not be prevented, it was a duty to watch our own constant transformation in order to direct and orient it. In this sense, education was the most important aspect of society.[62]

Henríquez Ureña believed that in Bergson's system, evolution replaced necessity through the continuous intrusion of unexpected events, "contingency was the birth of becoming, evolution creates. Over an undefined perspective the universe is developed."[63] The understanding of evolution as free from determination furthered Rodó's philosophical interests, and in *Los Motivos de Proteo* he carefully avoided philosophical systematization, which by then was associated with the evils of positivism. He saw the collapse of Spencerian philosophy as the end of big systems in favor of a fragmented philosophy. In this book he also developed the analysis of time as the greatest innovator and a conception of being as multiple. In his view, we are not "one, but many," and for this reason we are constantly creating ourselves. For Rodó existence was change, and this was a continuous process of creating ourselves.[64] Following Guyau, Rodó also insisted in the importance of love in the process of self-transformation.

In 1912 García Calderón published an article in Buenos Aires' newspaper *La Nación*, reporting on his experience after attending a lecture by Bergson at the university in Paris. He described Bergson as a true creator, always communicating through a "metaphysics close to poetry" that created a music that "revealed the subtle presence of Próspero in *Ariel*."[65] He continued his narration explaining how Bergsonism was growing in France among the most diverse people, from the unionists to moderate Catholics. More importantly, "The youth [was] Bergsonian" everywhere, and there was a way to think and a style that were also the result of the work of this philosopher.[66] Bergson had provided a path to escape the past. Calderón claims,

> What did the philosophy of the past teach? The perfect correlation between reason and nature, the universal rule of the mechanistic laws, the determinism that made impossible any contingency in the realms of matter and spirit, the faith in science, the psychological automatism that did not know the importance of conscious life and saw in it, like [Théodule-Armand] Ribot, a luxury phenomenon, an epiphenomenon without which the interior mechanism would work perfectly well.[67]

García Calderón synthesized the new philosophy as a new view of life that opened up the possibility of universality and assimilation, ideas that had been circulating among Spanish American intellectuals who had read Fouillée and Guyau. Vasconcelos was the lead intellectual in developing a philosophy that mixed Guyau and Bergson with the intention of addressing concerns about race and identity. His most well-known work is the *Cosmic Race*, but his most directly relevant philosophical work was devoted to aesthetics. In 1916 he published an article in the influential Cuban journal *Cuba Contemporánea*, in which he explained the way in which nature was judged as dual; on one side there was the rational/scientific perspective and, on the other, there was the aesthetic judgment that defined "this is beautiful" ("*así es lo bello*").[68] In this context he defined the relationship between the material and the aesthetic. For him, beauty was "a rhythmic coincidence between the natural movement of the spirit and the already reformed movement of things." It was not the result of causality, but "of an internal accommodation, a conversion to the spirit."[69]

Vasconcelos takes from Bergson the idea of continuity and becoming. Indeed, he mentions Bergson while criticizing those who were more interested in describing movement at the expense of understanding the value of movement itself.[70] This notion of continuity and becoming avoids the essentialism and determinism of scientific materialism, and seemed to emphasize practice, something that was very useful for Vasconcelos after the civil war that transformed the country after 1910. It is for this reason that Mexican Bergsonism continued to be influential even after it lost its ascendency in the 1930s. In 1941 a book was published to explain Bergson's influence in the country; in the words of Vasconcelos, Bergson was attractive because he provided "concrete ideas" that were not the usual abstractions, and his solution "conquered" the intellectuals' wills because it was based on the "*idée force.*"[71]

Ontologically, the notion of being that is developed in Mexico is about "a concrete being, and, at the same time invisible; an operating being that in the same way performed by the Creator, was manifested in its results." This was not formal or abstract content, but "dynamic and alive."[72] Unlike the positivist time in which the invisible natural law worked to make unwanted matter extinct, this notion of being was based on the possibilities of becoming, and on the restitution of metaphysics. Vasconcelos affirmed that for those like him, essence was not "an abstract sign," but the basic reality where what was "sensible and invisible developed each one their own world, the worlds of consciousness."[73] For us, Vasconcelos writes, "the essence is not an abstract sign, it is the basic reality where the sensible and the invisible partake developing each its own world; the worlds of consciousness."[74] Abandoning the idealism that had begun the process of removing materialism from philosophical concerns, Vasconcelos mentioned that those like him "affirmed being in absolute realism." But this was a realism of the spirit, realism that was the "transubstantiation of the inferior substance," the "triumph of the consciousness over the wide infinity of the Cosmos."[75] In this sense, Bergson was for Vasconcelos a philosopher above the traditional divisions of materialism and idealism. Bergson "defined the essence as a portion of life" and denied that it could be identified with ways of knowing, whether Platonism, scholasticism, or "the false essentialist phenomenalism that came after these."[76] The understanding of being as dynamic and multiple allowed for a new conception of nation that refuted the deterministic views of race associated with positivism and science.

The relevance of Bergson was, obviously, not the same in every Spanish American country. Since his philosophy was open-ended, there were many interpretations that circulated. Those in countries in which scientific institutions had acquired a position of political relevance were more involved in defending the principles of materialism. In Argentina, for example, there was an interpretation of Bergson's work as materialistic. José Ingenieros, a leading Darwinian psychologist and philosopher, wrote in 1910 that it was foolish to see Bergson and James as good sources for saving spiritualist and neo-idealist philosophical approaches. In his view, these two philosophers shared a dynamic conception of the mental life that it was in no way contradictory to the ideas of scientific psychology. In this view, the foundations of "radical empiricism" or "pure experience" were not opposed to the natural sciences, since they still considered psychological events as manifestation of live matter that was continuously evolving, which fit perfectly the goals of a biological and evolutionist psychology.[77]

The understanding of Bergson as materialist, in the sense that he admitted to the biological formation of the psyche, did not interfere with the emergence of racial ideas that were not defined by matter. In 1906 Leopoldo Lugones, a leading poet and intellectual from Argentina, wrote an article to explain the influence of French ideas in his country that was published by the *Mercure de France*. In it he mentioned that the "problem of the races" has been simplified in his lifetime. Even the word "race" was losing its anthropological meaning to mean "something better," namely, the "spiritual community" of certain human groups through the view of "traditions and general aspirations" that were generated by the similarities in character that resulted in mutual sympathy. Accordingly, "race" meant at this time "a great friendship."[78] The nation was not built around racialized bodies, but around affinities that sanction the recovery of the concept of national assimilation.

Bergson's interpretations worked very well to articulate different views on racial difference among those who were considered inferior and not representable. Bergson's popularity grew enormously in Spain and Spanish America, and the philosopher himself visited a students' residence in Madrid to give a speech in 1916. The following year, the Spanish philosopher Manuel García Morente published a book that included Bergson's speech and the ones that he had delivered about the latter's philosophy. This work was rapidly circulated among intellectuals in Spanish America, and was very influential in the growing popularity of this philosophy. Paying attention to Bergson's speech there is a clear recognition of the admiration felt by the French for Spanish art and literature, and the contributions of this country's culture to the sciences and civilization. He also emphasized the "sympathies" that existed between the two nations, showing recognition for Spain as a civilized nation that was opposed to the views predominant at the end of the nineteenth century.[79]

According to García Morente, the new philosophy was not idealist, realist, materialist, or spiritualist. Its novelty was, precisely, in its ability to avoid old philosophical problems. This was possible because it was inspired in an aestheticism that opened the door to a new humanism that ultimately favored universality and oneness, and a common goal for humanity. While some in the past, like the Spanish writer Azorín, had tried to find in "the ruins," and in the "spirit of the race" the life force "that lasted longer than time," Bergson's philosophy allowed García Morente's generation to find an answer to "this diffuse and confusing desire for spirituality that characterized the end of the nineteenth century." On one side, it "limited the intellect in its pretention to have absolute domination"; and, on the other, it discovered and used "a new psychic activity, intuition," in order to provide a new foundation for "the venerable work of metaphysics."[80] The dynamism and mobility of this new form of consciousness drastically contrasted with the frozen and deterministic view of racialized bodies that characterized the end of the nineteenth century.

The Uruguayan Carlos Vaz Ferreira (1872–1958) wrote a commentary about reading Verlaine, the model poet of Bergsonians, and explained that thanks to Bergson and James, psychism (*psiquismo*) was now not understood as discourse, but "as a fluid mental reality" that was not an expression of logic. It was the expression of what was not representable in the traditional understanding of rationality, even when it "was common to all men" and was the true treasure of humanity. But Vaz Ferreira also recognized that the capture of the flow of life through nondiscursive methods complicated the desire for truth, and even promoted among some who practiced it "fraud, exaggeration, artifice, *pose*, and *snobism*."[81] He noticed that the emphasis that Bergsonism gave to subjectivity might be extremely dangerous, particularly in the view of those devoted to the hard sciences and materialism.

The placing of Bergsonism in a borderline position regarding its true scientific value was not only a concern of Vaz Ferreira. After all Bergson was awarded the Nobel Prize in Literature in 1927, even though he had never written any work of fiction. But in the explanation for the award the committee wrote that his book, *Creative Evolution*, was considered a master poem, "a cosmogony of great scope and unflagging power, without sacrificing a strictly scientific terminology."[82] Partly this might have been connected to the 1922 public debate between Albert Einstein and Bergson about time and how the latter's idea fit the new theory of relativity, which seemed to indicate, again, the supremacy of the hard sciences.[83] Einstein's rejection of Bergson's ideas on time and memory are in part the reason for the decline in popularity of the latter's work in Spanish America by the 1930s.[84]

An article written by the Argentine psychologist Aníbal Ponce (1908–38) in 1928 provides us with a good example of how the debate between Einstein and Bergson was viewed in this region. Discussing Bergson's Nobel Prize,

Ponce mentioned with disappointment that news agencies felt obliged to explain he was given the award in the less relevant category of literature, "since a Nobel prize for philosophy did not exist." But Ponce did not share this sense of shame, since Bergson had realized Guyau's almost unattainable ideal of becoming an "artist-philosopher."[85] This defense of Bergson, though, changes toward the end of the article, where Ponce revealed his fears regarding Bergson's legacy. He explained that only the discussion of Einstein's theory of relativity had prompted the French philosopher to speak and debate openly after a long period of silence. But for those who, like Ponce, loved him and admired him, Bergson's decision had been a mistake. The aftermath of the confrontation showed that the future "will not respect [Bergson's] work." According to Ponce, Einstein's rejection of Bergson's ideas seemed to indicate that "from the scientific framework that Bergson had created and used to impress" others, something that he "enjoyed" doing, nothing would remain in the near future.[86] A few years later, an intellectual renewal led by physics instead of biology spread quickly in Spanish America, and with it a form of materialism that was less dangerous than those of the past. Biological materialism in the analysis of humans led, as we saw, to the conformation of the body and, as a result, racial differences. The materialistic standing of those who were interested in physics moved away from the body and race and more into the understanding of time, cosmos, and energy and matter. Materialism, then, was embraced in a less problematic way than in the past.

In 1925 Einstein traveled to Argentina, Uruguay, and Brazil, lecturing to both specialized and general audiences about the theory of relativity and its meaning.[87] This ignited an interest in physics and in what this discipline might say about the philosophical problems at stake. A report published in 1924 by the Sociedad Científica Argentina deals exclusively with the study of physics, and according to it the main concerns of the time were related to Einstein's theory of relativity, Planck's work on radiation, and Bohr's theory of the atom.[88] An essay published in 1931 by the college of Physics and Mathematics of the La Plata University shows how questions of causation and determination that had been central to the intersection between the social sciences and biology were now addressed through physics, particularly in the analysis of Bohr's negation of causality and its philosophical and scientific significance.[89] Bergson's philosophy entered a decline after the challenges coming from physics, and even writers and artists who had been his stronger supporters saw in physics a new path to develop inquiry. Curiously, both Spencer and Bergson ended their lives under the cloud of suspicion after new scientific developments attacked their philosophies' core ideas.

As in the past, new ideas were not only relevant for the sciences, but also over time began to overlap with views about different societies and cultures. Niels Bohr himself explained this in 1938, while giving an address to participants at the International Congress of Anthropological and Ethnological Sciences that met in Copenhagen. Bohr acknowledged the radical transformation introduced by the new physics, which could be illustrated "by the fact that even the principle of causality, so far considered as the unquestioned foundation for all interpretation of natural phenomena," was proven "too narrow a frame to embrace the peculiar regularities governing individual atomic processes."[90] So, scientists had to do "with a rational development" of the means of "classifying and comprehending new experience which, due to its very character, finds no place within the frame of causal description suited only to account for the behaviour of objects so long as this behaviour is independent of the means of observation."[91]

In an analogous way, the observation of human psychology posed an epistemological problem by the intersection of language and difference. Bohr pointed out that the obstacles "to an unprejudiced attitude towards the relation between various cultures" was connected to the "deep rooted differences of the traditional backgrounds on which the cultural harmony in different human societies is based and which exclude any simple comparison between such cultures."[92] Taking a page from quantum physics, he proposed that "different human cultures" were complimentary to each other: "Indeed, each such culture represents an harmonious balance of traditional conventions by means of which latent potentialities of human life can unfold themselves in a way which reveals to us new aspects of its unlimited richness and variety."[93] Finally, he emphatically requested to recall the idea that the mixing of the populations worked "for the advancement of human civilization." Humanistic studies, according to Bohr, should aid in transforming the history of cultural development to erase all forms of prejudice: "the common aim of all science." This proposal presented a new perspective on how to bring together science, materialism, and social development.[94]

Conclusion: Neo-Idealism and New Materialism

At the end of the twentieth century, advances in evolutionism and genetics again brought concerns about human evolution, differences among humans as expressed through race, tensions between notions of representation and the "real," and a renewed quarrel among those interested in sciences and philosophy. More importantly, the need to balance the new scientific progress against philosophical concerns about emancipation and the meaning of what is human, led to new strains of materialism. If the philosophical renewal of the 1900s was accomplished through neo-idealism, in the twenty-first century new materialist approaches seem to be attempting the same. More importantly, the decline of universal and humanistic systems created a pessimism that in many ways mirrored what had happened in the 1890s, particularly regarding the obsession with extinction and the problems of continuity for human beings.

Whereas by the 1890s the plasticity of life was seen, with regard to race, as a problem that created dangerous differences, now the plasticity of matter welcomes the possibility of decentering conceptions of the human. As Hannah Landecker has noted, the development of biotechnology in the present has raised an important question: "What is the social and cultural task of being biological entities—being simultaneously biological things and human persons—when the 'biological' is fundamentally plastic?"[95] This question is not that different from the one that, as we saw, Spanish American intellectuals were trying to answer. The sameness implied in the concept of humanity was quite irreconcilable in the context of an ever-changing nature, particularly when some humans were racialized. Bergsonism, as we saw, allowed for new ways to address this problem. The materiality of the body worked to ultimately favor sameness through evolutionary changes that eliminated unneeded differences.

In the present time, materiality is not studied along neo-idealist concerns, but the philosophical vitalism that was behind the renewal of humanistic conceptions by the 1900s remains extremely important among those identified as "new materialists." According to Coole and Frost, given "the immanence of matter associated with new materialisms, it is unsurprising that they should be emerging contemporaneously with a new vitalism."[96] But this event is not a historical novelty. The opposition analyzed in the previous section between mechanistic and vitalist perspectives in Spanish America is still important for the development of philosophical inquiry today. As Coole and Frost have recognized, hostilities "have traditionally been staged as an opposition between mechanistic and vitalist understandings of (dead versus lively) matter. Typically, they were resolved by distinguishing between the sort of mechanical, inorganic matter described by physicists and the evolving organic systems described by biologists."[97] The new materialists often "discern emergent, generative powers (or agentic capacities) even within inorganic matter, and they generally eschew the distinction between organic and inorganic, or animate and inanimate, at the ontological level."[98] This perspective shows clearly that Darwin's philosophical implications continue to have an impact today. Biological changes still "have significant implications for our understanding of the human as a distinctive biological or moral entity."[99] It is for this reason that the debates we saw taking place after the 1870s are very important to those interested in new philosophical understandings of materialism, particularly today's feminist theorists. It seems that those whose bodies/matter were not representable share a philosophical concern about the intersection of materiality and culture in the context of Enlightenment or post-Enlightenment politics.

Grosz's work on Darwin and Bergson is a good example of this continuity. She is interested in "an understanding of the real or the universe that does not reduce what is there to matter, but is capable of conceptualizing the nuances and layers of ideality that matter carries within itself."[100] According to her, this ontology "does not give us a politics (or an ethics) in itself, but it does orient us toward political and ethical action."[101] In a similar way to the intellectuals discussed in the previous section, Grosz is not interested in the ways in which freedom is connected with emancipation from oppression, but in developing "a concept of life where freedom is conceived not only or primarily as the elimination of constraint or coercion, but more positively as the condition of, or capacity for, action."[102] It is here, just as before, that the philosophy of Bergson becomes very useful, and maybe the labels of neo-idealism and new materialism are a disservice to the intentions of those who wanted to escape the constraints established by a philosophy defined before the existence of important scientific evidence.

In many ways today's concerns are not different to those expressed by Vaz Ferreira about the uses of Bergson and the problems of reconciling science and social theory, or how to define the relationship between representation and matter. Karen Barad is a good example of this approach. Concerned about the consequences of the "linguistic turn" among scholars interested in social development, she asked important questions: "How did language come to be more trustworthy than matter? Why are language and culture granted their own agency and historicity while matter is figured as passive and immutable, or at best inherits a potential for change derivatively from language and culture?"[103] In order to return to matter, Barad follows the work of the already mentioned physicist Niels Bohr as the basis of her work, which is centered on the study of the practices of knowledge. Barad refuses "the representationalist fixation on "words" and "things" and the problem of their relationality." Instead she proposed "*a causal relationship between specific exclusionary practices embodied as specific material configurations of the world* (i.e., discursive practices/(con)figurations rather than "words") and specific material phenomena (i.e., relations rather than 'things')."[104] This causal relationship results in "intra-action," a term that signifies "the mutual constitution of entangled agencies."[105] Her "agential realism" attempts to clarify "the nature of the casual relationship between discursive practices and material phenomena."[106]

Her goal was to grasp and attend "to the political possibilities for change, the responsible practice of science, and the responsible education of scientists," all of which are objectives shared with the scientists analyzed in this chapter.[107] Barad brings together the analysis of social formation within the realm of materiality, a connection that remained elusive in the period analyzed in this chapter and even today. After all, those labeled as not representable in the realm of reason tried, and continue trying today, to reframe oppressive ideas of difference that were articulated in the context of representation first, and later through biological evolution. The case of Spanish American intellectuals could be extremely useful to examine the true political emancipatory practices that this approach can have in our present time.

Notes

1. Elizabeth Grosz, *Becoming Undone: Darwinian Reflections on Life, Politics, and Art* (Durham, NC: Duke University Press, 2011), 1.

2. Diana Coole and Samantha Frost, "Introducing the New Materialisms" in *New Materialisms: Ontology, Agency, and Politics*, ed. Diana Coole, and Samantha Frost (Durham, NC: Duke University Press, 2010), 4.

3. The term *Latin America* groups all the geographical areas that were part of the French, Spanish, and Portuguese colonial system. Since the historical development of the ex-French and -Portuguese colonies follow a different path regarding ideology and periodization, in this chapter I will analyze the Spanish American experience.

4. Daniel Mesa Gancedo, "El poema extenso como institución cultural forma poética e identidad americana en Bello, Heredia y Echeverría" in *Nueva revista de filología hispánica* (2008): 87–122.

5. Carl Mitcham, *Thinking through Technology: The Path between Engineering and Philosophy* (Chicago: University of Chicago Press, 1994), 296.

6. Carlos Calvo, *Anales históricos de la revolución de la América Latina, 1: acompañados de los documentos en su apoyo desde al año 1808 hasta el reconocimiento de la independencia de ese extenso continente*, vol. 1 (Paris: A. Durand, 1864), lxxvi. Emphasis in the original.

7. Manuel Carrasco Albano, "Memoria presentada . . . sobre la necesidad i objetos de un congreso Sud-Americano," in *Comentarios sobre la Constitución Política de 1833* (Santiago, Chile: Librería del Mercurio, 1874), xxv.

8. Ibid., xxii.

9. Ibid., xxv.

10. For an example of this historical and linguistic view in the United States, see Thomas Jefferson, *An Essay towards Facilitating Instruction in the Anglo-Saxon and Modern Dialects of the English Language* (New York: John F. Trow, 1851).

11. Charles Darwin, *The Descent of Man, and Selection in Relation to Sex* (London: John Murray, 1871).

12. For a more detailed account on the relationship between evolution, race, and heredity, see Adriana Novoa and Alex Levine, *From Man to Ape* (Chicago: Chicago University Press, 2010).

13. Carlos O. Bunge, *La Educación* (Buenos Aires, Argentina: D. Jorro, 1903), vii.

14. Pascal Blanchard, Sandrine Lemaire, Nicolas Bancel, and Dominic Thomas, eds. *Colonial Culture in France since the Revolution* (Bloomington: Indiana University Press, 2013), 2.

15. Alfred Fouillée, *Education from a National Standpoint*, trans. and ed. W. J. Greenstreet (London: Edward Arnold, 1892), 8. French Edition: *L'enseignement: au point de vue national* (Paris: Hatchette, 1891), xvii.

16. The original was published after Guyau's death, in 1889.

17. Jean-Marie Guyau, *Education and Heredity: A Study in Sociology*, trans. W. J. Greenstreet (London: Walter Scott Publishing, 1903), 276.

18. Alfred Fouillée, *Education*, 123.

19. Laurent Dobuzinskis, "Non-welfarism Avant la Lettre: Alfred Fouillee's Political Economy of Justice," *European Journal of the History of Economic Thought* 17, no. 4 (2010): 841n5. The original French text comes from Alfred Fouillée, *La psychologie des idées forces*, vol. 1 (Paris: Alcan, 1893), 359.

20. Ibid.

21. Kapteyn Gertrude, "Translator's Preface," *Jean-Marie Guyau: A Sketch of Morality Independent of Obligation or Sanction* (London: Watts & Co., 1898), ix. On feminist realism, see Molly Youngkin, *Feminist Realism at the Fin de Siècle: The Influence of the Late-Victorian Woman's Press on the Development of the Novel* (Columbus: Ohio State University Press, 2007).

22. Kapteyn, "Translator's Preface," ix.

23. Ibid., x

24. Geoffrey C. Fidler, "On Jean-Marie Guyau, Immoraliste," *Journal of the History of Ideas* 55n1 (January, 1994): 82.

25. Gertrude Kapteyn, "Translator's Preface," 3.

26. Geoffrey C. Fidler, "On Jean-Marie Guyau, Immoraliste," 82.

27. Ibid., 80.

28. Jean-Marie Guyau, *A Sketch of Morality Independent of Obligation or Sanction* (London: Watts, 1898), 208.
29. Ibid.
30. Ibid., 208–9.
31. See Rafael Montoro, "Kant: El neo-kantianismo y los neokantianos españoles," *Revista de Cuba* 4 (1878), 77–89, 188–200.
32. Ibid., 216–17.
33. Ibid., 49.
34. There is a permanent overlapping of the ideas generated in the Americas and Europe during the second half of the nineteenth century and the beginning of the twentieth. Certain aspects of the work of Emile Durkheim, for example, resemble the ethics of Dewey, and the same happens with the work of Fouillée and Guyau. See Hans Joas, "The Problem of the Emergence of New Morality and New Institutions as a Leitmotif in Durkheim's Oeuvre" in *Emile Durkheim: Sociologist and Moralist*, ed. Stephen Turner (New York: Routledge, 1993), 223. J. M. C. Chevalier, "Pragmatisme et idées-forces. Alfred Fouillée fut-il une source du pragmatisme américain?" *Dialogue* 50 (2001): 633–68.
35. Carlos O Bunge, *Principes de psychologie individuelle et sociale* (Paris: Félix Alcan, 1903).
36. Gertrude Kapteyn, "Translator's Preface," xi.
37. José Enrique Rodó, *Obras completas*, ed. Emir Rodríguez Monegal (Madrid, Spain: Aguilar, 1957).
38. Eugenio M. Hostos, *Tratado de Sociología* (Madrid, Spain: Imprenta de Bailly-Baillière, 1904).
39. Enrique Llauría, *Evolución super-orgánica: la naturaleza y el problema social* (Madrid, Spain: Fernando Fé, 1905).
40. Pedro Henríquez Ureña, "Estudio de Llauría Sobre la Naturaleza y el Problema Social," *Ensayos Críticos* (Havana, Cuba: Imprenta Esteban Fernández, 1905), 91.
41. Francisco Garcia Calderón, "Les courants philosophiques dans l'Amérique latine," *Revue de Métaphysique et de Morale* (1908): 674–81, 679.
42. In this chapter I analyze only the works that relate Bergsonism with racial ideas. For a complete study of Bergson in Latin America, see Alfredo Coviello, *El proceso filosófico de Bergson y su bibliografía*, 2nd ed. (Tucumán, Argentina: Revista Sustancia, 1941); Alfredo Coviello, "Bergson en América" in Horacio González *¿Inactualidad del Bergsonismo?* (Buenos Aires, Argentina: Colihue, 2008).
43. Francisco García Calderón, "Dos Filósofos Franceses, Bergson and Boutroux,"*El Comercio*, Lima, Peru, May 5, 1907.
44. Carlos Malagarriga, La Evolución Creadora (Madrid, Spain: Renacimiento, 1912).
45. Fernández corresponded with William James. See Jaime Nubiola, "Jorge Luis Borges y William James" in *Aproximaciones a la obra de William James: la*

formulación del pragmatismo, ed. J. de Salas y F. Martín (Madrid, Spain: Biblioteca Nueva, Universidad Complutense de Madrid, 2005): 201–18. Jorge L. Borges's father, a friend of Fernández, was also a devoted follower of both, which explains this writer's philosophical interests. See Bruno Bosteels, "The Truth Is in the Making: Borges and Pragmatism" in *Romanic Review* 98, no. 2/3 (2007): 135.

46. Francisco Romero, *La Filosofía en América* (Buenos Aires, Argentina: Raigal, 1952), 16.

47. See Marisa A. Muñoz, "Bergson y el bergsonismo en la cultura filosófica argentina" in *Cuadernos Americanos: Nueva Epoca* 2, no. 140 (2012): 103–22.

48. Carlos O. Bunge, *El Derecho. Ensayo de una teoría jurídica integral*, vol. I (Buenos Aires, Argentina: Valerio Abeledo, 1915), 72.

49. In this section Bunge analyzed the following editions: William James, Henri Bergson, and Emile Le Brun, *Le pragmatisme* (Paris: Flammarion, 1911); Henri Bergson, *L'évolution créatrice* (Paris: Félix Alcan, 1913).

50. Carlos O. Bunge, *El Derecho*, 75.

51. Ibid., 78.

52. Most intellectuals and scientists read Bergson in French, but translations of work in Spanish started to appear by the beginning of the twentieth century. For example, *Materia y Memoria. Ensayo sobre la relación del cuerpo con el espíritu*, translated by Martín Navarro, was published in Madrid in 1900.

53. Víctor A. Belaúnde, "Prólogo," Mariano Ibérico, *La Filosofía de Enrique Bergson* (Lima, Peru: Sanmartí, 1916), iii.

54. Ibid.

55. Ibid.

56. Mariano Ibérico, *La Filosofía de Enrique Bergson* (Lima, Peru: Sanmartí, 1916), x.

57. Ibid.

58. For an analysis of Mexican philosophy, see José Gaos and Alain Guy, "L'actualité Philosophique au Mexique," *Les Études philosophiques Nouvelle Série* 13, no. 3, *Aspects de la Pensée Ibéro-Américaine* (Juillet/Septembre 1958): 289–301.

59. Alfonso Reyes, *Pasado Inmediato y Otros Ensayos* (Mexico D.F.: Fondo de Cultura Económica, 1941), 23.

60. Pedro Henríquez Ureña, "La Revolución y la Cultura en México," *Revista de Filosofía* xi, no. 1 (Buenos Aires, Argentina: Enero 1925), 125–32.

61. Pedro Henríquez Ureña, "La Obra de José Enrique Rodó," *Conferencias del Ateneo de la Juventud* (Mexico D.F.: Universidad Nacional Autónoma de Mexico, 2000), 62.

62. Ibid.

63. Ibid.

64. José Rodó, *Los Motivos de Proteo* (Buenos Aires, Argentina: Tecnibook Ediciones, 2011), 1.

65. Francisco García Calderón, "El Bergsonismo" in *Gonzalez, Horacio. ¿Inactualidad del Bergsonismo?* (Buenos Aires, Argentina: Ediciones Colihue SRL, 2008), 371.
66. Ibid.
67. Ibid., 372.
68. José Vasconcelos, "Pitágoras: Una teoría del Ritmo, part 2," *Cuba Contemporánea* 12, 205. The first part of this article is in the same volume, pp. 66–94.
69. Ibid., 206.
70. Ibid., 207.
71. José Vasconcelos, *Homenaje a Bergson* (Mexico D.F.: Imprenta Universitaria, 1941), 137.
72. Ibid., 138.
73. Ibid., 142.
74. Ibid.
75. Ibid.
76. Ibid., 52.
77. José Ingenieros, "La psicología biológica," *Anales de la Sociedad de Psicología* 1 (1910): 9–34.
78. Leopoldo Lugones, "La République Argentine et l'influence française" in *Mercure de France*, LX (September 15, 1906), 183–200. This was an influential article that was reproduced in several Spanish American countries. See Ismael López, "A propósito de un artículo de Lugones," *Trofeos* 1, no. 13 (1906): 145–51.
79. Henri Bergson, "Discurso de M. Henri Bergson," ed. Manuel García Morente, *La Filosofía de Henri Bergson* (Madrid, Spain: Residencia de Estudiantes, 1917), 20.
80. Manuel García Morente, *La Filosofía de Henri Bergson*, 34.
81. Carlos Vaz Ferreira, "Leyendo a Verlaine," *Nosotros* 2, no. 9 (April 1908): 165–66. Emphasis in the original.
82. "Presentation speech by Per Hallström, President of the Nobel Committee of the Swedish Academy, on December 10, 1928." http://www.nobelprize.org/nobel_prizes/literature/laureates/1927/press.html.
83. See Jimena Canales, *The Physicist and the Philosopher: Einstein, Bergson, and the Debate That Changed Our Understanding of Time* (Princeton, NJ: Princeton University Press, 2015).
84. Bergson published his ideas on relativity in *Durée et imultanéité: à propos de la théorie d'Einstein*, published in 1922. The reception of this book was quite negative and contributed to the decline of Bergson popularity.
85. Aníbal Ponce, "Henri Bergson y el premio Nobel de Literatura," Horacio Gonzalez, *¿Inactualidad del Bergsonismo?* (Buenos Aires, Argentina: Ediciones Colihue SRL, 2008), 349.
86. Ibid., 351.
87. Alfredo T. Tolmasquim and Ildeu C. Moreira, "Einstein in Brazil: The Communication to the Brazilian Academy of Science on the Constitution of Light"

in *History of Modern Physics—Proceedings of the XXth International Congress of History of Science*, 2002, pp. 229–42.

88. Ramón G. Loyarte, *Evolución de las ciencias en la República Argentina: La Evolución de la Física* (Buenos Aires, Argentina: Imprenta Coni, 1924).

89. Enrique Gaviola, *Contribución al Estudio de las Ciencias Físicas y Matemáticas: Dualidad y Determinismo* (La Plata, Argentina: Facultad de Ciencias Fisicomatemáticas, 1931). For another good example of the relationship between philosophy and physics, see Rafael García Bárcena, "¿A dónde va el universo físico?" *Revista Cubana de Filosofía* 1 no. 3 (January–December 1948), 27–40.

90. Niels Bohr, "Natural Philosophy and Human Cultures," *Nature* 143 (February 18, 1939): 268.

91. Ibid., 270.

92. Ibid., 271.

93. Ibid.

94. Ibid., 272.

95. Hannah Landecker, *Culturing Life: How Cells Became Technologies* (Cambridge, MA: Harvard University Press, 2009), 235.

96. Coole Diana and Samantha Frost, "Introducing the New Materialisms," 9.

97. Ibid.

98. Ibid.

99. Ibid., 17.

100. Elizabeth Grosz, "Significant Differences. An Interview with Elizabeth Grosz," *Interstitial Journal* (March 2013), 1. https://interstitialjournal.files.wordpress.com/2013/03/grosz-interview1.pdf.

101. Ibid.

102. Elizabeth Grosz, *Becoming Undone*, 71.

103. Karen Barad, "Posthumanist Performativity: Toward an Understanding of How Matter Comes to Matter," *Signs* 40, no. 1 (2014), 801.

104. Ibid., 814.

105. Karen Barad, *Meeting the Universe Halfway: Quantum Physics and the Entanglement of Matter and Meaning* (Durham, NC: Duke University Press, 2007), 33.

106. Ibid., 34.

107. Ibid.

Chapter 7

Bergsonism in Postrevolutionary Mexico

Antonio Caso's Theory of Aesthetic Intuition

ANDREA J. PITTS

This chapter is an examination of Mexican philosopher Antonio Caso's (1883–1946) conception of aesthetic intuition and its relationship to Bergsonism. Caso was a founding member of a group of philosophers in early-twentieth-century Mexico known as the *Ateneo de la Juventud* ("Athenaeum of Youth"). The *Ateneo* began to meet in 1909, just before the start of the Mexican Revolution, and was comprised of writers, politicians, and educators who sought to develop a critical response to a form of positivism that characterized the followers of the then-president Porfirio Díaz.[1] Among the theoretical resources that Caso and the *Ateneo* turned to in an effort to critique the Porfiriato's exaltation of the natural sciences were the writings of Henri Bergson.[2] Caso adapted Bergson's views to develop what he hoped would be a new role for art and a new form of aesthetics in postrevolutionary Mexico. Aesthetics, for Caso, offered not only a way to reshape national identity, but, philosophically speaking, was the foundational link between the moral and natural orders of the human being.

While readers of Caso throughout the twentieth and twenty-first centuries have noted the influence of Bergson in his writings on science, metaphysics, and morality, less attention has been paid to the underpinnings of vitalism within Caso's aesthetics. Some scholars of Caso, however, do note that his theory of aesthetic intuition closely follows the account of intuition found in the writings of Bergson.[3] In this vein, Rosa Krauze de Kolteniuk has even stated, in agreement with Patrick Romanell, that Caso is more consistent in bearing out the philosophical implications of Bergsonism in *Existence as Economy, as Disinterest, and as Charity* (*Existencia como economía, como desinterés y como caridad*) than Bergson is himself in *Les deux sources de la morale et de la religion*. Yet, the manner in which Caso adapts Bergson's writings and the lenses though which interpreters of Bergson have read *Les deux sources de la morale et de la religion* may leave contemporary readers of both figures with unanswered questions. I thereby attend to the manner in which Caso interprets Bergson's writings on intuition and the function that aesthetic intuition plays in his overarching philosophical system.

To elaborate these views, in what follows, I first introduce the context of Caso's writings and the work of the *Ateneo*. Then, in the second section, I explore his conception of aesthetic intuition and its role in his broader conceptions of metaphysics, science, and morality. I aim to demonstrate that Caso's understanding of resistance to Porfirian positivism makes his view strongly complimentary to Bergson's political views as found in *Les deux sources de la morale et de la religion*. Such overlap thus presents Caso as a significant figure to study alongside Bergson, and this rich set of connections undergirds the relevance of his work for contemporary philosophical questions. The final section of the chapter thus takes up several examples of such contemporary concerns.

El Ateneo and Antipositivism

The formation of the *Ateneo de la Juventud* in 1909 marked a pivotal series of events in the history of philosophy in Mexico. Prior to this, the period of roughly 1876 to 1911 was a time when much of the land, major industries, and significant shares of the nation's natural resources were under the control of foreign investors. These market practices then served, in turn, as the financial means for Díaz to achieve his goals of industrializing and "modernizing" Mexico.[4] In addition, under the educational reforms of Gabino Barreda during the 1860s and 1870s, guided by then-president Benito Juárez, the theoretical underpinnings of positivism were considered "the instrument that was needed to put an end to the era of disorder and anarchy that had befallen the Mexican nation."[5] The method for progress according to scholars and politicians under the Porfiriato, referred to as the *Científicos*, was Comtean in nature,[6] and appealed to science for all national matters, including the economic, social, and educational affairs of the state.

Members of the *Científicos* adapted views of evolution to defend, in their eyes, the rightful place of Porfirio Díaz. The reasoning, as applied to the political realm, was that if only the "fittest" were able to survive in the natural order of things, then Díaz's successful political campaigns provided evidence that he was the most "fit" to rule and benefit the nation.[7] Also, more generally, while Díaz's economic reforms led to an increase in wealth for investors and elites in the nation, the introduction of foreign capital in the nation served to lessen the value of goods produced by the country's poor indigenous and mestizo peasantry. Moreover, under the Porfiriato, the economic and political developments of the United States and Europe were used as metrics by which Mexico's cultural and industrial changes were being measured. Later philosophers and historians, such as Leopoldo Zea, would note that this form of comparison and competition led to the establishment of unattainable and disingenuous ideals for the nation.[8]

The Mexican Revolution in 1910 brought about sweeping changes in the political, educational, and cultural landscapes of the country, and Caso's writings and teachings impacted nearly every generation of philosophers thereafter. Although instructors at the National Preparatory School would introduce Caso to the philosophical tenets of positivism, it was through the mentorship of Justo Sierra that Caso would develop a deep skepticism of positivism's dismissal of metaphysics, theology, and nonempirically based forms of moral philosophy.[9] In this sense, Caso and the *Ateneo de la Juventud* were opposed to the Porfiriato's exaltation of science, the imposition of foreign economic influence in the nation, and the implications of erasing theology, moral theory, and metaphysics from the educational curricula of the nation.

For instance, in 1910, the *Ateneo* began staging a series of public lectures through which they aimed to reach public audiences beyond the wealthy elite who benefited from the prior educational system available during the Porfiriato. The lectures and the new educational curricula designed by the *Ateneo* intended to reach the poor peasantry who had been disregarded by Díaz's regime. For example, Jesus Acevedo of the *Ateneo* established a series titled *La Sociedad de Conferencias* in which members staged public meetings to discuss literature, poetry, philosophy, art, and politics.[10] The primary aim of these meetings, wrote the *Atenista* Alfonso Reyes, was "to have direct dealings with the public, to talk to them."[11] Caso was a prominent participant in these meetings. In addition to his role as a public intellectual, he was also primarily a defender of state-sponsored education as a means to connect with the public. Throughout his life, he taught at various institutions, including the Universidad Nacional de Mexico, the Escuela Nacional Preparatoria, the Escuela Nacional de Jurisprudencia, and the Colegio de Mexico.

With these political motivations in mind, we can consider John Haddox's claims regarding Latin American philosophy. Haddox argues that a great deal of Latin American philosophy is marked by its groundedness in cultural transformation and political life. Writing in response to notable theorists such as José Gaos and Francisco Romero, Haddox claims that philosophers such as Caso and José Vasconcelos were writers whose thought was intended to be "readily accessible to all, [and] not [narrow specialists] who can be understood only by other professional philosophers."[12] Caso too presumably would have been in agreement with the spirit of this claim regarding philosophy. Caso writes that "philosophical activity is not something independent of life and action, or art and science" and that philosophy should be marked by an ability and vigor to grapple with the struggles of human existence.[13]

Caso thus distinguishes between two approaches to philosophy: the heroic and the discrete. Heroic philosophical endeavors are marked by inventiveness, enthusiasm, intrepidity, striving, and problematization, and are personified through the work of figures such as Plato, Plotinus, Augustine, Pascal, Bergson, and Scheler.[14] Discrete philosophy is characterized by objectivity, calmness, abstraction, logic, and practical impotency, and can be situated among the writings of theorists such as Aristotle, Descartes, Kant, and Husserl.[15] Caso considered himself and his mentors and colleagues, such as Sierra, heroic philosophers, who sought social and political change alongside and in conjunction with their philosophical pursuits.[16] In a critical voice against both the methodology of positivism and a proposed exceptionalism for discrete approaches to philosophy, he claims, as Haddox notes, that a theory of existence "is incomplete without a theory of the value of existence."[17] Accordingly, Caso writes critically of the endeavor to exact a rational science of existence:

> Let us suppose that we know everything. We have deciphered the mysteries of the most distant nebulae. We know the most hidden composition of matter, the enigma of force, the intimacy of motion, the nature of light, heat, and electricity, the enigma of life, the arcane of consciousness [. . .] Our mathematics possesses irresistible analytical procedures, such that infinitesimal calculus becomes a boring instrument. Our physics and chemistry are perfect; our biology without defect; even our psychology is

perfect [. . .] Nevertheless, we would still be dumbfounded by the question: What is the value of the universe?[18]

Thus, fundamental for Caso's philosophical views are axiological and aesthetic concerns regarding the value of existence.

Such a view provides the methodological orientation for understanding Caso's aesthetics. Namely, following the positivist teachings of his upbringing and the antipositivist convictions he strengthened through the *Ateneo*, Caso develops a systematic theory of philosophy that while grounded in experience, offers an expansive role for moral theory, metaphysics, and aesthetics. At the most general level, for Caso, aesthetics serves as a philosophical bridge between nature and normativity. His views on the relationship between aesthetics, metaphysics, morality, and experience appear throughout his oeuvre, and his most systematic treatment of his views appear in *La existencia como economía, como desinterés y como caridad*. Initially the work was published as a short essay in 1916 as *La existencia como economía y como caridad: Ensayo breve de la esencia de Cristianismo*, and expanded into five chapters in 1919, under the title of *La existencia como economía, como desinterés y como caridad*, with no subtitle. The text's final edition was published in 1943. There are many important historical and biographical events in Caso's life that emerged between the first edition of this text and the final edition; however, one notable feature of the newer editions is that they appear during or following two world wars. This, as Haddox has noted, may have been an important reason why we see Caso's shifting philosophical views. In particular, Caso's theory of humanism is significantly developed throughout the three editions of the text, and appears most strongly in the third edition.[19]

Romanell notes that we see a change in Caso's thinking between the earlier and later periods of his writings. Romanell argues that Caso's earlier works, such as *El concepto de la historia universal en la filosofía de los valores* (1923) and the 1916 and 1919 versions of *La existencia*, each illustrate an affinity with the pragmatist thought of William James. Namely, we see James's influence appear in these earlier writings of Caso, including what Romanell notes as Caso's "social objectivism," whereby all value and truth is determined through that which is considered socially useful.[20] Thus, Caso rejects subjectivism and what he describes as "ontologism" (perhaps drawing the critique from another work influenced by James, Max Scheler's *Der Formalismus in der Ethik und die materiale Wertethik*), wherein the existence of values is posited as distinct from lived reality. Caso proposed instead that truth, beauty, and goodness are determined through the ability of such values to satisfy the collective desires of a society.[21]

However, by the 1943 publication of *La existencia*, Caso no longer relies on James and instead adopts Husserl as a primary figure for understanding value, and more importantly for the purposes of this chapter, for developing his theory of intuition. In the 1920s and 1930s, many prominent philosophers in Mexico began paying a great deal of analytical attention to German phenomenology. Caso was part of this intellectual trend, which included delivering a series of lectures on Husserl and Scheler, and eventually publishing *La filosofía de Husserl* in 1934. With the shift in his thought between James and Husserl, Caso seeks to address another complicated philosophical relationship: that of Husserl and Bergson on the topic of intuition. He proposes that both theorists are incomplete without the other and that his conception of intuition brings together their respective philosophical insights.[22] Accordingly, among the major changes made between the 1919 version of *La existencia* and the 1943 version is the addition of a form of perspectivism, notably influenced by José Ortega y Gasset,[23] and the replacement of Jamesian pragmatism with Husserlian phenomenology.[24]

As Rigel Olivares Vargas notes regarding Caso's intuitionism, "Intuitionism is the cornerstone of Caso's philosophy, and the means by which his work continued to meet the diverse philosophical concerns that he had throughout his life: the critique of positivism, the problem of transcendence, values, the refounding of metaphysics, and so on."[25] First, to understand the role of intuition in Caso's thought, it is important to note his conception of life. In the early 1916 version of *La existencia*, Caso begins the essay by discussing the relationship between being and living. He states, quoting the French biologist Félix Le Dantec, that "to be is to struggle, to live is to overcome."[26] To bear out the significance of this quotation, the essay proceeds by tracing Darwinian evolutionary theory and Bergsonian vitalism. From Darwin, Caso takes up a claim based loosely on natural selection that not all forms of possible life survive.[27] Thus, not all possible existence is made actual. Second, given a competition for resources and the tendency of living organisms to "persist in their being" (i.e., via reproduction and nutrition), Caso interprets this struggle for existence as self-interested and as a form of *egoísmo*.[28] Positioning his conception of life against Kantianism, Caso proposes in the 1919 version of *La existencia* that life cannot be grounded in the order of reason.[29]

This coincides with Bergson's rejection of Kant's conception of rationality as well. Intelligence to facilitate actions for the human animal, according to

Caso, emerges as part of the adaptability of the human species to survive, which includes tool usage. Such intelligence arises not because of some special feature of the human animal above and beyond other forms of life, but rather because instinct is insufficient for sustaining the human animal, according to this Bergsonian reading.[30] From these premises, Caso describes life as economic, and proposes the following equation for understanding life: "Life = Minimum effort × Maximum benefit."[31] This equation echoes both the Malthusian influence on Darwin,[32] as well as the formulation in Bergson that "life tends toward the utmost possible action, but that each species prefers to contribute the slightest possible effort."[33] This conception of life functions for all forms of life according to Caso, and implies that the striving of life is an attempt to balance the least expenditure of effort for maximal gain. Of the vital energy of human animals, Caso writes, "Life is always interested. It is an assimilating and dissimilating, economic, [and] selfish activity. To nourish, to grow, to reproduce, to play, to make tools, to die, all of this, as we have already seen, is pure economics, the pure effect of *egoísmo*, [and] of formless imperialist effort."[34] However, what remains inexplicable within all empirical research on the human animal, Caso proposes, is the existence of the specifically human form of *disinterested* inquiry into the nature of beauty and the good. Thus, art, for Caso becomes the exemplification of the possibility of nonegoistic intuition. Caso also draws from James and Bergson to propose in the 1916 version of *La existencia* that the same vital energy that seeks to conserve itself also has a surplus [*tiene un surplus*] in the human animal.[35] That surplus, he argues, gives rise to both play and art. Art, as I examine below, becomes the bridge between human animal being and human moral being.

Aesthetic Intuition and Bergsonism

In Caso's attempt to bridge nature and normativity, he distinguishes between play and art. Yet, we must first distance Caso's account of play from Spencer's infamous "surplus energy theory,"[36] a distinction which Caso himself makes explicitly in *Principios de Estética* (1944). In that text, Caso quotes Leo Tolstoy's work *What Is Art?* [1897] and asks his readers to consider the value of Spencer's hypothesis on play.[37] With Spencer, Caso agrees that art and play arise from a surplus of animal energy that is not expended through practical activities for survival. However, given Caso's commitments to Friedrich Schiller's adaption[38] of Kant's conception of the "free play of the imagination" and the moral significance of aesthetic experience, Caso seeks to develop a conception of art that is distinct from play. This notion of art, though, remains connected to a conception of the surplus energy of the human animal.[39] Namely, Caso asks his readers to consider Spencer's claim that play and art *both* arise from surplus energy that has not been expended by an animal's instinctual activities. For Spencer, play arises first to expend excess energy, and then later art, as a form of play, arises for the human animal. Thus, both art and play are the result of the casting off of excess vital energy.

Caso argues against Spencer, and states that Schiller's notion of play was "developed and disfigured" by Spencer. He turns to the work of Karl Groos, a German psychologist and philosopher, as someone who will allow him articulate a theory of play that maintains a noninstrumentalist function for both play and art. Groos proposes that art and play are more similar than practical activities and art. While Spencer proposes that practical activities of the animal are on a continuum with art, Groos claims that what distinguishes play and art from practical activities of the animal is that both play and art arise from *disinterested* activities of the animal, that is, purposelessness (unlike uninterestedness wherein the animal derives no pleasure). Groos, following Schiller as well, proposes that play and art operate as both disinterested and self-interested inclinations in the animal. While Groos's ultimate distinction between human and nonhuman animals rests on a psychological distinction, Caso draws largely on the nature of disinterested activity and its role in artistic creation to defend a morally transcendent role for art in the human animal.[40] This crucial difference between play and art thus allows Caso to more tightly link his own theory of aesthetic intuition back to conceptions of morality and freedom (i.e., more closely with Schiller).

From this conception of art, Caso attempts to bridge the natural being of the human animal with the normative existence of human life. Artists, for Caso, point to the ability of the human animal to transcend its mere instinctual being. The reason for this is because the artist personifies the possibility of aesthetic intuition, which for Caso is a kind of profound recognition of particularity. Unlike instinctual intuition or theoretical intelligence, aesthetic intuition considers "the individual, the being, the animal, or the situation" in itself.[41] As Haddox notes on this point, "As Caso explains it, for practical purposes, the scientist, the theoretician, and the mathematician abstract from the individual certain concepts that they can schematize, organize, and put to use, while in contrast, the artist, the poet, and the musician present a distinctive, intrinsically valuable picture of the concrete individual."[42] Aesthetic intuition is thus the noninstrumental, that is, disinterested, element of the human animal's activities that when combined with creative expression gives rise to art.

Here we can see a connection between Caso's conception of intuition and that of Bergson. Conceiving of intuition as the apprehension of concrete particulars is a view well-supported by Bergson. Regarding Bergson's notion of intuition, Elizabeth Grosz notes that intuition is not a "concrete and well-formed concept."[43] Rather it is "more a 'shadow,' a 'swirling of dust.'"[44] Grosz states that "intuition is an emergent and imprecise movement of simplicity that erupts by negating the old, resisting the temptations of intellect to understand the new terms of the language and concepts of the old."[45] This imprecise movement of intuition has two tendencies for Bergson. The first tendency corresponds with Caso's conception of disinterested vital energy. Bergsonian intuition is a movement inward "into a depth beyond practical utility, available to use at those moments of reflection when we can perceive our own inner continuity above and beyond action and definable results."[46] The second tendency of intuition is the ability to see the particularity of intuition in the durational flow of all life, which derives from self-reflection on the inward movement of the first tendency.[47] Bergson writes in *L'évolution créatrice*, "By intuition I mean instinct that has become disinterested, self-conscious, capable of reflection upon its object and of enlarging it indefinitely."[48] This outward movement is a direct experience of the connections between life and matter, duration and space, the object and the subject.[49] Through intuition, the particularity of the human intellect connects to the universality of duration, which is to say, a universal quality of becoming. Leonard Lawlor describes Bergson's notion of duration as comprised of two simple ideas: "The first is perhaps at the heart of Bergson's philosophy: the past survives. The second follows from the first: the moment coming from the future is absolutely new."[50] Intuition's connection to duration requires the double tendency mentioned above, and highlights the inherent creativity of existence. Moreover, duration, in this sense, implies a direct contrast to the positivist claims that human social change can be understood through the persistent efforts of scientific rationality. As mentioned above, the claims of the *Científicos* that all moral, social, and political progress would be reducible to scientific inquiry and the availability of empirically verified predictions are directly challenged by this conception of an underlying ontological form of differentiation and change. Namely, what we will see below is that a lack of human self-interest and instrumental reasoning (including the rejection of any kind of calculus regarding human prudential self-interests) is what characterizes the emergence of morality for Caso.

To understand Caso's conception of intuition, we can clarify his views on the existence of values. Regarding this point, Michael Candelaria argues in *The Revolt of Unreason* that Caso is a Platonist. Candelaria states, "In Caso's view, values are Platonic forms grasped by the intuition. As Platonic forms they exist objectively."[51] Candelaria then proceeds to argue in the following chapter why this is the case on his reading. However, another examination of Caso's writings on aesthetics suggests that this reading of the existence of values cannot be correct. Namely, in *Principios de estética*, Caso cites Bergson as an inspiration for his own view that "abandons, definitively, all Platonism, and explains to us the object of contemplation, without leaving the field of experience."[52] Caso praises Bergson for developing a theory of intuition that does not require the presupposition of an immaterial realm of ideas.

Moreover, in the chapter of *Principios* titled "Platonism and Empathy," Caso reiterates the tremendous vision of Plato, as a heroic philosopher, who proposes a "philosophy of love."[53] Plato's philosophy of love connects the intuition of beauty to truth and the good. Caso then refers to Plotinus's conception of love as kind of "mystical transportation" that takes up the insights of Plato.[54] Last, connecting mystical transportation to German philosophy, Caso situates discussions of *Einfühlung*, or what is often translated as "empathy," within his analysis. Through this connection to German philosophy, Caso brings together "something practical and concrete [that] diverges from pure logical thought and metaphysical idealism."[55] The differences between art and mysticism are of degree, not essence, he claims. In this sense, certain features of Platonism can be relevant for Caso's own views on the concrete experience of objects of intuition; however, this does not imply a kind of *metaphysical* commitment to the existence of a separate immaterial order of existence. Rather, the emergence of *Einfühlung* is itself an outgrowth of the natural capacities of the human animal.

We can thus turn back to Bergson as an important figure for Caso's conception of intuition and for his axiological views. In particular, Bergson proposes that intuition moves outward into the durational flow of time, including human history. To clarify aesthetic intuition, Caso discusses aesthetic values such as beauty, grace, tragedy, comedy, and the sublime. He holds, as Haddox notes, that the concept of beauty "is outside the realm of good and evil."[56] Moreover, beauty and the values of the artist are also outside the economic calculus of everyday necessity. For example, in a discussion of Bergson's *Le rire: Essai sur la signification de comique*, Caso analyses Bergson's discussion of comedy as a general treatise on the object of art and the principles of aesthetics. He proposes, alongside Bergson, that were intuition as common as some critics have proposed, we would all be artists. However, the kind of intuition that he is developing, and that he draws from Bergson, is one that is not commonplace. He writes,

> If reality, Bergson states, was enough to directly affect our senses or our consciousness, and we could enter into immediate communication with the outside world and ourselves, we would all be artists. But between nature and our person; more so, between us and our own consciousness, stands a veil. This obstacle is heavy for ordinary people; light, or rather, almost transparent for the artist and the poet. Why?[57]

The reason for this Caso explains is that survival often requires considering one's own needs, and this requires becoming adept at understanding how the world can help us meet our own needs. Our impressions of the world guide us toward self-directed action, which means that objects are not usually taken in their specificity, but rather as general members of objects for our use. Following Bergson, he cites this passage from *Le rire*:

> The INDIVIDUALITY of things or of beings escapes us, unless it is materially to our advantage to perceive it. Even when we do take note of it—as when we distinguish one man from another—it is not the individuality itself that the eye grasps, i.e., an entirely original harmony of forms and colours, but only one or two features that will make practical recognition easier.[58]

Here, Bergson notes that even the perceptual practices involved in our understandings of the world are themselves derived from a kind of instrumental interestedness.[59] Such a view supports the Kantian conception of aesthetic disinterestedness, while at the same time pointing to the disruption of the Kantian conception of the modern subject that seeks to secure its own rational stability. Rather, as Claire Colebrook argues, "Bergson places the aesthetic sense close to an overcoming of active synthesis."[60] Thus, as she argues, aesthetic intuition is the capacity for reorienting the human animal away from relationships of subject-object, and toward creative difference.[61]

Bergson's conception of art and intuition enters into this discussion again when Caso cites the following passage:

> From time to time, however, in a fit of absentmindedness, nature raises up souls that are more detached from life [. . .] Were this detachment complete, did the soul no longer cleave to action by any of its perceptions, it would be the soul of an artist such as the world has never yet seen. It would excel alike in every art at the same time; or rather, it would fuse them all into one. It would perceive all things in their native purity: the forms, colours, sounds of the physical world as well as the subtlest movements of the inner life. But this is asking too much of nature. Even for those of us as she has made artists, it is by accident, and on one side only, that she has lifted the veil. In one direction only has she forgotten to rivet the perception to the need. And since each direction corresponds to what we call a SENSE—through one of his senses, and through that sense alone, is the artist usually wedded to art. Hence, originally, the diversity of arts. Hence also the specialty of predispositions.[62]

This passage points to the limitations of the artist, that even artists and poets are not fully immersed in vital duration or in all aspects of the specificity of the object of their creation. While they may be directly intuiting the specificity of the colors, sounds, rhythms, tones, and shapes of their particular object or moment, their media for expression are limited. The reason for this derives not from the concrete materiality of artistic creation, but rather from the claim, according to Caso, that the artist's disinterest serves aesthetic values rather than moral ones. This means that although aesthetic intuition is connected to eternal duration through the experience of the sublime, for example, it does not provide the crucial intuitive link necessary to feel empathy, that is, feelings for other human animals.

This topic raises a complicated set of issues in Caso's theory. Namely, he holds moral values above aesthetic values, and defends *caridad* (charity) as the highest moral value. In *Principios de estética*, the German notion of *Einfühlung* becomes the critical link between morality and aesthetics. Turning to the works of Theodor Lipps, Caso explains that when properly understood, *Einfühlung* is the link between aesthetics and moral action, and provides a theory of empathy that links artistic disinterestedness to moral selflessness. Unfortunately, a full analysis of this concept and its function within Caso's aesthetics and his moral theory exceeds the scope of this chapter. What is important to highlight in this discussion is the moral value of *caridad* for Caso, and its functioning within his philosophical worldview.

Caridad, for Caso, is an opposing potentiality that exists within the human animal, that is, a vital energy that works against its egoistic tendencies. If the maxim listed above for the interest of life was that the least amount of effort should be offered for the maximal gain, under the value of *caridad*, this maxim is inverted. Caso proposes that *caridad* is comprised of the greatest amount of effort for even the most minimal benefit. Such selfless and difficult acts thereby preserve nobility and holiness. One reason for this, he proposes, is that aesthetic values are not sufficient to explain human progress. We see this discussion emerge primarily in the 1919 and 1943 editions of *La existencia*. There, Caso explains several types of human progress and contends that neither physical progress nor artistic progress can account for the betterment of the human animal. Because there are many ancient ways of living that exceed even the highest forms of excellence in the current day, he proposes that these cannot be progressive activities for the human animal. Here he cites cave paintings, ancient Egyptian art, and aboriginal Australian dance as more perfectly disinterested forms of art than those that exist in modernity.[63] The reason for this is because contemporary art, for Caso, always retains an element of self-interest, both in terms of the financial benefits and esteem afforded to artists for their work.

Yet, it is the possibility of rejecting egoism completely through sacrifice, *caridad*, and what today we would call *altruism* that provide the possibility for universal human progress. Caso is careful, however, to note that such forms of selflessness are not commonplace in individual human acts, nor in the mere aggregation of human individuals at the level of the species. At the level of the species, he claims, all the pains, desires, and acts only serve the ends of the species.[64] Some form of existence above and beyond the natural being of the human animal is necessary. This possibility for progress thereby exceeds the human animal's and species' existence as an interested being. Thus, the possibility for freedom lies in the human ability to sacrifice one's own interests for the good of others, according to this view.

Caso then proceeds to debate theoretical proposals that would challenge his view, for example, those of Nietzsche and Schopenhauer. He also rejects the Kantian moral law. He states that rationality does not compel us to be selfless. He writes, "The good is not a categorical imperative, a law of reason, as Kant thought, but is an excitement. It does not command, it never commands, it inspires. It does not impose, it does not come from outside, it flows from intimate consciousness, from a feeling that strengthens its roots in the depths of spiritual existence."[65] *Caridad* and sacrifice are described as "supernatural," but quoting Sierra he writes that this form of love for humankind "is supernatural which feels like the most natural thing on earth."[66] This link between *caridad* and the "naturalness" of the sentiment of selflessness indicates a bridging concept for Caso between the biological being of the human animal and its moral being.

Here we have another interesting connection to Bergson's work. Namely, Caso is often interpreted as a stark dualist for the claim regarding the supernatural form of charity that he invokes as the highest moral order of the human animal. Moreover, he analyzes in great detail the figure of Jesus Christ as an example of this form of love for humankind. That is, he analyzes Christ's martyrdom as a supreme act of human selflessness. Having such an exemplar thus undergirds the belief and emotional resonance in humans that extreme selflessness is possible. This faith and optimism for human goodness that he proposes against Schopenhauer is spiritually connected to the eternal duration of existence. The capacity is universal, and therefore also irreducible to any one particular religion or doctrine. Interestingly, despite his devotion to Christ as a perfect moral figure, Caso states in an interview in 1921: "I am a Christian and a follower of the Gospels, though not a member of any church or communion."[67] He also dedicates a chapter of *La existencia* to Tolstoy and the relationship between religion and politics. He vehemently resisted Catholic dogma and debated with his contemporaries regarding the possibility of a proof for the existence of God (about which Caso was skeptical) and the ability to comprehend God (about which Caso rejected any rational access to God). God appears to be, in Caso's own words, "A person [. . .] the most personal of all persons, the most real of all realities, the most fully existent of all existents."[68] He also states that "God is charity" and "Without good actions there is no God."[69] The suggestion here is that God is actional, that is, an unfolding force for differentiation, and that God is not outside of nature, but immanent in nature.[70]

Leaving aside the many theological implications of his view, these statements connect his work to Bergson. As I mention above, Romanell states that Bergson is more Bergsonist in *La existencia* than Bergson is in *Les deux sources*. Romanell claims that Bergson holds two views that are in tension between *L'évolution créatrice* and *Les deux sources*. In *L'évolution créatrice*, Romanell claims, Bergson concludes that God is unceasing life. However, by *Les deux sources* Bergson claims that God is love.[71] The two views, Romanell argues, are not consistent, namely, because life and love need not be viewed as interchangeable terms. He claims moreover that Bergson's invocation of mysticism in *Les deux sources* avoids offering any arguments for a defense of the new claim that God should be viewed as a spiritual form of love. Caso, he states, does offer a series of arguments that attempt to make this connection. Also, rather than attempting to derive a conception of divine love from the "metaphysical biologism" that Bergson proposes in *L'évolution créatrice*, Caso claims that morality is nonbiological to make his shift to divine love more theoretically expedient.[72]

To challenge Romanell's reading, we can take a brief look at contemporary readings of the political significance of *Les deux sources*. For example, Keith Ansell-Pearson and Jim Urpeth propose a version of Bergson's defense of "God as life" that is much more compatible with Caso. They state that Bergson develops a conception of God as the "divine force [that] is the creative energy at work in the evolution of life [. . .] on the line of life that culminates in the human, or something like it, we can conceive of a superhuman or super-life possibility. As Deleuze puts it, Bergson introduces a capacity for 'scrambling the planes, of going beyond his own plane as his own condition, in order to finally express naturing Nature.'"[73] Under this reading, God is conceived as supernatural through the divine's incarnation in human action, a view that draws very near to the invocation of the "supernatural" God of Caso. Moreover, Lawlor focuses on Bergson's conception of *unjust charity* in *Les deux sources*. Although space does not permit a full analysis of this concept alongside that of Caso, it is important to note that Lawlor examines Bergson's notion of unjust charity as a "command for justice [that is] most unnatural, most cheats nature, what is least naturalistic [. . .] Unconditionally, it commands justice for everyone."[74] While the book-length version of *La existencia* was published in 1919, *and Les deux sources* in 1932, the overlapping ideas are notable and call for an extended analysis of these works.

Contemporary Philosophical Issues in Caso's Bergsonist Aesthetics

As I mention in the previous section, much more analytical attention will be necessary to explore the relationship between Caso's philosophical views and those of Bergson. Such analysis should be welcomed by recent scholars of Bergson especially, given the newly renewed interest in his work by political philosophers, philosophers of religion, and ethicists. Similarly, exploring other contemporary philosophical issues that can be raised or revisited through his work would exceed the remaining few pages of this chapter. In what follows, I simply set the stage and offer several examples of ways in which Caso's work connects to several contemporary philosophical concerns.

First, Caso's and Bergson's writings emphasize that egoism and the biologization of the human animal can lead to an amoral, if not immoral, conception of human animal life. For example, Caso's distinction between human animals and nonhuman animals appears to not consider an expanded moral sense toward animals. However, if we examine his theoretical views, namely, that altruism and empathy distinguish the realms between the moral and the natural, we may find a much more expansive view for animal philosophy. For example, Kelly Oliver, in *Animal Lessons: How They Teach Us to Be Human*, examines the notion of *Einfühlung* and its functions in the writings of Martin Heidegger, Edmund Husserl, and Maurice Merleau-Ponty. She explores how this notion and its placement as a theory of empathy between humans and nonhuman animals and among humans operates according to these various thinkers. She also examines how it points toward each author's ontological and moral distinctions regarding the place of the human animal in the natural world. As I mentioned above, the notion of *Einfühlung* in Caso requires more attention, and so too does his understanding of how the human animal relates morally to nonhuman animals based on this reading of empathy and perception. While a number of contemporary readers of Bergson have been examining his work within discussions of "New Materialism" and philosophy of biology,[75] I contend, that understanding Caso's views of play, empathy, moral imagination, and imperial dominance may also challenge and extend our philosophical understandings of animal-human relationships. While his emphasis on personhood may appear to limit him to merely a defense of a kind of human exceptionalism, as Haddox points out, his defense of personalism may have stemmed from the belief that self-interested forms of "animality" were the causes of the atrocities of World Wars I and II.[76] Thus, his work expresses an optimism for the existence of a moral order that wrests free of such forms of individual and collective self-interested, instrumental reasoning.

Second, recall that the historical setting for Caso's work is to defend the study of morality, aesthetics, and metaphysics in the face of the trenchant positivism of the Porfiriato. While philosophical debates regarding naturalist readings of normativity are commonplace, we can also turn to contemporary political debates regarding the role of the humanities in public education more generally. For instance, Brad Petitfils argues in *Parallels and Responses to*

Curricular Innovation: The Possibilities of Posthumanistic Education that research universities in the United States are privileging STEM fields (i.e., science, technology, engineering, and mathematics) over the humanities because these disciplines help reiterate the narrative that the United States will be better suited to compete in a global market if students pursue these fields.[77] Thus, while the shift from nineteenth-century positivism to twenty-first-century neoliberal educational systems would require much further argumentation, Caso's adaptation of Bergsonian ideas regarding the value of intuition and of axiology, more generally, remain pressing concerns.

Third, an extended analysis of the humanism of Caso's writings would require an elaborate study of his conceptions of imperialism, his critiques of communism, and his defense of *mestizaje*. While he was vocally against conquest, he proposed measures that would support assimilationist models of culture for indigenous groups in Mexico. His writings also remain limited in terms of their usefulness for feminist analysis, as Francisco Nodar Manso argues in "Antonio Caso: *El mito de su liberal mentalidad político-social*."[78] Yet, to focus on feminist philosophy in the context of Mexico, the role of Caso in the development of Mexican humanism may remain significant, and contemporary work by feminist scholars have begun to note the impact of the *Ateneo* and other early-twentieth-century philosophers in Mexico. For example, Rubí de María Gómez Campos in *El sentido de sí: Un ensayo sobre feminism y la filosofía de la cultura* (2004) develops an account of Mexican philosophy of culture that focuses on women's philosophical relevance for postrevolutionary Mexico. Interestingly, her work takes up the theoretical gaps and trajectories of prominent Mexican philosophical projects aimed at questions regarding the relationship between culture and existence. Such feminist work need not directly connect to figures like Caso or other twentieth-century men in philosophy, but it is certainly able to critically challenge traditional narratives of Mexican philosophy and demonstrate their inadequacy by highlighting the prominent work done by women as cultural producers alongside and, at times, against prominent men in the nation.

Finally, one additional connection to contemporary philosophical work is that of contemporary humanist proposals among decolonial thought. While Caso may seem to be a strange fit within decolonial thought, his anti-imperialism, humanism, and interest in the relationship between science and philosophy may place him in conversation with decolonial theorists today. Consider, for example, Sylvia Wynter's articulation of humanism in "Unsettling the Coloniality of Being/Power/Truth/Freedom: Towards the Human, After Man, Its Overrepresentation—An Argument," wherein the author explores contemporary neuroscience, literary theory, theories of emotion from psychology, and evolutionary biology to propose a universalizing humanism that could combat the ontological excision of colonized peoples, for example, excision through genocide, cultural assimilation, and historical erasure. Such an analysis of the relationship between particularity and universality would be well paired with the form of perspectivism, concrete universalism, and theory of vitalism that Caso proposes. While there may be significant differences between these theorists in terms of Caso's conceptions of race, indigeneity, and human social groups, a study of these tensions and points of divergence would help distinguish contemporary decolonial theorists from previous theoretical articulations of anti-imperialism and of the possibilities for national culture among *mestizo* and colonized peoples. In addition, such analysis would demonstrate the diverse ways in which Bergson's ideas took shape outside European and Anglo-American geopolitical contexts, which, as we see through Caso's work and his subsequent impact on Mexican culture, led to many and varied forms of philosophical innovation.

Notes

1. Positivism within Mexico took the form of two general tendencies that were both endorsed under the banner of the Comtian motto of "Order and Progress." Leopoldo Zea, "Preface to the English Translation," in *Positivism in Mexico* (Austin, TX: University of Texas Press, 2014), 1–2. These two tendencies were "to subordinate politics to science, to see politics as a tool of sociology, and [. . .] to conceive this social technology as a science that must be guided by biological principles," Eduardo Mendieta, "The Death of Positivism and the Birth of Mexican Phenomenology" in *Latin American Positivism: New Historical and Philosophical Essays*, ed. Gregory D. Gilson and Irving W. Levinson (Lanham, MD: Lexington Press, 2013), 4.

2. Other prominent members of the *Ateneo* included Pedro Henríquez Ureña, Alfonso Reyes, and José Vasconcelos.

3. See, for example, Michael Candelaria, *The Revolt of Unreason: Miguel de Unamuno and Antonio Caso on the Crisis of Modernity* (New York: Rodopi, 2005). John Haddox, *Antonio Caso: Philosopher of Mexico* (Austin, TX: University of Texas Press, 1971); Rosa Krauze de Kolteniuk, *La filosofía de Antonio Caso* (Mexico City: Universidad Autónoma de México, 1961); Patrick Romanell, *Making of the Mexican Mind: A Study in Recent Mexican Thought* (Lincoln: University of Nebraska Press, 1952).

4. Haddox, *Antonio Caso*, 4.

5. Leopoldo Zea, *El positivismo en México: Nacimiento, apogeo y decadencia* (Mexico City: El Colegio de México, 1943), 56. All texts cited in English have been translated from the original Spanish by the author unless otherwise noted.

6. The core commitment of Comtean positivism was that science would be capable of perfecting all aspects of human society, including its moral and political dimensions.

7. Haddox, *Antonio Caso*, 4.

8. For example, Zea offered the seemingly paradoxical critique that the concept of "originality" has been proposed as the only trait that Latin America must "copy" from Europe, Leopoldo Zea, *The Role of the Americas in History* (Lanham, MD: Rowman & Littlefield, 1992), 4–5.

9. Sierra in a notable address in 1908 distances himself from Díaz and from the philosophical positivism of the Porfiriato. Sierra begins attending the lectures of the *Ateneo* in 1910 and eventually reformulates his views of positivism and social Darwinism. Romanell, *Making of the Mexican Mind*, 59–60.

10. Michael Candelaria, *The Revolt of Unreason*, 95.

11. Ibid.

12. John Haddox, "Latin American Personalist: Antonio Caso" in *The Personalist Forum* 8, no. 1 (1992): 109.

13. Antonio Caso, *Filósofos y doctrinas morales* (Mexico City: Librería Porrúa, 1915), 11–13. Quoted and translated in Haddox, "Latin American Personalist," 110.

14. Haddox, *Antonio Caso*, 14.

15. Ibid.

16. This form of philosophizing (i.e., as holding both a public political role and intellectual role simultaneously) has been common within various traditions in Latin American and Africana philosophy. For an analysis of the relationship between the philosophical commitments of Caso and his political and educational careers, see Haddox, "Latin American Personalist: Antonio Caso."

17. Haddox, Antonio Caso, 14.

18. Antonio Caso, *Obras completas, Tomo 6: Historia y antología del pensamiento filosófico. Evocación de Aristóteles. Filosofía*, ed. Rosa Krauze de Kolteniuk (Mexico City: Universidad Nacional Autonoma de Mexico, 1972b), 7. Quoted and translated in Candelaria, *The Revolt of Unreason*, 108.

19. Haddox, *Antonio Caso*, 30–31.

20. Romanell, *Making of the Mexican Mind*, 73.

21. Ibid.

22. Antonio Caso, *Obras completas, Tomo 3: La existencia como economía, como desinterés y como caridad*, ed. Rosa Krauze de Kolteniuk (Mexico City: Universidad Nacional Autonoma de Mexico, 1972a), 62.

23. Ortega's overarching view is that "perspective is one of the components of reality." Andrew Dobson, *An Introduction to Politics and Philosophy of José Ortega*

y Gasset (New York: Cambridge University Press, 2009), 145). This commitment attempts to dissolve the problem of the object-subject distinction by way of accepting a version of ontological pluralism, and rejecting any aperspectival notion of reality.

24. Romanell, *Making of the Mexican Mind*, 78.

25. Rigel Olivares Vargas, "El concepto de *intuición* en Antonio Caso. *Iztapalapa* 58 (2005): 172.

26. Caso, *Obras completas, Tomo 3*, 8.

27. Ibid., 8–9.

28. Ibid., 9.

29. Ibid., 46–47.

30. See Leonard Lawlor, "Asceticism and Sexuality: 'Cheating Nature' in Bergson's *The Two Sources of Morality and Religion*," *Bergson, Politics, and Religion*, ed. Alexandre LeFebvre and Melanie White (Durham, NC: Duke University Press, 2012).

31. Caso, *Obras completas, Tomo 3*, 11.

32. It has been well documented that Darwin read Malthus's *Essay on the Principle of Population* and that the text influenced his views on natural selection. For example, Vorzimmer notes that there were a number of resources in Malthus's *Essay* that would have provided a mathematical demonstration for the relationship between the rate of growth in a given human population and the potential scarcity of available food sources for that population Peter Vorzimmer, "Darwin, Malthus, and the Theory of Natural Selection," *Journal of the History of Ideas* 30 (1969): 537–38. This would, in Darwin's hands, lead to the articulation of a theory of natural selection, which, although different from Malthus's concerns with overreproduction, would retain a significant impact on his thinking.

33. Henri Bergson, *Creative Evolution*, trans. Arthur Mitchell (Mineola, NY: Dover, 1998), 128–29.

34. Caso, *Obras completas: Tomo 3*, 70.

35. Ibid., 12.

36. Spencer's surplus energy theory of play was predicated on the idea that the function of noninstrumental activities, including art and recreation in animals, was to release or expend unused vital energy. Gordon Burghardt, *The Genesis of Animal Play: Testing the Limits* (Cambridge, MA: MIT Press, 2005), 28–29.

37. Caso, *Obras completas, Tomo 5: Estética* (Mexico City: Universidad Nacional Autonoma de Mexico, 1971), 84.

38. From Schiller, this discussion can be found in *Über die ästhetische Erziehung des Menschen* (1795).

39. Caso, *Obras completas, Tomo 5*, 81–82.

40. Groos does not defend a firm ontological distinction between human and nonhuman animals. Rather, he proposes at the end of *The Play of Animals* that an "artistic germ" may exist in nonhuman animals, thereby making his distinction one of degree, and not in kind. Karl Groos, *The Play of Animals*, trans. Elizabeth L. Baldwin (New York: Appleton, 1898), 327–28.

41. Caso, *Obras completas, Tomo 5*, 85.
42. Ibid., 44–45.
43. Elizabeth Grosz, "Bergson, Deleuze and the Becoming of Unbecoming," *Parallax* 11, no. 2 (2005): 4–13, 8.
44. Ibid.
45. Ibid.
46. Ibid.
47. Ibid.
48. Bergson, *Creative Evolution*, 176.
49. Grosz, "Bergson, Deleuze, and the Becoming of Unbecoming," 8.
50. Leonard Lawlor, *The Challenge of Bergsonism: Phenomenology, Ontology, Ethics* (New York: Continuum, 2003), 80.
51. Candelaria, *The Revolt of Unreason*, 109.
52. Caso, *Obras completas, Tomo 5*, 96.
53. Ibid., 105.
54. Ibid.
55. Ibid., 106.
56. Haddox, *Antonio Caso*, 46.
57. Haddox, *Antonio Caso*, 95. "The veil" in this passage appears to refer loosely to instrumental reasoning, both at the conceptual and practical levels. Caso seems to suggest that by some unknown (or perhaps unknowable) natural inclination, humans are granted the capacity to extend beyond their self-driven interests.
58. Caso, *Obras completas, Tomo 5*, 95. Quoting Henri Bergson, *Laughter: An Essay on the Meaning of the Comic*, trans. Cloudesley Brereton and Fred Rothwell (New York: Macmillan, 1911), 152–53.
59. Language too relies on such generalizations, he claims, and thus the figure of the poet serves as the concrete possibility for human life to strive beyond its usual sets of generalizations and forms of instrumental reasoning.
60. Claire Colebrook, "The Art of the Future," *Bergson, Politics, and Religion*, eds. Alexandre LeFebvre, and Melanie White (Durham, NC: Duke University Press, 2012), 85–86.
61. Ibid., 86–87.
62. Caso, *Obras completas, Tomo 5*, 97.
63. Caso, *Obras completas, Tomo 3*, 95. Such a comment here is also indicative of the form of indigenismo that Caso supported, which included a romanticized conception of indigeneity.
64. Ibid., 94.
65. Ibid., 96.
66. Ibid., 97.
67. Haddox, *Antonio Caso*, 57. Haddox cites an interview with Caso printed in *La crónica* in Lima, Peru, July 16, 1921.
68. Caso, *Obras completas, Tomo 3*, 113.

69. Ibid., 102, 114.

70. Such a reading invites comparative work between Caso and Spinoza.

71. Romanell, *Making of the Mexican Mind*, 77.

72. Ibid., 77–78.

73. Keith Ansell-Pearson and Jim Urpeth, "Bergson and Nietzsche on Religion: Critique, Immanence, and Affirmation," *Bergson, Politics, and Religion*, ed. Alexandre LeFebvre and Melanie White (Durham, NC: Duke University Press, 2012), 253.

74. Lawlor, "Asceticism and Sexuality," 156–57.

75. For example, William Connolly, Alia Al-Saji, Claire Colebrook, and Elizabeth Grosz are among the contemporary theorists working on various strands of "New Materialism" and Bergson studies.

76. Haddox, "Latin American Personalist," 112.

77. Brad Petitfils, *Parallels and Responses to Curricular Innovation: The Possibilities of Posthumanistic Education* (New York: Routledge, 2014), 67.

78. Nodar analyses Caso's ovarian-testicular theory of sexual difference, and shows poignantly how it reiterates harmful pedagogical claims and biologized conceptions of women's capacities.

Chapter 8

Antagonism and Myth

José Carlos Mariátegui's Revolutionary Bergsonism

JAIME HANNEKEN

In an article published the year before his death, in which he gives an overview of the world events of the preceding quarter century, José Carlos Mariátegui (1894–1930) writes, "Historically, the philosophy of Bergson has coincided, as no other intellectual element, with the ruin of bourgeois idealism and rationalism and with the death of the old absolute [. . .] for that reason, it represents a season in the trajectory of modern thought" ("Históricamente, la filosofía de Bergson ha concurrido, como ningún otro elemento intelectual, a la ruina del idealismo y racionalismo burgueses y a la muerte del antiguo absoluto [. . .] Por este hecho, representa una estación en la trayectoria del pensamiento moderno").[1] The passage represents one of only a handful of direct references Mariátegui's written oeuvre makes to Bergson, despite the amply recognized influence the vitalist thinker held over his own ideas. Even this brief mention captures the French philosopher's prodigious impact on the heterodox socialist tradition from which Mariátegui would derive his most important interventions, and which argued forcefully against the teleological absolutism underwriting bourgeois notions of progress.

One of the most radical and prominent twentieth-century exponents of Peruvian socialism and *indigenismo*, Mariátegui is best known for his affirmation of the potential for national political renewal contained in native customs, what he characterized—following the anarcho-syndicalist Georges Sorel's own Bergsonian formulation—as a myth of indigenous socialism. The enduring popularity of Mariátegui's signature concept has gone hand in hand with a critical ambivalence surrounding his affinities with vitalism: although a substantial, long-standing body of scholarship has painstakingly documented the references, allusions, and encounters that would signal his Bergsonism, in part such attention has been aimed at distancing and diminishing the presence of any irrationalist tendencies that might stain Mariátegui before more contemporary sensibilities as an exoticist or mystic. For the historical materialism of midcentury Marxism and the poststructuralism of postcolonial and cultural studies, the ongoing relevance of Mariátegui's legacy, no matter how indisputable its importance, depends on the recovery of a properly rational interpretation of his thought from which notions like "myth" or "spirit" can be logically deduced, or dismissed altogether.[2]

The critical opportunity at hand in the task of reflecting on Mariátegui's Bergsonism today, then, is to generate a more precise awareness of the conceptual consistencies between the two within the terms of vitalism itself rather than through the lens of theoretical viewpoints that are extraneous or even opposed to it. With that in mind, I have focused the following analysis on the broad presence of Bergsonian notions like duration, qualitative difference, and the virtual in Mariátegui's core proposals, especially as they adhere to the Sorelian model of vitalism through which they were conveyed. My study is centered loosely on the themes of myth and antagonism: not only do these topics arguably serve as the cornerstones of Mariátegui's main interpretive schemes; what is perhaps more important, because myth and antagonism are conceits meant at bottom to isolate the time of life as change and resistance, they also represent sites where the Bergsonian thread of his reasoning finds its fullest expression. Teasing out the vitalist patterns of reason at work in them, I argue—with the help of Ernesto Laclau's theorization of hegemony—reveals a more comprehensive picture of Mariátegui's political logic as a strategic and ultimately hegemonic mobilization of time.

Although Mariátegui is the Peruvian writer of his time most closely associated with Bergsonism, he was by no means responsible for importing it to local contexts. Vaguely defined invocations of intuition and the *élan vital* were current among Peru's intellectual circles by the end of World War I: indeed, in the same article cited by my opening quote, Mariátegui credits Bergson, among other things, with producing "the mental confusion of Latin American university students" ("la confusión mental de los universitarios latinoamericanos").[3] Bergsonism constituted, as Aníbal Quijano put it, an "ideological watering hole" ("bebedero ideológico")[4] that in 1920s Peru resonated deeply with the climate of antipositivism driving the incipient formation of popular nationalism and cultural democratization.[5] Peruvian nationalism, like that of many Latin American republics, had unfolded during the nineteenth century under the liberal arrangements of neocolonialism: based on the export—mainly to Great Britain—of raw materials and mass-produced agricultural crops, liberal capitalism in Peru concentrated wealth and power in a miniscule oligarchic elite, reducing the nation's indigenous and mestizo majority to perpetual destitution. The consolidation of the latifundio-based land-tenure system, accentuating dependency on foreign investment and exacerbating the already vast economic disparity produced by semifeudal labor conditions, left Peru vulnerable to the instability of world markets after the turn of the century. The proliferation of worker strikes and protests, the circulation of anarcho-syndicalist rhetoric introduced by European immigrant laborers, and the emergence of popular student movements all announced an urgent need for the democratic opening of the nation's economic and political structures.[6] But such a transformation, as Peru's intellectual class realized, could not be achieved in material terms alone, without a profound revision of the cultural, institutional, and philosophical edifices that had sustained neocolonial dependency, in short, a reinvention of Peru's historical identity, one able to account for the ethnic and cultural reality of its heretofore silenced indigenous masses.

Where the nineteenth century's reigning philosophical models of liberalism and positivism compelled Peruvian elites to assess their society's lack of "progress" through the rationalist view of the Hegelian march of history or of social Darwinism, vitalism legitimized a nonlinear, nonrational conception of modernity. This conception was in line with widespread convictions about the "Decline of the West" and European decadence inspired by the outbreak of World War I. Furthermore it allowed for the revalorization of non-Occidental, premodern, and "primitive" cultures that science and reason had pronounced naturally and irrefutably inferior. Vitalism's divorce of time from history not only freed the analysis of Peruvian society from the premise of modernity's empty, universal, and irreversible development, according to which all of Latin America was inevitably categorized as backward or even ahistorical. It concomitantly provided the intellectual framework for theorizing indigenous and rural communities—groups whose non-European beliefs, practices, and racial makeup made them, from a rigidly rationalist view, not just premodern but quite literally frozen in the past—as contemporary citizens and modern national subjects.[7] It was amid such an atmosphere of social crisis and national revitalization that Mariátegui returned to Peru in 1923 from three years of exile spent traveling and studying in Europe, steeped in the philosophies and polemics of interwar socialism.

Sorel and the Myth of the General Strike

Mariátegui's European sojourn, spent mainly in Italy, brought him into contact with contemporary luminaries like Benedetto Croce and Romain Rolland, and with the protagonists of the period's main left-wing factions, most notably Piero Gobetti and other members of the *Ordine Nuovo* group. The presiding conflict of European leftism, namely the ideological split between the social democratic tenets of parliamentary socialism and anarcho-syndicalist voluntarism and the respective conceptions of history, class structure, and worker consciousness informing each—would color his eventual examination of Peruvian reality. Amid the considerable and varied collection of intellectual leaders from this context analyzed or implicitly referenced in Mariátegui's essays, his deepest debt belongs to Sorel. Sorel was an eclectic and by some accounts erratic figure, who is generally acknowledged as the forebear of various anarcho-syndicalist, as well as fascist branches of thought. His main target in *Decomposition of Marxism*, *Reflections on Violence*, and *The Illusions of Progress* (all from 1908) was what he viewed as the quietism of mainstream socialism that operated under the leadership of thinkers like Jean Jaurès and Eduard Bernstein. Both Juarés and Bernstein endorsed official doctrines that oriented policy to the incorporation of worker constituencies into party platforms. Parliamentary socialism's emphasis on compromise, negotiation, and gradual reform signaled to Sorel its conservative, antirevolutionary essence, which for him could be traced to a reliance on decrepit Enlightenment principles of analysis and synthesis. Such primacy of reasoned discourse, he argued, was geared to the neutralization of proletarian concerns in the interest of bourgeois control: resolution and synthesis amounted to stasis and stagnation. As David Ohana explains, "The purpose of Sorel's radical analysis was to reveal the dangers of the bourgeois state of mind: the search for harmony, illusions of progress, democracy, rationalism and optimism were a cover for class interest, attempts to temper conflict, appease strife, suppress vitality and harmonise the reality of conflict."[8]

Against the harmony advocated by parliamentary socialism, Sorel positioned himself as the theorist of conflict. Visibly melding Bergson's notions of duration and qualitative difference with Nietzsche's will to power and Jean-Pierre Proudhon's syndicalist proposals of proletarian activism, his treatises consistently sought to privilege social factors of antagonism, action, and creation as the core of revolutionary change. The most forceful and controversial articulation of Sorel's philosophy, which patently employs Bergsonian principles of time, difference, and action, is his theory of the myth of the general strike.[9] He describes myth, significantly, as an "image" that, gathering the proletariat's collective memory and experience of exploitation ("painful memories of particular conflicts"),[10] incites them to revolutionary combat in the interest of life. In its images "are found all the strongest inclinations of a people, of a party or of a class, inclinations which recur to the mind with the insistence of instincts in all the circumstances of life, and which give an aspect of complete reality to the hopes of immediate action upon which the reform of the will is founded."[11]

The myth of the general strike uses Bergson's fundamental precepts to alter the traditional dialectical understanding of historical movement as internal contradiction and synthesis, in two important ways. First, it conceives antagonism in Bergsonian fashion as a function of qualitative difference. Myth presents proletarian opposition to the existing order as absolute and instantaneous rather than calculated and relative. Like duration, myth conjures myriad instances of the socialist struggle into a complete and indivisible whole, that is, it "concentrat[es] the whole of socialism in the drama of the general strike; there is thus no longer any place for the reconciliation of opposites through the nonsense of official thinkers."[12] Sorel expressly contrasts the qualitative dimension of myth with parliamentary socialism's more idealist, "utopian" vision of change in terms that highlight their separate understandings of time. While myths, he writes, "Are not descriptions of things but expressions of a will to act," "a utopia is, on the contrary, an intellectual product; it is the world of theorists who, after observing and discussing the facts, seek to establish a model to which they can compare existing societies in order to estimate the amount of good and evil they contain."[13] The charge leveled here against reformist socialism is intimately tied to its espousal of rationalist maxims of order and progress: the impulse to isolate and compare social phenomena as data that can be fixed and juxtaposed, after the fact, on a single plane of analysis, conceives the time of change as space. Weighing unmet worker demands against a preestablished ideal as though it were plotting the variables of an equation, Sorel contends, socialism misconstrues the singular, irreversible nature of antagonism and action. By spatializing change, it projects and produces stasis.

The quality of duration Sorel imputes to his social myths as instantaneous and complete products of time equally pertains to the second and corollary Bergsonian feature of his theory: as occurrences of duration, myths are necessarily virtual. For the same reason that they cannot be planned or held up to an abstract ideal, their outcomes cannot be assessed at the level of historical particulars. There is no knowing how myth will relate to future reality or evaluate its correctness. Sorel insists that such concerns are beside the point, because the future created in the image of myth is always already imminent. Existing reality can only perceive it as catastrophe: "It must never be forgotten," Sorel claims, "that the perfection of this method of representation would vanish in a moment if any attempt were made to resolve the general strike into a sum of historical details: it must be taken as an undivided whole and the passage from capitalism to socialism conceived as a catastrophe whose development defies description."[14]

As Chantal Mouffe and Laclau point out in their classic analysis of hegemony, Sorel's social myth—and in particular, we might add, that which this idea owes to Bergson—introduced a decisive shift in the development of twentieth-century socialism insofar as it gave a precise theorization to the contingency and heterogeneity at play in the formation of social conflict. Where fin de siècle revolutionary thinkers hesitated to abandon the Marxist narrative that attributed historical necessity to class division and production, the myth of the general strike provided a meaningful formulation for the multifarious social factors that could agglutinate one group against another. From this perspective, Mouffe and Laclau write, "It matters little whether or not the general strike can be realized: its role is that of a regulating principle, which allows the proletariat to think the *mélange* of social relations as organized around a clear line of demarcation; the category of totality, eliminated as an objective description of reality, is reintroduced as a mythical element establishing the unity of the workers' consciousness."[15] Their account not only helps to explain how Sorel's theories managed to reconcile a vitalist conceptualization of the absolute with classically dialectical definitions of antagonism; it also illustrates why his heterodox formulations were to prove so instructive for Mariátegui's examination of Peru, where heterogeneity and contingency had shaped social relations in ways that orthodox ideas about "uneven and combined development" could only partially grasp.

Clarifying Peruvian History

Undoubtedly, the themes of antagonism and action as treated by Sorel correspond to the most Bergsonian moments of Mariátegui's analysis of Peruvian reality, culminating, of course, in his translation of the myth of the general strike to indigenous activism: as he writes in 1927, in the prologue to Luis E. Valcárcel's *Tempestad en los Andes*, "It is not the civilization or the alphabet of the white man that is lifting the soul of the Indian. It is the myth, the idea of the socialist revolution."[16] But it is Mariátegui's earlier commentaries on the European political scene, published in a series of articles soon after his return from abroad that most directly emulate Sorel's perspective. One of these, titled "Two Conceptions of Life" ("Dos concepciones de la vida"), diagnoses the stagnation of leftist thought since the war. Against the material comforts of postbellum prosperity that suggest a return to belle epoque ethics of "living gently"—an ethics that imbued bourgeoisie and proletariat alike with "a superstitious respect for the idea of progress"—he declares that "life, more than thought, now wishes to be action, that is, struggle. Modern humanity has need of faith. And the only faith that can fill its deepest self is a combative faith."[17] In another, called "Man and Myth" ("El mito y el hombre"), he pronounces—alluding to Vico and Nietzsche as much as Sorel—the ineptitude of reason before the power of myth: "Neither reason nor science can be myth. Reason itself has been charged with demonstrating to humanity that it is not enough, that only myth possesses the precious virtue of satisfying its deepest self."[18] And in an homage to the successes of the Bolshevik revolution, titled "The Final Struggle" ("La lucha final"), Mariátegui reaffirms the immediate and absolute, indeed virtual, nature of the socialist myth: "The uneducated man does not worry about the relativity of his myth. It would not even be possible for him to understand it [. . .] Because he must act, he acts. Because he must fight, he fights. He knows nothing of the relative insignificance of his effort in time and space" ("El hombre iletrado no se preocupa de la relatividad de su mito. No le sería dable siquiera comprenderla [. . .] Puesto que debe actuar, actúa. Puesto que debe combatir, combate. Nada sabe de la relativa insignificancia de su esfuerzo en el tiempo y en el espacio").[19]

The favoring of action over knowledge, the denunciation of the frailness and conservativism of reason, confidence in the vital role played by myth in social life, all of these mainstays of Sorel's thought inflect Mariátegui's writing on Peru. After 1924, and most pointedly with regard to the near-enslavement of the indigenous population—what he later terms *el problema del indio*—this inflection gives shape to the unifying thread of Mariátegui's work as a whole, namely, the ongoing task of reconceptualizing and clarifying Peruvian history. His approach to this endeavor employs a peculiar adaptation of Bergson's ideas about time. Rather than understanding national history as a series of successive data that naturally give way from one event to the next, Mariátegui attempts to isolate the purely temporal dimension of historical phenomena. That which is in the phenomena provokes change and action—or alternatively, fails to substantively alter the fabric of society—form the interpretative armature of his alternative history.

While this interpretive departure from materialism certainly serves to challenge Marxism's more stagist assumptions about economic determinism, more saliently for the contemporary Peruvian context it aimed to refute the overtly nostalgic attitude that predominated in literary and scholarly representations of the past, which at one point Mariátegui accusingly labels *pasadismo*. "The spirit of our people," he writes, "is *pasadista*; but it is not historical" ("El espíritu de nuestra gente [. . .] es pasadista; pero no es histórico").[20] Indeed, much literary production of the early twentieth century, caught up in the popular trends of *costumbrismo* and *perricholismo*, reduced Peruvian history to its colonial period, reproducing with romantic sentimentalism detailed tableaus of the *criollo* customs, personalities, and landscape of eighteenth-century Lima.[21] Where literature or social commentary portrayed pre-Columbian society at all, it was through the specialized and often primitivist optic of archeology and early anthropology, effectively discarding out of hand any historical continuity between the preconquest period and modern-day society. Mariátegui sees the prevalent "melancholy" of national literature as an imaginary support and counterpart of the overwhelming recidivism of national politics. Colonial nostalgia contrived to perpetuate contemporary social problems by masking their material causes, causes that become visible, and can be addressed only through appreciation of the fluid links between present, past, and future. Such a realization is at the crux of his "revolutionary thesis of tradition" ("tesis revolucionaria de la tradición"), according to which "the ability to think history and the ability to make it or create it, are identical: the revolutionary has an image of the past that is perhaps a little subjective, but animated and living, while the *pasadista* is incapable of representing it to himself in its turbulence and fluidity. Whoever cannot imagine the future, in general cannot imagine the past either" ("La facultad de pensar la historia y la facultad de hacerla o crearla, se identifican: El revolucionario, tiene del pasado una imagen un poco subjetiva acaso, pero animada y viviente, mientras que el pasadista es incapaz de representárselo en su inquietud y su fluencia. Quien no puede imaginar el futuro, tampoco puede, por lo general, imaginar el pasado").[22] The key difference between *pasadismo* and historicism, then, hinges on the latter's investment in the future. Mariátegui implies that the past only truly exists as a function of time in the Bergsonian sense, as part of a will to act and create. He reiterates, in "*Pasadismo* and Futurism" ("Pasadismo y futurismo") that "the capacity to understand the past is solidary with the capacity to feel the present and to worry about the future" ("La capacidad de comprender el pasado es solidaria de la capacidad de sentir el presente y de inquietarse por el porvenir").[23]

The points made above help us better to qualify the crucial revision Mariátegui's work undertakes of Peruvian *indigenismo*, a revision that is not straightforwardly materialist but, in his own formulation, "material idealist."[24] Unlike earlier pro-indigenous initiatives, which construed indigenous suffering as a result of lack of education, legislative negligence, or even ethnic primitiveness, Mariátegui's objective is to demonstrate their rootedness in socioeconomic structures. His entire intellectual project rests on the demand to reframe Peruvian dependence and inequality, especially the perennial destitution and abuse of its indigenous majority, in the "unmistakable and clearcut terms" of material reality.[25] His most ambitious effort to that effect, the *Seven Interpretive Essays on Peruvian Reality* (*Siete ensayos de interpretación de la realidad peruana*) (1928), in fact, assumes the traditional schematic division between base and superstructure. The first three essays, dedicated to economic issues of land and relations of production, are followed by four examinations of the institutional structures of education, religion, regionalism and centralism, and literature. Yet despite the unflagging rigor of these analyses, which on the surface remain faithful to the developmental stages laid out by historical materialism, what becomes apparent in the texture of Mariátegui's argument is the desire to spotlight, through these formal constraints, that Peruvian history has produced or has the potential to produce change. In sum, the overarching thesis of the *Seven Essays* is precisely that Peru does *not* change. Its failure to establish itself as a modern nation, to secure material progress, and to assimilate indigenous populations must be understood in his eyes first and foremost as a failure to act, to actualize as motive force the qualitative differences that conquest, colonization, and independence imposed on the Peruvian socius. Without the mobile, we may say spiritual, engagement of these differences, Peruvian history reveals nothing but a string of purely formal and ultimately static contradictions.

Any reader of the *Seven Essays* will be familiar with the principal among these contradictions: the conquest destroyed imperial Incan institutions without replacing them with an equally viable system of sustenance and social control. Spanish colonizers implanted in Peruvian society a morality of treasure hunters and rent collectors, which dominated political discourse under the mercantile capitalism of the viceroyalty. Absent the ethical foundations of capitalism, the oligarchy continued to rule Peru's liberal republic with the mentality of feudal lords. And finally, the lack of a true bourgeoisie leaves no structural ground from which a revolutionary socialist consciousness might emerge. It is impossible to disregard here the presence of certain commonplaces of classic modes-of-production narratives. But the apparent economic determinism of Mariátegui's ideas distracts us from the real point he wishes to make, that the arrival of successive "new" economic and ideological forces over the four centuries since the Spanish conquest have precipitated no transformation of Peruvian society. In Peru, liberalism and rationalism have amounted to meaningless shells of progress, because their governing ideas have no bearing on the activities and lives of the subjects they claim to manage. The empty rhetoric of rational autonomy and free enterprise is met on the ground with latifundios, *gamonalismo*, and coercive labor practices held over from bygone eras. Capitalism's existence as data, as physical phenomena, does not transcend the merely spatial realm of neocolonial dependence.

In effect, Mariátegui is arguing that a crass materialism is inadequate for comprehending the trajectory of modern societies, whose advance cannot simply be counted and recorded. An earlier analysis of this problem, in *Peruanicemos al Perú*, stresses the same distinction: even paragons of capitalist development like the United States should not be measured by the size of their achievements but by the vital nature of their progress, their human energy: "History teaches us that the roots and spiritual and physical impulses of the North American phenomenon are entirely found in its biological matter. It teaches us, moreover, that in this matter quantity has been less important than quality [. . .] The North American phenomenon appears, in its origin, not only quantitative but also qualitative" ("La historia nos enseña que las raíces y los impulsos espirituales y físicos del fenómeno norteamericano se encuentran íntegramente en su material biológico. Nos enseña, además, que en este material el número ha sido menos importante que la calidad [. . .] El fenómeno norteamericano aparece, en su origen, no sólo cuantitativo sino también cualitativo").[26] The persistence of the human factor in economic development, Mariátegui reasons, also explains the error of those who would "reduce Peruvian progress to a problem of hard capital [. . .] as though there did not exist, with a right to priority in the debate, a problem of human capital" ("reducen el progreso peruano a un problema de capital aúreo [. . .] como si no extisiese, con derecho a prioridad en el debate, un problema de capital humano").[27]

Contradiction and Antagonism

The theme of "qualitative" progress is revived in the *Seven Essays*, where over and over again Mariátegui attempts to trace Peru's material backwardness to the moral lassitude of its human institutions. This is the main failing, for example, of the Catholic Church: because of its historic focus on the administration and pacification of colonial subjects, evangelization in Spanish America contented itself with coercing the outward signs of piety rather than carrying out the spiritual conversion of its flock. The importation of Catholicism to Peru can be considered an ecclesiastical venture, Mariátegui argues, but it is not properly religious, because "the religious spirit is tempered only in combat, in suffering."[28] In much the same way, public education has historically served to prepare Peru's rarified elite for lives of technocratic posturing rather than original enterprise, instilling in them the obsession with "moving words instead of things." He writes, "Almost all of us look with horror on the active professions that require energy and [the spirit of struggle], because we do not want to fight, suffer, take risks, and make our own way to prosperity and independence" ("Casi todos miramos con horror las profesiones activas que exigen voluntad enérgica y espíritu de lucha, porque no queremos combatir, sufrir, arriesgar y abrirnos paso para nosotros mismos hacia el bienestar y la independencia").[29] In the end, what accounts for Peru's historic torpor is not the ongoing material fact of economic disparity, but a social attitude of spiritual immobility, the lack of a will to struggle and suffer. In Laclau's terminology, in Peru there exist contradictions, but not antagonism.

It is true that Laclau could not by any measure be considered a Bergsonian philosopher; however, his ideas are useful in this context because of their strategic translation of Sorel's main theses concerning social myth.[30] Laclau takes the distinction between contradiction and antagonism to be an essential step for grasping the heterogeneous and contingent nature of hegemony. As he explains, contradiction, on the one hand, describes the types of change that result from the material logic of production. It is what happens when "relations of production [. . .] have become a brake on any further development of productive forces."[31] Antagonism, on the other hand, describes the motivations for human resistance to existing material conditions, which originate in a variety of milieus of social interaction and cannot be fully explained within the objective structure of economic reality. As such, a "constitutive outside" is at play in any antagonistic relationship. Marxism's long-standing assumption that contradiction necessarily implies antagonism—that the logic of the former subsumes the latter—manages to convert history into a "rational and coherent process," but in doing so it limits social transformation to a predetermined horizon where all possible developments are already accounted for in advance. What the mechanical outlook of contradiction misses, Laclau, like Mariátegui, notes, is precisely capitalism's human component. As he puts it, "The wage worker does not count as a concrete person, of flesh and blood, but as a seller of labor power."[32] In other words, under the dictates of "economic determination in the last instance," the set of possible motives for action of any social agent do not extend beyond the position she or he occupies in the structure of economic relations. Contradiction thus reflects the "utopian" features of reformist socialism—analysis, mechanistic emplotment of change, and so on—abhorred by Sorel: like them, it presumes a formal reconciliation of opposites, while antagonism entails combat, resistance.

Using the distinction posed by Laclau, it is easy to see why Mariátegui refuses to explain the predicament of Peruvian modernity in the terms of contradiction alone, and why he appears to discount the brute facts of contradiction as decidedly inert or at least secondary factors in the nation's development. Not coincidentally, the one place he discovers the antagonism missing from Peruvian history, and with it the seeds of revolutionary praxis, is in the indigenous communities of the rural interior, which, in the face of the dehumanizing labor conditions of the latifundio, retain practices of cooperation handed down from the pre-Columbian *ayllu*:

> In Indian villages where families are grouped together that have lost the bonds of their ancestral heritage and community work, hardy and stubborn habits of cooperation and solidarity still survive that are the empirical expression of a communist spirit. The "community" is the instrument of this spirit. When expropriation and redistribution seem about to liquidate the "community," indigenous socialism always finds a way to reject, resist, or evade this incursion.[33]

The characterization of indigenous resistance marks the climax of Mariátegui's revolutionary project: the affirmation of an indigenous socialist spirit is simultaneously his most provocative and problematic proposal, a paradox that is evidenced by the perpetual and critical tension surrounding it, and which can be explained, I want to suggest, by the dual notion of time it employs. On the one hand, of course, the time of indigenous myth is thoroughly Bergsonian: its antagonism toward dominant society is expressed as a function of endurance and vital impulse, as habits of memory that persist, tenacious and robust, in the interest of survival. In Bergson's words, "The organism which lives is a thing that endures, its past, in its entirety, is prolonged into the present, and abides there, actual and acting."[34] Yet, on the other hand, and by means of an imperceptible shift in perspective, Mariátegui appears to pass from the pure time of myth to a mythical timelessness. His words also intimate that the "communities" resist in virtue of their stasis, that indigenous culture has stayed intact for centuries, something that elsewhere is not merely suggested but stated outright: "It can [. . .] be assumed that in four centuries the Indian has undergone very little spiritual change [. . .] [Under the weight of these four centuries, the Indian has stooped morally and physically.] But the dark depths of his soul have hardly altered" ("No es aventurada [. . .] la hipótesis de que el indio en cuatro siglos ha cambiado poco espiritualmente [. . .] Bajo el peso de estos cuatro siglos, el indio se ha encorvado moral y físicamente. Mas el fondo oscuro de su alma casi no ha mudado").[35] In such moments of Mariátegui's analysis, the radical historicity of antagonism becomes indistinguishable from the ahistoricism of a prelapsarian revival. How are we to understand this conflation of the two types of time associated with myth, the apparent collapse between pure time and pure space? Let us return again briefly to Laclau, who provides, I think, an instructive interpretation of the political and discursive existence of social myth.

For Laclau, as was summarized above, the proper comprehension of political struggle rests on the distinction between contradiction and antagonism which, it logically follows, is also a distinction of space and time. The dislocations occasioned by antagonism in established social structures are pure time because of their constitutive exteriority to social discourse; said discourse, in turn, is responsible for reducing "the variation [of social events] to an invariable nucleus which is an internal moment of the pre-given structure," and is therefore purely spatial.[36] To the reordering of elements emerging from antagonism's dislocation of the spatial field of discourse, Laclau gives the name myth. It is "a principle of reading of a given situation, whose terms are external to what is representable in the objective spatiality constituted by the given structure."[37] Just like Sorel, Laclau intends to pinpoint the role of indeterminacy in the production of social meaning—in short, its qualitative dimension. But the point he adds to Sorel's conclusions is that myth, in promising a better world, cannot be fully separate from the objective social realm it critiques, because "any representation of a dislocation involves its spatialization. The way to overcome the temporal, traumatic and unrepresentable nature of dislocation is to construct it as a moment in permanent structural relation with other moments, in which case the pure temporality of the 'event' is eliminated."[38] At issue here is the difference between the content of myth, the radicality of the event it apprehends, and its political function, which is carried out through representation. But, Laclau clarifies, the respatialization undertaken by myth is also the unavoidable measure by which politics lives on. In the mediation of time and space, the absent fullness of the alternative society myth serves as a constant reminder that the space of social objectivity is never fully constituted and remains contingent: "Politics only exists insofar as the spatial eludes us."[39]

Mythic Potential

Laclau's insights help to unravel the temporal paradox at the heart of Mariátegui's indigenous myth by requiring us to separate the event it denotes—according to Mariátegui's own interpretation, its existence as duration—from the rhetorical role it plays in his intellectual project, which is from the start resolutely political. As the *Seven Essays* makes clear, Mariátegui's purpose is to respatialize the mythic potential of indigenous communities' resistance by envisioning it, not just as an ideological touchstone for national unity, but also as a force of material, economic processes, quite concretely as the spiritual revitalization of production. The antagonistic gesture conveyed by the communities' habits of cooperation, it should be noted, is not singled out and praised solely for its enduring spirit, but conjointly because of its capacity to convert indigenous laborers into a modern workforce. Unlike the semifeudal latifundio, a recalcitrant system that is "constitutionally incapable of technical progress," indigenous enclaves, Mariátegui says, have been proven to "spontaneously transform" into socialist cooperatives when presented with the opportunity for commercial innovation.[40] He writes, "The 'community' on one hand shows effective capacity for development and transformation and on the other constitutes a system of production that keeps alive in the Indian the moral incentives necessary for his maximum output as a worker" ("La "comunidad" [. . .] de una parte acusa capacidad efectiva de desarrollo y transformación y de otra parte se presenta como un sistema de producción que mantiene vivos en el indio los estímulos morales necesarios para su máximo rendimiento como trabajador").[41] The "change" Mariátegui seeks in Peruvian history, then, does not exclusively refer to the vital adaptiveness of the communities, but also and indissociably their capacity for modern progress, not only antagonism but also contradiction. At the confluence of the content of indigenous myth and its material manifestation lies its political dimension. The stylized, arrested portrait of the indigenous is discursively static but politically mobile insofar as it sets in motion once again a reminder of the nonclosure of the social within the existing parameters of objective reality.

What an earnest attention to the vitalist component of Mariátegui's thought yields is perhaps, above all, an appreciation for the ongoing political survival of myth, the most compelling proof of which is his own social legacy. Mariátegui's actions, even more than his theories, make clear that he took struggle and faith to be constituent elements of any emancipatory program. It is not arbitrary that he is so often qualified by critics as an "agonistic" figure. Probably drawing on Miguel de Unamuno's "agony of Christianity," he confessed in an interview to being an "agonic soul" ("un alma agónica"), referring both to his religious faith and to the personal and political turmoil of his own life path.[42] In fact, the years of productive fervor during which Mariátegui conceives and elaborates indigenous myth coincide with a series of intense conflicts both political and personal, which would culminate in his death in 1930, including government censorship and harassment, confrontations with official Latin American communist organizations, the amputation of his right leg, and the precipitous decline of his health. The intellectual initiatives he carried out at the same time doubtless partook of the same struggle, which it would not be exaggerated to call, in more than one sense, a battle for life. As historian Alberto Flores Galindo remarks, there is no locating the key to Mariátegui's thought in a text or quotation, in his representations alone, because "it was not elaborated patiently at a desk, but in the interior of life itself, in struggle and conflict, day by day" ("no se elaboró pacientemente en un escritorio, sino al interior de la vida misma, en la lucha y el conflicto, día a día").[43] There is reason to argue, then, that myth and antagonism themselves represent the most enduring part of Mariátegui's oeuvre, that which, as Bergson had it, continues to abide in the present, "actual and acting."

Notes

1. José Carlos Mariátegui, *Historia de la crisis mundial* (Lima: Empresa Editora Amauta, 1959), 199. Unless otherwise indicated, all English translations are my own. Where published English translations are not available or have been altered, I include the original language text of quotes.

2. The leading critics of the Marxist tradition of literary criticism in Latin America unanimously downplay the role of myth in Mariátegui's thought. Angel Rama and Aníbal Quijano, in particular, situate Mariátegui as a precursor to later, more incisive formulations of *indigenismo* precisely because of the vitalist trappings of myth. See also, from this period, the studies of Robert Paris, especially his polemical exchange with Luis Villaverde Alcalá-Galiano on the Sorelian influence in his work (Luis Villaverde Alcalá-Galiano, "El sorelismo de Mariátegui," *Aportes* 22 (1971): 166–77; Robert Paris, "Mariátegui: un 'sorelismo' ambiguo." *Aportes* 22 (1971): 178–84. The postcolonialist and cultural studies reception of Mariátegui has similarly attempted to rationalize the theory of indigenous myth: notable here is Neil Larsen's reading, which proposes that it constitutes a momentary "leap of faith" similar to Spivak's "strategic essentialism," meant merely to establish the ideological foundation of Peruvian nationalism. For a more recent examination of Mariátegui's points of contact with postcolonialism, see Jaime Hanneken, "José Carlos Mariátegui and the Time of Myth," *Cultural Critique* 81 (2012): 1–30, 2012.

3. José Carlos Mariátegui, *Historia*, 199.

4. Aníbal Quijano. Reencuentro y debate: Une introducción a Mariátegui (Lima: Mosca Azul, 1981), 78.

5. According to Jesús Chavarría, Bergson was introduced to the Peruvian scholarly community by Mariano Ibérico Rodríguez, who in 1916 completed his doctoral thesis on the French thinker. The careers of other prominent figures of early twentieth-century Peru, such as José de la Riva Agüero and Víctor Andrés Belaúnde, were similarly molded by Bergsonism. See Jesús Chavarría, *José Carlos Mariátegui and the Rise of Modern Peru 1890–1930* (Albuquerque: University of New Mexico Press, 1979), chapter 2; Paris, "Mariátegui," 22–23.

6. Analogous phenomena during the same period forced revolutionary or reformist democratization in Mexico, Uruguay, Argentina, and Chile. In Peru, social unrest took the form of an ambitious worker-student alliance that oversaw the creation of the APRA (Alianza Popular Revolucionaria Americana) movement headed by Víctor Raúl Haya de la Torre and of the Universidad Popular González Prada, an institution dedicated to worker education, where Mariátegui himself lectured in 1923–24. For a general overview of the Peruvian context during these years, see Chavarría, chapter 1; for the continental context, see Tulio Halperín Donghi, *The Contemporary History of Latin America*, ed. and trans. John Charles Chasteen (Durham, NC: Duke University Press, 1993).

7. The various shapes assumed by the Latin American rejection of positivism include movements as early as *arielismo* and the Mexican *Ateneo de la juventud* and encompass the later emerging discourses of *mestizaje* and transculturation. The most radical of the antipositivist proposals, such as José Vasconcelos's prediction of the emergence of a melded "cosmic race," or Ricardo Rojas's theories about the revival of an indigenous aesthetic system in Argentina, merely invert the scientific thesis about non-European timelessness by positing a resuscitation of preconquest cultures. For a general overview of the "revolt against scientism," see Martin Stabb, *In Search of Identity: Patterns in the Spanish American Essay of Ideas, 1860–1960* (Chapel Hill: University of North Carolina Press, 1967), chapter 3.

8. David Ohana, "Georges Sorel and the Rise of Political Myth" in *History of European Ideas* 13, no. 6 (1991): 736.

9. Bergson himself, as Ohana also notes (737), found Sorel's Marxist interpretation of his philosophy highly questionable. As he wrote to Sorel's disciple Edouard Berth in 1935, "[This] is without a doubt because his doctrine, very close to Hegelianism, as you have shown, is above all a construct, and I am irremediably wary of all philosophical constructs" ("c'est sans doute parce que sa doctrine très proche de l'hegelianisme, comme vous l'avez montré, est avant tout une construction, et que toute construction philosophique me rend irrémédiablement méfiant"), Sand, Shlomo, and Henri Bergson, "Quelques remarques sur Sorel critique de L'évolution creatrice. Quatre lettres inédites de Bergson à Sorel," *Cahiers Georges Sorel* 1 (1983): 110.

10. Georges Sorel, *Reflections on Violence*, ed. Jeremy Jennings (New York: Cambridge University Press, 1999), 118.

11. Ibid., 115.

12. Ibid., 113.

13. Ibid., 28.

14. Ibid., 40.

15. Ernesto Laclau and Chantal Mouffe *Hegemony and Socialist Strategy: Towards a Radical Democratic Politics*, 2nd ed. (New York: Verso, 2001), 40.

16. José Carlos Mariátegui, *"The Heroic and Creative Meaning of Socialism": Selected Essays* (Atlantic Highlands, NJ: Humanities Press International, 1996), 81.

17. Ibid., 139; 141–42.

18. Ibid., 142.

19. José Carlos Mariátegui, *El alma matinal y otras estaciones del hombre de hoy* (Lima, Peru: Empresa Editora Amauta, 1959), 27.

20. José Carlos Mariátegui, *Peruanicemos de Perú* (Lima, Peru: Empresa Editora Amauta, 1975), 33.

21. *Costumbrismo*, mainly associated with Ricardo Palma and his *Tradiciones peruanas*, was produced in short vignettes of colonial life published in periodicals from the 1870s on; *perricholismo*—named for the eighteenth-century actress Micaela

Villegas and her scandalous affair with the viceroy—refers to a more aggressively nostalgic style of sentimentalist literature focused on social intrigues and elite circles of colonial society. Mariátegui denounces *perricholismo*, but ironically defends Palma's *costumbrismo* in "El proceso de la literatura," the last of the *Seven Essays*.

22. Mariátegui, *Peruanicemos al Perú*, 164.

23. Ibid., 33.

24. Mariátegui introduces and defines this perspective in "El idealismo materialista," included in *Defensa del marxismo* (vol. 5 of his complete works).

25. Mariátegui, *Seven Peruvian Essays*, 32.

26. Mariátegui, Peruanicemos al Perú, 92.

27. Ibid., 91.

28. Mariátegui, *Seven Interpretive Essays*, 136.

29. Ibid., 80. Translation altered in José Carlos Mariátegui, *Siete ensayos de interpretacion de la realidad peruana* (Mexico City: Ediciones Era, 2001), 97.

30. In an interview, Laclau confirms the Sorelian signature of his early theories about hegemony, stating "if radical democracy is anti-utopian in that it does not advocate any blueprint for society, it can also only live and assert itself through the constant production of social myths [. . .] the structure of mythical identity as described by Sorel remains essentially valid," Ernesto Laclau, Judith Butler, and Slavoj Zizek, *Contingency, Hegemony, Universality: Contemporary Dialogues on the Left* (New York: Verso, 2000), 232.

31. Ernesto Laclau, *New Reflections on the Revolution of Our Time* (New York: Verso, 1990), 7.

32. Ibid., 9.

33. Mariátegui, *Seven Interpretive Essays*, 58.

34. Henri Bergson, *Creative Evolution*, trans. Arthur Mitchell (Mineola, NY: Dover, 1998), 15.

35. Mariátegui, *Seven Interpretive Essays*, 275; Mariátegui, *Siete ensayos* (2001), 307.

36. Laclau, *New Reflections*, 41.

37. Ibid., 61.

38. Ibid., 72.

39. Ibid., 68.

40. Mariátegui, *Seven Interpretive Essays*, 58.

41. Mariátegui, *Siete ensayos* (2001), 78 (my translation). Urquidi's translation of this passage is incomplete and fails to convey the quantitative dimension of production ("máximo rendimiento como trabajador") expressed in the original Spanish.

42. Quoted in Eugenio Chang-Rodríguez, *Pensamiento y acción en González Prada, Mariátegui y Haya de la Torre* (Lima, Peru: Fondo Editorial de la Pontificia Universidad Católica del Perú, 2012), 209.

43. Alberto Flores Galindo, *La agonía de Mariátegui. La polémica con la Komintern* (Lima, Peru: Desco, 1980), 11.

Bibliography

Adorno, Theodor. "Free Time." In *The Culture Industry: Selected Essays on Mass Culture*, edited by J. M. Bernstein. London: Routledge, 2001.
———. *History and Freedom*. Translated by Rodney Livingstone. Cambridge, UK: Polity Press, 2006.
———. *Negative Dialectics*. Translated by E. B. Ashton. New York: Continuum Publishing Company, 1973.
Adotevi, Stanislas. *Négritude et Négrologues*. Paris: Éditions Le Castor Astral, 1972.
———. "Négritude Is Dead: The Burial," *Journal of the New African Literature and the Arts* 7/8 (1969–70): 70–81.
Alcalá-Galiano, Luis Villaverde. "El sorelismo de Mariátegui." *Aportes* 22 (1971): 166–77.
Alcoff, Linda Martin. *Visible Identities: Race, Gender, and the Self*. Oxford, UK: Oxford University Press, 2005.
Alipaz, Daniel. "Bergson and Derrida: A Question of Writing Time as Philosophy's Other." *Journal of French and Francophone Philosophy* XIX, no. 2 (2011): 96–120.
Al-Saji, Alia. "Hesitation as Philosophical Method: Travel Bans, Colonial Durations, and the Affective Weight of the Past," *Journal of Speculative Philosophy* 32, no. 3 (2018): forthcoming.
An, Yanming. "Liang Shuming and Henri Bergson on Intuition: Cultural Context and the Evolution of Terms." *Philosophy of East and West* 47, no. 3 (1997): 337–62.
Anderson, Benedict. *Imagined Communities: Reflections on the Origin and Spread of Nationalism*. London: Verso, 2006.
Ansell-Pearson, Keith. "Bergson's Encounter with Biology." *Angelaki: Journal of the Theoretical Humanities* 10, no. 2 (2005): 59–72.
———. *Germinal Life: The Difference and Repetition of Deleuze*. New York: Routledge, 1999.
Antliff, Mark. *Inventing Bergson: Cultural Politics and the Parisian Avant-Garde*. Princeton, NJ: Princeton University Press, 1993.

Arendt, Hannah. *The Human Condition*. Chicago: University of Chicago Press, 1958.
———. *On Revolution*. London: Penguin Books, 1990.
Avineri, Shlomo. "The Problem of War in Hegel's Thought." In *The Hegel Myths and Legends*, edited by Jon Stewart, 131–41. Evanston, IL: Northwestern University Press, 1996.
Balibar, Étienne and Immanuel Wallerstein. "The Nation Form: History and Ideology." In *Race, Nation Class: Ambiguous Identities*, edited by Étienne Balibar and Immanuel Wallerstein, translated by Chris Turner, 86–107. London: Verso, 1991.
———. *Race, Nation Class: Ambiguous Identities*. London: Verso, 1991.
Barad, Karen. *Meeting the Universe Halfway: Quantum Physics and the Entanglement of Matter and Meaning*. Durham, NC: Duke University Press, 2007.
———. "Posthumanist Performativity: Toward an Understanding of How Matter Comes to Matter." *Signs* 40, no. 1 (2014): 801.
Bartov, Omer, and Phyllis Mack. *In God's Name: Genocide and Religion in the Twentieth Century*. Translated by Arthur Mitchell. New York: Dover Publications, 1907.
Bergson, Henri. "Bergson à P. Masson-Oursel, 8 septembre 1932." *Correspondances*. Paris: Presses Universitaires de France, 2002.
———. *Creative Evolution*. Translated by Arthur Mitchell and W. S. Palmer. Mineola, NY: Dover Publications, 1998.
———. *The Creative Mind: An Introduction to Metaphysics*. Translated by Mabelle L. Andison. Mineola, NY: Dover, 2007.
———. *Les deux sources de la morale et de la religion*. Paris: Presses Universitaires de France, 1932.
———. *Discurso de M. Henri Bergson*. Madrid, Spain: Residencia de Estudiantes, 1917.
———. *L'évolution créatrice*. Paris: Presses Universitaires de France, 1907.
———. *L'évolution créatrice*. Paris: Félix Alcan, 1913.
———. *Henri Bergson: Key Writings*, edited by Keith Ansell-Pearson and John Mullarkey. New York: Continuum, 2002.
———. *Laughter: An Essay on the Meaning of the Comic*. Translated by Cloudesley Brereton and Fred Rothwell. New York: Macmillan, 1911.
———. *Materia y memoria: Ensayo sobre la relación del cuerpo con el espíritu*. Translated by Martin Navarro. Madrid, Spain: V. Suarez, 1900.
———. *Matière et mémoire: Essai sur la relation du corps à l'esprit*. Paris: Presses Universitaires de France, 1896.
———. *Matter and Memory*. Translated by N. M. Paul and W. S. Palmer. New York: Zone Books, 1991.
———. *The Meaning of the War: Life and Matter in Conflict*. Translated by H. Wilson Carr. London: T. Fisher Unwin, 1915.
———. *Mélanges*. Paris: Presses Universitaires de France, 1972.
———. *Mind-Energy: Lectures and Essays*. Translated by H. Wilson Carr. Westport, CT: Greenwood, 1920.

———. *Œuvres*. Translated by F. L. Pogson. Paris: Presses Universitaires de France, 1959.
———. *La pensée et le mouvant*. Paris: Presses Universitaires de France, 1938.
———. *Le Rire: Essai sur la signification du comique*. Paris France: Alcan, 1900.
———. *Time and Free Will*. Translated by F. L. Pogson. Mineola, NY: Dover Publications, 2001.
———. *The Two Sources of Morality and Religion*. Translated by R. Ashley Audra, Cloudesley Brereton, and W. Horsfall Carter. Notre Dame, IN: University of Notre Dame Press, 1977.
Bernasconi, Robert. "Lévy-Bruhl among the Phenomenologists: Exoticisation and the Logic of 'the Primitive.'" *Social Identities* 11, no. 3 (2005): 229–45.
Billig, Michael. *Laughter and Ridicule: Towards a Social Critique of Humor*. London: Sage, 2012.
Blanchard, Pascal, Lemaire Sandrine, Nicolas Bancel, and Dominic Thomas. *Colonial Culture in France since the Revolution*. Translated by Alexis Pernsteiner. Bloomington: Indiana University Press, 2013.
Bohr, Niels. "Natural Philosophy and Human Cultures." *Nature* 143 (1939): 268–72.
Boittin, Jennifer Anne. *Colonial Metropolis the Urban Grounds of Anti-Imperialism and Feminism in Interwar Paris*. Lincoln: University of Nebraska Press, 2010.
Bosteels, Bruno. "The Truth Is in the Making: Borges and Pragmatism." *Romanic Review* 98, no. 2/3 (2007): 135–51.
Brandom, Robert. *Making It Explicit: Reasoning, Representing, and Discursive Commitment*. Cambridge, MA: Harvard University Press, 1994.
Braudel, Fernand. *Civilization and Capitalism, Volume 3: 15th–18th Century: The Perspective of the World*. Los Angeles: University of California Press, 1982.
Brennan, Teresa, and Carole Pateman. "'Mere Auxiliaries to the Commonwealth:' Women and the Origins of Liberalism." *Political Studies* 27, no. 2 (1979): 183–200.
Brodwin, Paul. *Biotechnology and Culture: Bodies, Anxieties, Ethics*. Bloomington: Indiana University Press, 2000.
Brown, Wendy. *Walled States, Waning Sovereignty*. Cambridge, MA: MIT Press, 2010.
Bunge, Carlos O. *El Derecho. Ensayo de una teoría jurídica integral Vol. I*. Buenos Aires, Argentina: Valerio Abeledo, 1915.
———. *Principes de psychologie individuelle et sociale*. Paris: Felix Alcan, 1903.
Burghardt, Gordon M. *The Genesis of Animal Play: Testing the Limits*. Cambridge, MA: MIT Press, 2005.
Calderón, Francisco Garcia. "Les courants philosophiques dans l'Amérique latine." *Revue de Métaphysique et de Morale* (1908): 674–81.
Calvo, Carlos. *Anales históricos de la revolución de la América Latina, 1: acompañados de los documentos en su apoyo desde al año 1808 hasta el reconocimiento de la independencia de ese extenso continente*, vol. 1. Paris: A. Durand, 1864.
Campos Gomez, Rubi de Maria. *El sentido de sí: Un ensayo sobre el feminismo y la filosofía de la cultura en México*. Mexico City: Siglo Veintiuno, 2004.

Canales, Jimena. *The Physicist and the Philosopher: Einstein, Bergson, and the Debate That Changed Our Understanding of Time*. Princeton, NJ: Princeton University Press, 2015.

Candelaria, Michael. *The Revolt of Unreason: Miguel de Unamuno and Antonio Caso on the Crisis of Modernity*. New York: Rodopi, 2005.

Canovan, Margaret. "Arendt, Rousseau, and Human Plurality in Politics." *Journal of Politics* 45, no. 2 (1983): 285–302.

Čapek, Milič. *Bergson and Modern Physics: A Reinterpretation and Reevaluation*. Dordrecht, the Netherlands: D. Reidell Publishing Company, 1971.

Card, Claudia. *The Atrocity Paradigm: A Theory of Evil*. Oxford, UK: Oxford University Press, 2005.

Carrasco Albano, Manuel. "Memoria presentada . . . sobre la necesidad i objetos de un congreso Sud-Americano." In *Comentarios sobre la Constitución Política de 1833*. Santiago, Chile: Librería del Mercurio, 1874.

Caso, Antonio. *El concepto de la historia universal en la filosofía de los valores*. Mexico City: México Moderno, 1923.

———. *La filosofía de Husserl*. Mexico City: Imprenta Mundial, 1934.

———. *Filósofos y doctrinas morales*. Mexico City: Librería Porrúa, 1915.

———. *Obras completas, Tomo 3: La existencia como economía, como desinterés y como caridad*, edited by Rosa Krauze de Kolteniuk. Mexico City: Universidad Nacional Autonoma de Mexico, 1972a.

———. *Obras completas, Tomo 5: Estética*, edited by Rosa Krauze de Kolteniuk. Mexico City: Universidad Nacional Autonoma de Mexico, 1971a.

———. *Obras completas, Tomo 6: Historia y antología del pensamiento filosófico. Evocación de Aristóteles. Filosofía*, edited by Rosa Krauze de Kolteniuk. Mexico City: Universidad Nacional Autonoma de Mexico, 1972b.

Cavell, Stanley. *The Claim of Reason: Wittgenstein, Skepticism, Morality, and Tragedy*. Oxford, UK: Oxford University Press, 1979.

Césaire, Aimé. *Discourse on Colonialism*. Translated by Joan Pinkham. New York: Monthly Review Press, 2000.

———. *Cahier d'un Retour Au Pays Natal*. England: Bloodaxe Books, 1995.

Césaire, Aimé, and Euzhan Palcy. *Aimé Césaire une voix pour l'histoire: Aimé Césaire, a voice for history*. Paris: JMJ Productions, 2006.

Chang-Rodríguez, Eugenio. *Pensamiento y acción en González Prada, Mariátegui y Haya de la Torre*. Lima, Peru: Fondo Editorial de la Pontificia Universidad Católica del Perú, 2012.

Chavarría, Jesús. *José Carlos Mariátegui and the Rise of Modern Peru 1890–1930*. Albuquerque: University of New Mexico Press, 1979.

Chevalier, J. M. C. "Pragmatisme et idées-forces. Alfred Fouillée fut-il une source du pragmatisme américain?" *Dialogue* 50 (2001): 633–68.

Congdon, Matthew. "Epistemic Injustice in the Space of Reasons." *Episteme* 12, no. 1 (2015): 75–93.

Colebrook, Claire. "The Art of the Future." In *Bergson, Politics, and Religion*, edited by Alexandre LeFebvre and Melanie White. Durham, NC: Duke University Press, 2012.

Comte, Auguste. *The Positive Philosophy of Auguste Comte*, vol. 1. Translated by H. Martineau. London: John Chapman, 1853.

———. *System of Positive Polity*, vol. 1. London: Longmans, Green and Co., 1875.

Coole, Diana, and Samantha Frost. "Introducing the New Materialisms." In *Materialism: Ontology, Agency, and Politics*, edited by Diana Coole and Samantha Frost, 1–47. Durham, NC: Duke University Press, 2010.

Coviello, Alfredo. "Bergson en América." In *¿Inactualidad del Bergsonismo?*, edited by Horacio González. Buenos Aires, Argentina: Ediciones Colihue, 2008.

———. *El proceso filosófico de Bergson y su bibliografía*, 2nd ed. Tucumán, Argentina: Revista Sustancia, 1941.

Curle, Clinton. *Humanité: John Humphrey's Alternative Account of Human Rights*. Toronto, ON: University of Toronto Press, 2007.

Darwin, Charles. *The Descent of Man, and Selection in Relation to Sex*. London: John Murray, 1871.

Deleuze, Gilles. *Bergsonism*. Translated by B. Habberjam and H. Tomlinson. New York: Zone Books, 1988.

de Vries, Hent. *Religion: Beyond a Concept*. Bronx, NY: Fordham University Press, 2009.

Diagne, Souleymane Bachir. "Achieving Humanity: Convergence between Henri Bergson and Muhammad Iqbal." In *Muhammad Iqbal: Essays on the Reconstruction of Modern Muslim Thought*, edited by H. C. Hillier and Basit Bilal Koshul, 33–55. Edinburgh: Edinburgh University Press, 2015.

———. *African Art as Philosophy: Senghor, Bergson and the Idea of Negritude*. Translated by Chike Jeffers. New York: Seagull Books, 2011.

———. *Bergson postcolonial*. Paris: CNRS Éditions, 2011.

———. "Bergson in the Colony: Intuition and Duration in the Thought of Senghor and Iqbal." *Qui Parle* 17, no. 1 (2008): 125–45.

———. "Bergson dans les colonies: Intuition et durée dans la pensée de Senghor et Iqbal." Translated by Yala Kisukidi. *Annales bergsoniennes V: Bergson et la politique, de Jaurès à aujourd'hui*, edited by Frédéric Worms. Paris: Presses Universitaires de France, 2012. 61–84.

———. "Rhythms: L. S. Senghor's Négritude as a Philosophy of African Art." *Critical Interventions: Journal of African Art History and Visual Culture* 1, no. 1 (2007): 51–68.

Dictionnaire de l'Académie française, 8th ed. (1932–35). Accessed January 15, 2017, https://artfl-project.uchicago.edu/content/dictionnaires-dautrefois.

Dobson, Andrew. *An Introduction to Politics and Philosophy of José Ortega Y Gasset*. New York: Cambridge University Press, 2009.

Dobuzinskis, Laurent. "Non-Welfarism Avant La Lettre: Alfred Fouillee's Political Economy of Justice." *The European Journal of the History of Economic Thought* 17, no. 4 (2010): 837–64.
Durkheim, Émile. *The Rules of Sociological Method*. New York: The Free Press, 1982.
Edwards, Brent Hayes. *The Practice of Diaspora: Literature, Translation, and the Rise of Black Internationalism*. Cambridge, MA: Harvard University Press, 2003.
Fabian, Johannes. *Time and the Other: How Anthropology Makes Its Object*. New York: Columbia University Press, 1983.
Fanon, Frantz. *Oeuvres*. Paris: Découverte, 2011.
———. *The Wretched of the Earth*. Translated by Constance Farrington. New York: Grove Press, 1968.
Fidler, Geoffrey. "On Jean-Marie Guyau, Immoraliste." *Journal of the History of Ideas* 55, no. 1 (1994): 75–97.
Flores Galindo, Alberto. *La agonía de Mariátegui. La polémica con la Komintern*. Lima: Desco, 1980.
Forman-Barzilai, Fonna, *Adam Smith and the Circles of Sympathy: Cosmopolitanism and Moral Theory*. Cambridge, UK: Cambridge University Press, 2010.
Fouillée, Alfred. *Education from a National Standpoint*. Translated by W. J. Greenstreet. London: Edward Arnold, 1892.
———. *L'enseignement: au point de vue national*. Paris: Hatchette, 1891.
———. *La psychologie des idées forces*, vol. 1. Paris: Alcan, 1893.
Fraser, Nancy, and Axel Honneth, *Redistribution or Recognition? A Political-Philosophical Exchange*. New York: Verso, 2003.
Gaos, José, and Alain Guy. "L'actualité Philosophique au Mexique." *Les Études Philosophiques* 13, no. 3 (1958): 289–301.
García Bárcena, Rafael. "¿A dónde va el universo físico?" *Revista Cubana de Filosofía* 1, no. 3 (1948): 27–40.
García Calderón, Francisco. *Dos Filósofos Franceses, Bergson and Boutroux*. Lima, Peru: El Comercio, 1907.
———. *El Bergsonismo*, edited by Horacio Gonzalez. Buenos Aires, Argentina: Ediciones Colihue, 2008.
García Morente, Manuel. *La Filosofía de Henri Bergson*. Madrid, Spain: Residencia de Estudiantes, 1917.
Gellner, Ernest. *Nations and Nationalism*. Ithaca, NY: Cornell University Press, 2008.
Goddard, Jean-Christophe. *Mysticisme et folie: Essai sur la simplicité*. Paris: Desclée de Brouwer, 2002.
Gray, John. *False Dawn: The Delusions of Global Capitalism*. New York: The New Press, 1998.
Greene, Joshua. *Moral Tribes: Emotion, Reason, and the Gap between Us and Them*. London: Penguin, 2013.
Groos, Karl. *The Play of Animals*. Translated by Elizabeth L. Baldwin. New York: Appleton, 1898.

Grosz, Elizabeth. *Becoming Undone: Darwinian Reflections on Life, Politics, and Art.* Durham, NC: Duke University Press, 2011.
———. "Bergson, Deleuze and the Becoming of Unbecoming." *Parallax* 11, no. 2 (2005): 4–13.
———. *The Nick of Time: Politics, Evolution, and the Untimely.* Durham, NC: Duke University Press, 2004.
———. "Significant Differences: An Interview with Elizabeth Grosz." *Interstitial Journal: A Journal of Modern Culture and Events* (March 2013), 1–5. Accessed July 20, 2017. https://interstitialjournal.files.wordpress.com/2013/03/grosz-interview1.pdf.
Guerlac, Suzanna. *Thinking in Time: An Introduction to Henri Bergson.* Ithaca, NY: Cornell University Press, 2006.
Guilhaumou, Jacques. "Sieyès et le non-dit de la sociologie: du mot à la chose." *Revue d'histoire des sciences humaines, Naissance de la science sociale (1750–1850)* 15 (2006): 117–34.
Guillaume, Paul, and Thomas Munro. *Primitive African Sculpture.* New York: Harcourt, Brace and Company, 1926.
Gutting, Gary. *French Philosophy in the Twentieth Century.* Cambridge, UK: Cambridge University Press, 2001.
Guyau, Jean-Marie. *Education and Heredity: A Study in Sociology.* Translated by W. J. Greenstreet. London: Walter Scott Publishing, 1903.
———. *A Sketch of Morality Independent of Obligation or Sanction.* London: Watts, 1898.
Haddox, John. *Antonio Caso: Philosopher of Mexico.* Austin: University of Texas Press, 1971.
———. "Latin American Personalist: Antonio Caso." *The Personalist Forum* 8, no. 1 (1992): 109–18.
Hallström, Per. "Presentation Speech." Speech presented at the Nobel Committee of the Swedish Academy, 1928.
Halperín Donghi, Tulio. *The Contemporary History of Latin America.* Translated by John Charles Chasteen. Durham, NC: Duke, 1993.
Hampton, Jean. *Contract and Consent.* Malden, MA: Blackwell, 1993.
Hanneken, Jaime. "José Carlos Mariátegui and the Time of Myth." *Cultural Critique* 81 (2012): 1–30.
Hardimon, Michael O. *Hegel's Social Philosophy: The Project of Reconciliation.* Cambridge, UK: Cambridge University Press, 1994.
Harvey, Elizabeth. *Senghor's Shadow: Art, Politics, and the Avant-Garde in Senegal, 1960–1995.* Durham, NC: Duke University Press, 2004.
Harney, Stefano, and Fred Moten. *The Undercommons: Fugitive Planning and Black Study.* London: Minor Compositions, 2013.
Hegel, G. W. F. *Elements of the Philosophy of Right.* Cambridge, UK: Cambridge University Press, 1991.

Henríquez Ureña, Pedro. "Estudio de Llauría Sobre la Naturaleza y el Problema Social." *Ensayos Críticos* (1905).
———. *Homenaje a Bergson*. Mexico D.F.: Imprenta Universitaria, 1941.
———. *La Obra de José Enrique Rodó*. Mexico D.F.: Universidad Nacional Autónoma de Mexico, 2000.
———. "La Revolución y la Cultura en México." *Revista de Filosofía* xi, no. 1 (1925): 125–32.
Hiddleston, Jane. *Decolonizing the Intellectual: Politics, Culture, and Humanism at the End of the French Empire*. Liverpool, UK: Liverpool University Press, 2014.
Honneth, Axel. *Reification: New Look at an Old Idea*. Oxford, UK: Oxford University Press, 2008.
———. *The Struggle for Recognition: The Moral Grammar of Social Conflicts*. Cambridge, MA: MIT Press, 1995.
Hostos, Eugenio. *Evolución super-orgánica: la naturaleza y el problema social*. Madrid, Spain: Fernando Fé, 1905.
———. *Tratado de Sociología*. Madrid. Spain: Imprenta de Bailly-Bailliere, 1904.
Hume, David. *An Enquiry Concerning the Principles of Morals*. Chicago: Open Court Publishing Co., 1912.
Hunt, Lynn. *Inventing Human Rights: A History*. New York: W. W. Norton, 2007.
Hymans, Louis. *Léopold Sédar Senghor: An Intellectual Biography: An Intellectual Biography*. Edinburgh: Edinburgh University Press, 1971.
Ibérico, Mariano. *La Filosofía de Enrique Bergson*. Lima, Peru: Sanmartí, 1916.
Ingenieros, José. "La psicología biológica." *Anales de la Sociedad de Psicología* 1 (1910): 9–34.
Iqbal, Muhammad. *The Reconstruction of Religious Thought in Islam*. Stanford, CA: Stanford University Press, 2012.
Irele, Abiola. *The African Experience in Literature and Ideology*. London: Heinemann, 1981.
———. *The Négritude Moment: Explorations in Francophone African and Caribbean Literature and Thought*. Trenton, NJ: African World Press, 2011.
Isaacs, Harold Robert. *Idols of the Tribe: Group Identity and Political Change*. Cambridge, MA: Harvard University Press, 1975.
James, William, Henri Bergson, and Emile Le Brun. *Le pragmatisme*. Paris: Flammarion, 1911.
Jankélévitch, Vladimir. *Henri Bergson*. Translated by Nils F. Schott. Durham, NC: Duke University Press, 2015.
———. *Henri Bergson*. Paris: Presses Universitaires de France, 1959.
Jay, Martin. *Downcast Eyes: The Denigration of Vision in Twentieth Century French Thought*. Berkeley: University of California Press, 1993.
Jefferson, Thomas. *An Essay towards Facilitating Instruction in the Anglo-Saxon and Modern Dialects of the English Language*. New York: John F. Trow, 1851.

Jones, Donna V. *The Racial Discourses of Life Philosophy: Négritude, Vitalism, and Modernity.* New York: Columbia University Press, 2010.

Jules-Rosette, Bennetta. *Black Paris: The African Writers' Landscape.* Urbana: University of Illinois Press, 1998.

Kebede, Messay. "Negritude and Bergsonism." *Journal of African Philosophy* Issue 3 (2003): 1–18.

Keck, Frédéric. "Le primitif et le mystique chez Lévy-Bruhl, Bergson et Bataille." *Methodos: Savoir et textes* 3 (2003): 137–57.

Kedourie, Elie. *Nationalism.* Malden: Blackwell, 1993.

Kelley, Robin D. G. "Black Study, Black Struggle," *Boston Review: A Political and Literary Forum* (March 2016). Accessed June 17, 2017. http://bostonreview.net/forum/robin-d-g-kelley-black-study-black-struggle.

Kisukidi, Nadia Yala. *Bergson ou l'humanité créatrice.* Paris: CNRS Éditions, 2013.

Kisukidi, Yala. "Présentation: Penser un Bergson postcolonial?" In *Annales bergsoniennes V: Bergson et la politique, de Jaurès à aujourd'hui,* edited by Frédéric Worms. Paris: Presses Universitaires de France, 2012, 49–59.

Krauze de Kolteniuk, Rosa. *La filosofía de Antonio Caso.* Mexico City: Universidad Autónoma de México, 1961.

Laclau, Ernesto, and Chantal Mouffe. *Hegemony and Socialist Strategy. Towards a Radical Democratic Politics,* 2nd ed. New York: Verso, 2001.

Laclau, Ernesto. *New Reflections on the Revolution of Our Time.* New York: Verso, 1990.

Laclau, Ernesto, Judith Butler, and Slavoj Zizek, *Contingency, Hegemony, Universality: Contemporary Dialogues on the Left.* New York: Verso, 2000.

Landecker, Hannah. *Culturing Life: How Cells Became Technologies.* Boston: Harvard University Press, 2009.

Lapoujade, David. "Intuition and Sympathy in Bergson." *Pli* 15 (2004): 1–17.

La Revue Du Monde Noir: The Review of the Black World, 1931–1932: Collection Complete, 1 A 6. Paris: Jean-Michael Place, 1992.

Larsen, Neil. "Indigenismo y lo 'postcolonial': Mariátegui frente a la actual coyuntura teórica." *Revista Iberoamericana* 62, no. 176–77 (1996): 863–73.

Lawlor, Leonard. *The Challenge of Bergsonism: Phenomenology, Ontology, Ethics.* New York, NY: Continuum, 2003.

Lecky, W. E. H. *History of European Morals: From Augustus to Charlemagne.* London: Longmans, Green and Co., 1913.

Leech, Gary M. *Capitalism: A Structural Genocide.* London: Zed Books, 2012.

Lefebvre, Alexandre. "Human Rights and the Leap of Love." *Journal of French and Francophone Philosophy* 24, no. 2 (2016): 21–40.

———. *Human Rights as a Way of Life: On Bergson's Political Philosophy.* Stanford, CA: Stanford University Press, 2013.

Lefebvre, Alexander and Melanie White. *Bergson, Politics, and Religion.* Durham, NC: Duke University Press, 2012.

Levene, Mark. "Genocide in the Age of the Nation State." *The Meaning of Genocide* 4, no. 1. London: I. B.Tauris & Co., 2005.
Llauría, Enrique. *Evolución super-orgánica: la naturaleza y el problema social.* Madrid: Fernando Fé, 1905.
López, Ismael. "A propósito de un artículo de Lugones." *Trofeos* 1, no. 13 (1906): 145–51.
Loyarte, Ramón G. *Evolución de las ciencias en la República Argentina. La Evolución de la Física.* Buenos Aires, Argentina: Imprenta Coni, 1924.
Lugones, Leopoldo. "La République Argentine et l'influence française." *Mercure de France* LX 1, no. 13 (1906): 183–200.
Luxemburg, Rosa. *The Accumulation of Capital.* Translated by Agnes Schwarzschild. London: Routledge, 2003.
Mackie, John L. "Evil and Omnipotence." *Mind* 64 (1955): 200–12.
Malagarriga, Carlos. *La Evolución Creadora.* Madrid, Spain: Renacimiento, 1912.
Mann, Michael. "The Autonomous Power of the State: Its Origins, Mechanisms and Results." *European Journal of Sociology* 25, no. 2 (1984): 185–213.
Mariátegui, José Carlos. *El alma matinal y otras estaciones del hombre de hoy.* Lima, Peru: Empresa Editora Amauta, 1959.
———. *"The Heroic and Creative Meaning of Socialism": Selected Essays.* Translated by Michael Pearlman. Atlantic Highlands, NJ: Humanities Press International, 1996.
———. *Historia de la crisis mundial.* Lima, Peru: Empresa Editora Amauta, 1959.
———. *Peruanicemos de Perú.* Lima: Empresa Editora Amauta, 1975.
———. *Seven Interpretive Essays on Peruvian Reality.* Translated by Marjory Urquidi. Austin: University of Texas Press, 1971.
———. *Siete ensayos de interpretacion de la realidad peruana.* Mexico City: Ediciones Era, 2001.
Marrati, Paola. "Mysticism and the Open Society: Foundations of Bergsonian Politics." In *Political Theologies: Public Religions in a Post-Secular World,* edited by Hent de Vries and Lawrence Sullivan, 591–602. New York: Fordham University Press, 2006.
Marx, Karl. *The Economic and Philosophical Manuscripts of 1844 and the Communist Manifesto.* Translated by Martin Milligan. New York: Prometheus Books, 1988.
———. *Capital: A Critique of Political Economy,* vol I. Introduced by Ernest Mandel. Translated by Ben Fowkes. New York: Penguin Books, 1990.
McClintock, Anne. *Imperial Leather: Race, Gender, and Sexuality in the Colonial Conquest.* London: Routledge, 2013.
McDowell, John. *Mind and World.* Cambridge, MA: Harvard University Press, 1996.
Medina, Jose. *The Epistemology of Resistance: Gender and Racial Oppression, Epistemic Injustice, and the Social Imagination.* Oxford, UK: Oxford University Press, 2012.

Mendieta, Eduardo. "The Death of Positivism and the Birth of Mexican Phenomenology." In *Latin American Positivism: New Historical and Philosophical Essays*, edited by Gregory D. Gilson and Irving W. Levinson. Lanham, MD: Lexington Press, 2013.

Merleau-Ponty, Maurice. *Humanism and Terror: An Essay on the Communist Problem.* Translated by John O'Neill. Boston: Beacon Press, 1969.

———. *In Praise of Philosophy and Other Essays*. Translated by John Wild. Evanston, IL: Northwestern University Press, 1988.

Mesa Gancedo, Daniel. "El poema extenso como institución cultural forma poética e identidad americana en Bello, Heredia y Echeverría." *Nueva Revista de Filología Hispánica* 56, no. 1 (2008): 87–122.

Millet, Jean. "Bergsonian Epistemology and Its Origins in Mathematical Thought." In *Bergson and Modern Thought: Towards a Unified Science*, edited by Andrew Papanicolaou and Pete Gunter. New York: Harwood Academic Publishers, 1987.

Mills, Charles. "Race and the Social Contract Tradition." *Social Identities* 6, no. 4 (2000): 441–62.

———. *The Racial Contract*. Ithaca, NY: Cornell University Press, 1997.

———. "The 'Racial Contract' as Methodology." In *From Class to Race: Essays in White Marxism and Black Radicalism*, 219–49. Lanham, MD: Rowman & Littlefield Publishers, 2003.

———. "White Ignorance." In *Race and Epistemologies of Ignorance*, edited by Nancy Tuana and Sullivan, Shannon. Buffalo: State University of New York Press, 2007.

———. "White Right: The Idea of a Herrenvolk Ethics." In *Blackness Visible: Essays on Philosophy and Race*, 139–67. Ithaca, NY: Cornell University Press, 1998.

Mills, Charles, and Pateman, Carole. *Contract and Domination.* London: Polity Press, 2007.

Mignolo, Walter D. "The Geopolitics of Knowledge and the Colonial Difference." *South Atlantic Quarterly* 101, no. 1 (2002): 57–96.

Mitcham, Carl. *Thinking through Technology: The Path between Engineering and Philosophy.* 1st ed. Chicago: University of Chicago Press, 1994.

Montoro, Rafael. "Kant: El neo-kantianismo y los neokantianos españoles." *Revista de Cuba* 4 (1878): 77–89.

Moore, F. C. T. *Bergson: Thinking Backwards*. Cambridge, UK: Cambridge University Press, 1996.

Mudimbe, V. Y. *The Invention of Africa: Gnosis, Philosophy, and the Order of Knowledge*. Bloomington: Indiana University Press, 1988.

Muñoz, Marisa A. "Bergson y el Bergsonismo en la cultura filosófica Argentina." *Cuadernos Americanos: Nueva Epoca* 2, no. 140 (2012): 103–22.

Nayar, Pramond. *Frantz Fanon*. New York: Routledge, 2013.

Nodar, Manso. "Antonio Caso: El mito de su liberal mentalidad politico-social." *Canadian Journal of Latin American and Caribbean Studies* 9, no. 18 (1984): 31–55.

Novoa, Adriana, and Alex Levine. *From Man to Ape*. Chicago: Chicago University Press, 2010.

Nubiola, Jaime. "Jorge Luis Borges y William James." In *Aproximaciones a la obra de William James: la formulación del pragmatismo*, edited by J. de Salas y F. Martín. Madrid, Spain: Biblioteca Nueva, Universidad Complutense de Madrid, 2005.

Nussbaum, Martha C. *Creating Capabilities: The Human Development Approach*. Cambridge, MA: Belknap Press, 2011.

———. *Not for Profit: Why Democracy Needs the Humanities*. Princeton, NJ: Princeton University Press, 2010.

Ohana, David. "Georges Sorel and the Rise of Political Myth." *History of European Ideas* 13, no. 6 (1991): 733–46.

Olivares Vargas, Rigel. "El concepto de intuición en Antonio Caso." *Iztapalapa* 58 (2005): 171–93.

Omar, Saleh. "Philosophical Origins of the Arab Ba'th Party: The Work of Zaki Al-Arsuzi." *Arab Studies Quarterly* 18, no. 2 (1996): 23–37.

Oyěwùmí, Oyèrónké. "Visualizing the Body: Western Theories and African Subjects." In *African Gender Studies: A Reader*. New York: Palgrave Macmillian, 2005.

Paris, Robert. "Mariátegui: un 'sorelismo' ambiguo." *Aportes* 22 (1971): 178–84.

———. *El marxismo latinoamericano de Mariátegui*. Buenos Aires: Ediciones de Crisis, 1973: 9–44.

Parkin, John. "The Power of Laughter: Koestler on Bergson and Freud." *Laughter and Power*, edited by John Parkin and John Phillips. Oxford, UK: Lang, 2006.

Pateman, Carole. *Sexual Contract*. Palo Alto, CA: Stanford University Press, 1988.

Petitfils, Brad. *Parallels and Responses to Curricular Innovation: The Possibilities of Posthumanistic Education*. New York: Routledge, 2014.

Piketty, Thomas. *Capital in the 21st Century*. Cambridge, MA: Harvard University Press, 2014.

Pinker, Steven. *The Better Angels of Our Nature: Why Violence Has Declined*. New York: Viking Press, 2011.

Ponce, Anibal. "Henri Bergson y el premio Nobel de Literatura." In *¿Inactualidad del Bergsonismo?*, edited by Horacio González. Buenos Aires, Argentina: Ediciones Colihue, 2008.

Protevi, John, and Keith Ansell-Pearson. "Naturalism in the Continental Tradition." In *The Blackwell Companion to Naturalism*, edited by Kelly James Clark. Malden, MA: Blackwell, 2016.

Quijano, Aníbal. *Reencuentro y debate: una introducción a Mariátegui*. Lima, Peru: Mosca Azul, 1981.

Rae, Heather. *State Identities and the Homogenisation of Peoples*. Cambridge, UK: Cambridge University Press, 2002.

Rama, Angel. *Transculturación narrativa en América Latina*. Buenos Aires, Argentina: Ediciones el Andariego, 2007.
Reyes, Alfonso. *Pasado inmediato y otros ensayos*. Mexico: Fondo de Cultura Económica, 1941.
Rodó, José Enrique. *Los motivos de Proteo*. Buenos Aires, Argentina: Tecnibook Ediciones, 2011.
———. *Obras completas*. Madrid, Spain: Aguilar, 1903.
Roemer, Michael. *Shocked but Connected: Notes on Laughter*. Lanham, MD: Rowman & Littlefield, 2012.
Romanell, Patrick. *Making of the Mexican Mind: A Study in Recent Mexican Thought*. Lincoln: University of Nebraska Press, 1952.
Romero, Francisco. *La Filosofía en América*. Buenos Aires, Argentina: Raigal, 1952.
Rousseau, Jean-Jacques. "Discourse on the Origin of Inequality." In *Basic Political Writings*, edited by Donald A. Cress, 25–81. Indianapolis, IN: Hackett, 1987.
Russell, Bertrand. *History of Western Philosophy*. London: Routledge, 2004.
Sand, Shlomo, and Henri Bergson. "Quelques remarques sur Sorel critique de *L'évolution creatrice*. Quatre lettres inédites de Bergson à Sorel." *Cahiers Georges Sorel* 1 (1983): 109–23.
Sartre, Jean-Paul. *Basic Writings*, edited by Stephen Priest. New York: Routledge 2001.
———. "Black Orpheus." In *"What Is Literature?" and Other Essays*. Cambridge, MA: Harvard University Press, 1988.
———. *The Emotions: Outline of a Theory*. Translated by Bernard Frechtman. New York: The Wisdom Library, 1948.
Sembène, Ousmane. "Novelist-Critic of Africa." *West Africa* (September 1962).
Senghor, Léopold Sédar. "Constructive Elements of a Civilization of African Negro Inspiration." *Presence Africaine* 24–25 (February–May 1959): 262–94.
———. *Nationhood and the African Road to Socialism*. Translated by Mercer Cook. Paris: Presence Africaine, 1962.
———. "Negritude: A Humanism of the Twentieth Century." In *The African Reader*, edited by Wilford Cartey and Martin Kilson, 179–92. New York: Vintage Books, 1970.
———. *On African Socialism*. London: Pall Mall Press, 1964.
———. "What the Black Man Contributes." In *Race and Racism in Continental Philosophy*, edited by Robert Bernasconi, 287–301. Bloomington: Indiana University Press, 2003.
Senghor, Léopold Sédar, and Kaal, H. "On Negrohood: Psychology of the African Negro." *Diogenes* 10, no. 1 (1962): 1–15.
Sharpley-Whiting, T. Denean. "Femme Négritude: Jane Nardal, La Dépêche Africaine, and the Francophone New Negro." *Souls: A Critical Journal of Black Politics, Culture, and Society* 2, no. 4 (2000): 8–17.
———. *Negritude Women*. Minneapolis: University of Minnesota Press, 2002.
Shaw, Devin Zane. "The Vitalist Senghor." *Comparative and Continental Philosophy* 5, no. 1 (2013): 92–98.

Scholz, Sally. *Political Solidarity.* University Park: Pennsylvania State University Press, 2008.
Shuster, Martin. *Autonomy after Auschwitz: Adorno, German Idealism, and Modernity.* Chicago: University of Chicago Press, 2014.
———. "Humor as an Optics: Bergson and the Ethics of Humor." *Hypatia* 28, no. 3 (2013): 618–32.
———. "Loneliness and Language: Arendt, Cavell, and Modernity." *International Journal of Philosophical Studies* 20, no. 4 (2012): 473–97.
———. "Nothing to Know: The Epistemology of Moral Perfectionism in Adorno and Cavell." *Idealistic Studies* 44, no. 1 (2015): 1–29.
———. "On the Ethical Basis of Language: Some Themes in Davidson, Cavell, and Levinas." *Journal for Cultural and Religious Theory* 14, no. 2 (2015): 241–66.
Sinclair, Mark. "Bergson's Philosophy of Will and the War of 1914–1918." *Journal of the History of Ideas* 77, no. 3 (2016): 486–87.
Sitbon-Peillon, Brigitte. "Bergson et le primitif: entre métaphysique et sociologie." In *Annales bergsoniennes I: Bergson dans le siècle*, edited by Frédéric Worms, 171–94. Paris: Presses Universitaires de France, 2002.
Smith, Adam. *The Theory of Moral Sentiments*, 9th ed. London: T. Cadell and W. Davies Publishers, 1801.
Smith, Tony. "A Category Mistake in Piketty." *Critical Sociology* 41, no. 2 (2010): 401–10.
———. "Technological Dynamism and the Normative Justification of Global Capitalism." In *Political Economy and Global Capitalism: The 21st Century, Present and Future*, edited by Robert Albritton, Bob Jessop, and Richard Vestra, 25–43. London: Anthem Press, 2007.
Sorel, Georges. *Reflections on Violence*, edited by Jeremy Jennings. New York: Cambridge University Press, 1999.
Soulez, Philippe. *Bergson Politique.* Paris: Presses Universitaires de France, 1989.
Sourieau, Marie-Agnes. "La Revue du Monde Noir." *Concise Encyclopedia of Latin American Literature.* London: Fitzroy Dearborn Publishers, 2000.
Stabb, Martin. *In Search of Identity. Patterns in the Spanish American Essay of Ideas, 1860–1960.* Chapel Hill: University of North Carolina Press, 1967.
Stevens, Jacqueline. *Reproducing the State.* Princeton, NJ: Princeton University Press, 1999.
———. *States without Nations: Citizenship for Mortals.* New York: Columbia University Press, 2011.
Stewart, Jon. *The Hegel Myths and Legends.* Evanston, IL: Northwestern University Press, 1996.
Stoler, Ann. "Colonial Aphasia: Race and Disabled Histories in France," *Public Culture* 23 (2011): 121–56.
———. *Race and the Education of Desire: Foucault's History of Sexuality and the Colonial Order of Things.* Durham, NC: Duke University Press, 1995.

Soyinka, Wole. "Myth, Literature, and the African World." In *I Am Because We Are: Readings in Black Philosophy*, edited by Fred Lee Hord and Jonathan Scott Lee. Amherst: University of Massachusetts Press, 1995.

Taylor, Charles. "The Politics of Recognition." In *Multiculturalism: Examining the Politics of Recognition*, edited by Amy Gutmann. Princeton: Princeton University Press, 1992.

Thiong'o, Ngũgĩ wa. *Decolonising the Mind: The Politics of Language in African Literature*. Harare: Zimbabwe Publishing House, 1987.

Thiam, Cheikh. *Return to the Kingdom of Childhood: Re-envisioning the Legacy and Philosophical Relevance of Negritude*. Columbus: Ohio State University Press, 2014.

Tolmasquim, Alfredo T., and Ildeu C. Moreira. "Einstein in Brazil: The Communication to the Brazilian Academy of Science on the Constitution of Light." In *History of Modern Physics—Proceedings of the XXth International Congress of History of Science presented at the XXth International Congress of History of Science*. Brussels, Belgium: Brepols, 2002.

Towa, Marcien. *Léopold Sédar Senghor: Négritude ou Servitude*. Yaoundé, Cameroon: Éditions CLE, 1971.

Townsend, Susan. *Miki Kiyoshi 1897–1945: Japan's Itinerant Philosopher*. Boston: Leiden, 2009.

Travis, Hannibal. *Genocide, Ethnonationalism, and the United Nations: Exploring the Causes of Mass Killing since 1945*. London: Routledge, 2013.

Turner, Stephen. *Emile Durkheim: Sociologist and Moralist*. New York: Routledge, 1993.

Vasconcelos, José. *Homenaje a Bergson*. Mexico D.F.: Imprenta Universitaria, 1941.

———. "Pitágoras: Una teoría del ritmo, part 2." *Cuba Contemporánea* 12, no. 205 (1916): 66–94.

Vaz Ferreira, Carlos. "Leyendo a Verlaine." *Nosotros* 2, no. 9 (1908): 165–66.

von Joeden-Forgey, Elisa. "Gender and Genocide." In *The Oxford Handbook to Genocide Studies*, edited by Donald Bloxham and A. Dirk Moses. Oxford: Oxford University Press, 2010.

Vorzimmer, Peter. "Darwin, Malthus, and the Theory of Natural Selection." *Journal of the History of Ideas* 30 (1969): 527–42.

Wallerstein, Immanuel. *The Modern World-System I: Capitalist Agriculture and the Origins of the European World-Economy in the Sixteenth Century*. Los Angeles: University of California Press, 2013.

Waterlot, Ghislain. *Bergson et la religion: nouvelles perspectives sur les Deux Sources de la morale et de la religion*. Paris: Presses Universitaires de France, 2008.

Weber, Max. *The Protestant Ethic and the Spirit of Capitalism: And Other Writings*. Translated by Peter Baehr and Gordon C. Wells. New York: Penguin Books, 2002.

Wetherell, Margaret. "Trends in the Turn to Affect: A Social Psychological Critique." *Body & Society* 21, no. 2 (2014): 139–66.

Worms, Frédéric. *Annales bergsoniennes V: Bergson et la politique, de Jaurès à aujourd'hui.* Paris: Presses Universitaires de France, 2012.

———. *Bergson ou les deux sens de la vie.* Paris: Presses Universitaires de France, 2004.

Wynter, Sylvia. "Unsettling the Coloniality of Being/Power/Truth/Freedom: Towards the Human, After Man, Its Overrepresentation—An Argument." *New Centennial Review* 3, no. 3 (2003): 257–337.

Youngkin, Molly. *Feminist Realism at the Fin de Siècle: The Influence of the Late-Victorian Woman's Press on the Development of the Novel.* Columbus: Ohio State University Press, 2007.

Zea, Leopoldo. *El positivismo en México: Nacimiento, apogeo y decadencia.* Mexico City: El Colegio de México, 1943.

———. "Preface to the English Translation." In *Positivism in Mexico.* Austin: University of Texas Press, 2014.

———. *En torno a una filosofía americana.* Mexico City: El Colegio de México, 1945.

———. *The Role of the Americas in History.* Lanham, MD: Rowman & Littlefield, 1992.

Contributors

Alia Al-Saji is associate professor of philosophy at McGill University (Montreal, Canada). Her research brings together phenomenology, French philosophy, feminist philosophy, and critical philosophy of race. Running through her work is an abiding interest in themes of time, racialization, and embodiment, the intersection of which she seeks to elaborate. Some of her publications include "The Racialization of Muslim Veils: A Philosophical Analysis" (*Philosophy and Social Criticism*, 2010); "The Temporality of Life: Merleau-Ponty, Bergson, and the Immemorial Past" (*The Southern Journal of Philosophy*, 2007); and "Material Life: Bergsonian Tendencies in Simone de Beauvoir's Philosophy" in *Differences: Rereading Beauvoir and Irigaray* (Oxford University Press, 2018). Al-Saji's recent work argues for the philosophical, political, and lived importance of hesitation, notably in her essay: "A Phenomenology of Hesitation: Interrupting Racializing Habits of Seeing" (in *Living Alterities: Phenomenology, Embodiment, and Race*, State University of New York Press, 2014). She is currently completing a monograph that elaborates a philosophy of time as embodied, intersubjective, and racialized in light of the work of Henri Bergson, Frantz Fanon, and Maurice Merleau-Ponty and in dialogue with critical race and feminist philosophies. Al-Saji is editor of the Feminist Philosophy section of the journal *Philosophy Compass* and coeditor of the *Symposia on Gender, Race, and Philosophy*.

Jaime Hanneken is associate professor of Spanish and Portuguese studies at the University of Minnesota. Hanneken specializes in nineteenth- and twentieth-century Latin American culture, postcolonial approaches to literature and culture, Francophone literature, and critical theory. Her recent publications include "José Carlos Mariátegui and the Time of Myth" in *Cultural Critique* 81 and "Los pliegues de *Paradiso*" in *Revista de Estudios Hispánicos* 45. Her work has also appeared in *Paragraph*, *MLQ*, *Comparative Literature*, and *MLN*.

Clevis Headley is currently associate professor of philosophy at Florida Atlantic University. He has served in various positions during his tenure at Florida Atlantic University: chair of the Department of Philosophy, director of the Ethnic Studies Certificate Program, director of the Master's in Liberal Studies, and special assistant to the dean for Diversity. Professionally, he was a founding member and served as the first vice-president and treasurer of the Caribbean Philosophical Association. Headley has published in the areas of Critical Philosophy of Race, Africana/Afro-Caribbean philosophy, and Analytic philosophy.

Annette K. Joseph-Gabriel is a scholar of contemporary francophone Caribbean and African literature with interdisciplinary specializations in black transnational feminisms, African diaspora literature, and slavery in the Atlantic world. She is currently an assistant professor of French and Francophone studies at the University of Michigan, Ann Arbor. Her forthcoming book, *Decolonial Citizenship: Black Women's Resistance in the Francophone World*, examines black women's articulations of citizenship through their work in anticolonial movements in Francophone Africa and the Antilles.

Leonard Lawlor is Edwin Erle Sparks Professor of Philosophy and director of Philosophy Graduate Studies at the Pennsylvania State University. Lawlor is the author of *Early Twentieth-Century Continental Philosophy* (Indiana University Press, 2011), *This Is Not Sufficient: An Essay on Animality and Human Nature in Derrida* (Columbia University Press, 2007), *The Implication of Immanence: Towards a New Concept of Life* (Fordham University Press, 2006), *The Challenge of Bergsonism: Phenomenology, Ontology, Ethics* (Continuum Press, 2003), *Thinking through French Philosophy: The Being of the Question* (Indiana University Press, 2003), *Derrida and Husserl: The Basic Problems of Phenomenology* (Indiana University Press, 2002), and *Imagination and Chance: The Difference between the Thought of Ricoeur and Derrida* (State University of New York Press, 1992). He has also published "Asceticism and Sexuality: 'Cheating Nature' in Bergson's *The Two Sources of Morality and Religion*," in *Bergson, Politics, and Religion* (Duke University Press, 2012).

Adriana Novoa is associate professor of history at the University of South Florida. She is a cultural historian whose specialty is science in Latin America, and her recent books include *¡Darwinistas!: The Construction of Evolutionary Thought in Nineteenth Century Argentina* (Brill, 2012) and *From Man* to Ape: Darwinism in Argentina, 1870–1920* (University of Chicago Press, 2010), both cowritten with Alex Levine. Her articles have been published in *Journal of Latin American Studies*, *Science in Context*, the *Latin Americanist*, and *Revista Hispánica Moderna*, among other journals. She is currently completing another manuscript that examines the politics of evolutionism and its relationship to gender and race titled *From Virile to Sterile: Masculinity and Race in Argentina, 1850–1910*.

Andrea J. Pitts is assistant professor of philosophy at the University of North Carolina, Charlotte. Their research interests include critical philosophy of race, feminist philosophy, Latin American and U.S. Latinx philosophy, and critical prison studies. Their publications appear in *Hypatia*, *Radical Philosophy Review*, and *Inter-American Journal of Philosophy*.

Martin Shuster is assistant professor of and director of Judaic Studies at Goucher College, where he is a member of the Center for Geographies of Justice. In addition to many articles, he is the author of *Autonomy after Auschwitz: Adorno, German Idealism, and Modernity* and *New Television: The Aesthetics and Politics of a Genre*, both published by the University of Chicago Press, in 2014 and 2017, respectively. Most recently, with Daniela Ginsburg, he translated Jean-François Kervégan's *L'effectif et le rationnel: Hegel et l'esprit objetif*, published as *The Actual and the Rational: Hegel and Objective Spirit*, also by the University of Chicago Press in 2018.

Mark William Westmoreland is a doctoral candidate and instructor of philosophy and ethics at Villanova University and also teaches philosophy and religious studies at Penn State Brandywine and Rowan University. Westmoreland was the guest editor of a special issue of the *Journal of French and Francophone Philosophy* 24, no. 2 (2016) commemorating seventy-five years since the death of Bergson, and he curated "Bergson(-ism) Remembered" in the same issue. Westmoreland works in political philosophy, philosophy of race, ethics, and philosophy of technology and has published on Bergson, Derrida, pedagogy, and issues of race and racism.

Melanie White is senior lecturer in social theory in the School of Social Sciences at the University of New South Wales, Sydney, Australia. She coedited *Bergson, Politics, and Religion* (Duke University Press, 2012) with Alexandre Lefebvre.

Index

aboriginal peoples, stereotype of, xi. *See also* the "primitives"
absolute justice, 4–5, 22
Acevedo, Jesus, 173
Achille, Louis-Thomas, 122, 129, 131–32, 139n24, 139n39
action, 197, 198, 199, 200, 207
adaptability, 177
adaptation, 64, 131–32
Adorno, Theodor W., 37–38, 52n16
Adotevi, Stanislas, 91, 97–98
aesthetic disinterestedness, 181, 182–84
aesthetic intuition, 7, 171–92
aestheticism, 159–60
aesthetics, 144, 157, 171, 175, 185–88; aesthetic experience, 88–90, 102, 178; aesthetic intuition, 178; aesthetic values, 182–83; indigenous, 209n7; morality and, 182–83
Africa, philosophy in, 189n16
African art, 88, 102–103, 112–13
African culture, root metaphors of, 107
African diaspora, black identity in, 121
African epistemology, 80, 114; emotion and, 111–13; vs. European epistemology, 104–107; music and dance metaphors for, 107–108; normative status of reason in, 109–10; rhythm and, 107–108
African ontology, 80

African style of thinking, 114; vs. European style of thinking, 105–107, 110–112; intuition and, 110–112
African subject, vs. European subject, 104–105
agency, 44
"agential realism," 165
Algiers, 17
alienation, 124
altruism, 183, 186
analysis, 196, 197
anarcho-syndicalist voluntarism, 196
Anglo-Saxonism, 145–46, 151
animal-human relationships, 62–63, 186
animality, 186
animal societies, 62–63, 66
Ansell-Pearson, Keith, 82, 88, 185
antagonism, 197, 198, 199; contradiction and, 203–206; myth and, 193–210
anticolonialism, 30n1
anti-imperialism, 187
antinégritude discourse, condition of, 94
antipositivism, 7, 172–77, 195
aphasia, 27
APRA (Alianza Popular Revolucionaria Americana) movement, 208n6
Arango, José F., 150

231

Arendt, Hannah, 37, 56n80
Argentina, 7, 154, 158–59, 161, 208n6, 209n7
arielismo, 209n7
Aristotle, 174
art, 153, 171, 190n36; distinct from play, 178; as exemplification of possibility of nonegoistic intuition, 177; intuition and, 177, 181–82; mysticism and, 180; national identity and, 171; as noninstrumental, 179; play and, 177–78. *See also* aesthetics
artists, 178–79; limitations of, 182; values of, 180–81
Asian philosophical thought, 8–9n2
aspiration, 21–23
assimilation, 122, 127, 128–29, 132, 137–38n3, 140n52, 152, 153, 157, 159, 187
Association of Martinican Students, 132–33
Ateneo de la Juventud, 155, 156, 171, 172–77, 187, 188n2, 209n7
atomistic thinking, 46, 105
Augustine, 174
authenticity, 122, 127–32, 137
automatism, 157
axiology, 175, 180, 187
ayllu, 204
Azorín, 160

Balibar, Etienne, 31n6
Barad, Karen, 164–65
beauty, 176, 177, 180–81
becoming, 23, 83, 157–58, 179
Beethoven, Ludwig van, x
being, 158; attitudes toward, 91; as duration, 90; intuition and, 87; living and, 176; mobility of, 84; ontology of, 90; rhythm of, 90, 108
Belaúnde, Víctor Andrés, 155, 208n5

belonging, 64, 68, 69, 122; boundary-making and, 58–59; colonialism and, 132; experience of, 73; race and, 128, 129, 130, 132; spectacle of, 121–40; sympathy and, 58–59
Bergson, Henri, 143, 150, 154–56, 164, 174, 188, 193; antirationalism and, 16; Argentine intellectuals and, 154; as "artist-philosopher," 161; awarded Nobel Prize in Literature in 1927, 160–61; Caso and, 171–92; as chair of ICIC, 3; colonialism and, 16–18; on community, 46–48; condemns German imperialism but not French colonialism, 17–18; contemporary literature on, 16–17; in context, 80–81; criticisms of, 80; as critic of state system, 37; debate with Einstein, 160–61; decolonizing, 13–35; delivers lectures at Ateneo de Madrid, 2; diplomatic engagement of, 13, 37; distinct approach to philosophy, 44; as French emissary to Spain during World War I, 2; Guyau and, 149–50, 151; half-opening or decolonizing, 28–30; Husserl and, 176; impact in Spanish America, 154; influence on movements throughout the Americas, 7; on intellect, 81–82; intuition and, 176; legacy of, 161, 164; as liaison between France and United States during Paris Peace Conference, 2–3; as materialist, 158, 159; new materialist readings of, 16; on norms, 44–46; as philosopher of race and/or colonialism, 1; philosophy of time, 14; political career of, 2–3; popularity in Spain and Spanish America, 159, 160, 169n84; prejudices of, xi; "probabilistic" method of, 25;

readings of, 16–19, 32n22, 80; rejection of Kant's conception of rationality, 176–77; relevance in early twentieth-century Spanish America, 151; on science, 82–83; Senghor and, 79–119; spiritualism and, 16; theology and, 184–85; as transcending the divisions of materialism and idealism, 158; uncritical position on French colonialism, 32n15; varying interpretations of across Spanish America, 158–59; visits Spain, 159; visits United States, 2; during World War I, 13. *See also* Bergson, Henri, works of
Bergson, Henri, works of, 168n52; *Creative Evolution*, 20–23, 26, 28, 47, 66, 73–74n3, 154, 156, 160, 179; decolonization of, 6; *Durée et simultanéité: à propos de la théorie d'Einstein*, 169n84; *La pensée et le mouvant*, 16, 29–30; *Laughter: An Essay on the Meaning of the Comic*, 6, 121–23, 127–28, 131–35, 137, 181–82, 184–85; *Matter and Memory*, 27, 28; *The Meaning of the War*, 68; *Time and Free Will: An Essay on the Immediate Data of Consciousness*, viii–x, 99–100; *The Two Sources of Morality and Religion*, vii–viii, x–xi, 2–3, 6, 8, 14–15, 19–20, 28–29, 30n1, 32n19, 33n24, 34n40, 37, 39, 43, 47–49, 57–76, 172, 184–85
Bergsonism, 8, 19, 92, 155; aesthetic intuition and, 177–85; borderline position with respect to science, 160; decline of, 161; difference and, 151–62; emphasis on subjectivity, 160; English-language resurgence of, 16; growth of in France, 157;

impact in Spanish America, 154, 158, 171–92, 194–95, 208n5; Mexican, 158, 171–92; Négritude Movement and, 6; in Peru, 194–95, 208n5; racial difference and, 151–62; revolutionary, 193–210; seen as source for racialist narratives of early twentieth century, 18
Bergson studies, 16–18, 32n22, 59
Berkeley, George, 154
Berlin, Isaiah, 80
Bernasconi, Robert, 31n11
Bernstein, Eduard, 196
Berth, Edouard, 209n9
Billig, Michael, *Laughter and Ridicule: Towards a Social Critique of Laughter*, 125
biological materialism, 161
biological vitalism, Jones's critique of, 91–92
biologization, 186, 192n78
biology, 80, 152, 161, 186
biotechnology, 163
the black body, 6, 122–27, 129, 138n4
black homogeneity: myth of, 98; Négritude and, 98
black identity, in African diaspora, 121
black intellectuals, 129, 137; colonialism and, 137–38n3, 138n4; in Paris, 122
blackness, 125, 128; caricature of, 132; exoticization of, 130; otherness and, 131–32; in public spaces, 120–140; as spectacle, 131, 133, 136–37; white spaces and, 137; white viewers' fascination with, 131. See also *Négritude* movement
black peoples: dehumanization and commodification of, 9n10; hunting of, 3, 9n10
black psyche, colonialism and, 6

blacks: in France, 121–22; objectification of, 124–25; "thingification" of, 124–25; in white spaces, 120–40
the body: the black body, 6, 122–27, 129, 138n4; laughter and, 131; materiality of, 163; racialized, 160; representation and, 164; as the site of comedy, 122–27
Bohr, Niels, 83, 161, 162, 164
Born, Max, 83
boundary-making: belonging and, 58–59; sympathy and, 58–59
bourgeois, 196
Boutroux, Emile, 154, 156
Brazil, 161
Briand, Aristide, 2
Brown, Wendy, 51n10
Bunge, Carlos O., 146, 151, 154; *Principes de psychologie individuelle et sociale*, 151
Byron, George Gordon, 144

call and response, as sociality of mystics, 72
Calvo, Carlos, 144
"the Cameroons," xi
Candelaria, Michael, *The Revolt of Unreason*, 180
capitalism, 202–203, 204; as genocidal, 40; homogenization and, 49, 50–51; nationalism and, 43; neocolonial finance and, 4; as a normative project, 40; "pathological homogenization" and, 39–40; state system and, 39–40, 42, 43
Carbet, Marie-Magdaleine (Magd Raney), 122, 129–31, 132, 136, 139n36
care, 58, 185
caridad (charity), 182–84
Carrasco Albano, Manuel, 144
Caso, Antonio, 7, 154, 155, 171–92; *caridad* (charity) and, 182–84;

contemporary philosophical issues in Bergsonist aesthetics of, 185–88; decolonial theory and, 187–88; *El concepto de la historia universal en la filosofía de los valores*, 175; *Existence as Economy, as Disinterest, and as Charity* (*Existencia como economía, como desinterés y como caridad*), 172, 175, 176, 177, 183, 184, 185; humanism and, 187–88; *La filosofía de Husserl*, 176; ovarian-testicular theory of sexual difference, 192n78; as Platonist, 180; *Principios de estética*, 180; "social objectivism" of, 175; theology and, 184–85
Catholic Church, 203
causality, 88–89, 154, 157, 161, 164–65
Cavell, Stanley, 48–49; *The Claim of Reason*, 48–49
Césaire, Aimé, 5, 9n9, 124–25, 137–38n3; *Cahier d'un retour au pays natal*, 124, 136
change, 58, 83, 200; capacity to, 67–68; constancy of, 48, 68; open societies and, 68; revolutionary, 197; spatialization of, 198; tendency toward, 47
Châtelet theater, 136–37
Chavarría, Jesús, 208n5
childhood memory, 32–33n23
Chile, 7; democratization in, 208n6
Científicos, 172–73, 179
cinematographic method, science and, 83–85
civilization: "civilized" societies, 24; education and, 146–47; as embodied difference, 152
class, 59, 196, 198; Négritude and, 95, 99; in Peru, 202
the closed, 5, 13–35, 58–61; civilized societies and, 24; community and,

46–47; as indifference, 23; lack of, 29; language of, 37–55; of organism vs. of obligation, 26; primitive societies and, 24; radical contingency of, 47; state structure and, 50; in *The Two Sources of Morality and Religion*, 22–23. *See also* closedness; closed societies; closure; open/closed dichotomy
closedness, x. *See also* the closed; closure; open/closed dichotomy
closed societies, x, xi, 5, 20, 28, 48, 58–59, 70, 76n53; colonialism and, 13; exclusion and, 68; group solidarity and, 68; natural sympathy and, 58–68; vs. open societies, 15; progress in, 21; relative justice and, 4; sociality in, 71–72; suffering and, 50; *us-them* orientation of, 58
closure, 13, 15, 29, 62; language of, 5, 37–56, 71; lessening of, 50; tendency to, 20, 22–24, 26, 28, 65. *See also* closedness; completion
coevalness, 29
coexistence, 24, 29
Colebrook, Claire, 181
Colegio de Mexico, 174
collective identification, laughter and, 125–26
collective resistance, 8
colonialism, 1–7, 13–35, 39, 114, 121–40; belonging and, 132; black intellectuals and, 137–38n3, 138n4; Black psyche and, 7; closed societies and, 13; "colonial aphasia," 13, 17; colonial erasure, 132; colonial violence, 4, 6; drive toward homogenization and, 39–42; French, 32n15, 146; nationalism and, 42; Peru and, 200; in postcolonial contexts, 13–35; Senghor and, 93, 97; Spanish, 200, 202; state framework and, 37; temporal narratives justifying, 14
colonized subjects, 132, 188
color-blindness, 5
color lines, identification across, 125, 137
comedy, ideology and, 6
comical Negro trope, 6, 121–40
communism, 187. *See also* Marxism
community: Bergson on, 46–48; claim to, 48–49; "closed" belonging to, 46–47; community transformation, 7; language and, 48–50; "open" belonging to, 46–47; open communities, 49; possibility of closure and, 50; sympathy and, 67; two ways to view belonging to, 46–47
competition, 138, 145, 152, 176, 187
complete sympathy, 58, 59; learning as starting point for, 73; mystics and, 69, 71–72; vs. natural sympathy, 71–72; open societies and, 60, 68–72
completion, 26, 29
complicity between all things, 86
Comte, Auguste, 60, 172, 188n1
concepts, 160; judgment of, 30
conflict, 196–97
conformity, 62–63
Connolly, William, 14
conquest, 187, 202
"conscience of the species," 153
conscious life, 149–50, 151
consciousness, viii, 1, 149, 158; dual, 133; duration as, 85–86; emotion and, 114; heterogeneous multiplicities of, 92; incapable of quantitative, scientific study, 83
construction, language and, 49–50
consumption, 131, 136
contingency, 198

continuity, 157–58
continuous flow, viii. *See also* duration
contradiction, 197; antagonism and, 203–206
Coole, Diana, 144, 163
cosmopolitanism, 67
cosmos, 161
costumbrismo, 200, 209–10n21
Cousin, Victor, 150
creative difference, 181
creative emotions, vii, x, 21
Creative Evolution (Bergson), 20–23, 26, 47, 66, 160, 179; Bunge's reading of as rejection of mechanistic approach to life, 154; God as unceasing life in, 184; "metaphysical biologism" in, 185; Rodó and, 156; sympathy in, 73–74n3; translation into Spanish, 154
creativity, 18
criollo customs, 200
Croce, Benedetto, 156, 196
Crusoe, Robinson, 54n55
Cuba, 7, 150
Cuba Contemporánea, 157
culture(s), 147, 164; complementary, 162; cultural acquisitions, 25–26, 33n24; cultural transformation, 174; materiality and, 164; philosophy of, 187
Curle, Clinton, 2

D'Annunzio, Gabriele, 153
Darwin, Charles, 143, 164, 177, 190n32; *Descent of Man*, 145
Darwinian evolution: 143, 148, 164, 176; morality and, 150, 151; race and, 144–51; racism and, 145–46; social, 189n9, 195
death, culture of, 153
"Decline of the West," 195
decolonial theory, 9n9, 13–35, 187–88

deep self, 33n24
degeneracy, 145–46
dehumanization, laughter and, 137
De la Riva Agüero, José, 208n5
delay, 28
Deleuze, Gilles, 14, 185; *Bergsonism*, 1–2, 28
democracy, 196
democratization, 195, 208n6
Depestre, René, 91
Descartes, René, 82, 174
desire, 131, 136
determination, 161
determinism, 88, 146, 147, 151, 152, 154, 155, 157, 200, 202
Deustua, Alejandro, 153
Dewey, John, 166n34
Diagne, Souleymane Bachir, 18–19, 32n22, 93, 102–103, 108, 112–13; *Bergson postcolonial*, 18
Díaz, Porfirio, 171, 172, 173, 186–87, 189n9
difference, 5, 6, 81, 146, 147, 197; as affirmation, 81; Bergsonism and, 151–62; Bergson's embrace of, 81; civilization and, 152; as continuity, 81; as creation, 81; creative, 181; embodied, 152; human nature and, 144; identification across, 137; indifference to, 5; intuition and, 87; as invention, 81; language and, 162; nature and, 144; oppressive ideas of, 165; between "primitive" and "civilized" societies, 24–25; qualitative, 197; racial, 159, 162; reality as, 83; recognition across, 137; sameness and, 153, 163
discrete philosophy, 174
discursive practices, material phenomena and, 165
disequilibrium, viii
disguise, 122, 129, 135, 136
Dobuzinski, Laurent, 147

dress, 121, 122; cultural expression and, 132; race and, 127, 128–29
dual consciousness, 133
dualism, 28, 104, 106–107, 184
duality, 132–33, 157
duration, viii, xii, 20, 24, 28, 80–81, 83, 85–86, 179, 197–98, 206; being as, 90; comprised of two ideas, 179; energy and, 85; epistemology and, 85; eternal, 182, 184; experience and, 85; flow of, 86; immersion in, 86; incompleteness and unpredictability of, 26–27; intuition and, 179; motion and, 85; openness and, 23; pulsations of positive and negative charges and, 85; as pure consciousness, 85–86; as the real, 85; rhythmic profile of, 90; space and, 179; subjectivity and, 85–86; thinking in, 85, 86, 92, 93, 106; universality of, 179
durée, 28. *See also* duration
Durée et simultanéité: à propos de la théorie d'Einstein (Bergson), 169n84
Durkheim, Émile, 64, 166n34
dynamic religions, x–xi, 23–24
dynamism, x, xii, 84, 160

Éboué, Félix, 121
economic organization, modern forms of, 46
economy of exchange, 4
education, 147; civilization and, 146–47; humanities and, 186–87; positivism and, 187
Edwards, Brent, 140n43; *The Practice of Diaspora: Literature, Translation and the Rise of Black Internationalism*, 133, 134–35
egoísmo, 176–77, 183, 186
Einfühlung, 180, 182, 186. *See also* empathy
Einstein, Albert, 160–61, 169n84

"*élan d'amour*," 25
élan vital, 21, 25, 28, 34, 69–70, 150, 155, 160, 194
El Comercio, 154
emancipatory practices, 165
emotion(s), 96; African epistemology and, 111–13; consciousness and, 114; creative, vii, x; emotionalism, 99; in Négritude epistemology, 109–14; Sartre's conception of, 113; Senghor and, 111–14; source of, 69
empathy, 180, 182, 186; perception and, 186; race and, 125
empiricism, 159
energy, 161; duration and, 85
Enlightenment, 144, 164, 196
environment, evolution and, 146–47
epistemology, 79, 162, 164; African, 80; African vs. European approaches to, 104–105; Cartesian, 104; crisis in modern, 100–101; duration and, 85; "epistemology of ignorance," 41; metaphor of sign and vision and, 107; modern European, 99–101; Négritude and, 93, 101–102, 109–14; ontology and, 108; science and, 106; Senghor and, 100, 106; Western, 107
equality, 4–5
Escuela Nacional de Jurisprudencia, 174
Escuela Nacional Preparatoria, 174
essentialism, 6, 92, 157, 158; antinégritude discourse and, 94; Négritude and, 96–97, 99, 100
ethics, 153–54
ethnic cleansing, 38
ethnicity, "fictive," 42
ethnocentrism, xi, 4
Europe: cultural assimilation in, 120–40; Mariátegui in, 196; Mexico and, 173. *See also specific countries*
European culture and tradition, 105, 132

European epistemology, vs. African epistemology, 104–107
European leftism, 196
European style of thinking: vs. African style of thinking, 105–107, 110–12; intellect and, 110–12
European subject, vs. African subject, 104–105
evil, 55n67
evolution, 7, 143–70; environment and, 146–47; materialist views of, 151; racial, 152. *See also* Darwinism; evolutionism
evolutionism, 64, 143, 150, 151, 153, 162; Darwinian, 176; evolutionary psychology, 159; racial hierarchies and, 145–46, 151. *See also* Darwinism
exchange, economy of, 4
exclusion, 6, 37–55, 58, 65, 165; closed societies and, 68; "general politics of," 59; general tendency toward, 72; homogeneity and, 37–55; laughter and, 125–26; natural tendency toward, 59; race and, 137; reconfiguring problem of, 59; sympathy and, 58, 59, 68
existence: within duration, 106; inherent creativity of, 179; science of, 174–75; theory of value of, 174–75
expansion, capitalism and, 39–40
experience, 69, 149, 175; duration and, 85; instrumental manipulation of, 81; mystic, 70–71; pure, 159; spatialization of, 85; tendencies of, 27
experimental psychology, 154
extinction, 163

Fabian, Johannes, 29
faith, 199
family, 64–65
Fanon, Frantz, 91, 117n51, 124, 140n52; *Peau noir, masques blancs*, 124
feminism/feminist theory, 7, 14, 143–44, 164; feminist analysis, 187; in Mexico, 187; race consciousness and, 133
Fernández, Macedonio, 154, 166–67n45
Fidler, Geoffrey, 149
finitude, absolute, xii
fixed state identity, 38
Flores Galindo, Alberto, 207
fluidity, 82
"*fonction fabulatrice*," 23–24
"forward movement," 21
Fouillée, Alfred, 146, 147, 150–51, 157, 166n34; *The Criticism of Contemporary Moral Systems*, 148; *La psychologie des idées forces*, 147
France, 145, 151, 159; Bergsonism in, 157; blacks in, 121–22; French intellectual tradition, 79, 150; Third Republic of, 146. *See also* French colonialism
freedom, 1, 4, 164, 178
French colonialism, 17–18, 32n15, 146
French Declaration of the Rights of Man and Citizen, 67
Freud, Sigmund, 151
Frost, Samantha, 144, 163
fundamentalism, 15
future, xii; interpenetration of past, present future, 93; newness of, 179; openness of, xii; unknowability of, 48; unpredictability of, 29

gamonalismo, 202
Gaos, José, 174
García Calderón, Francisco, 153, 154, 156–57

García Morente, Manuel, 159–60
gender, 59
gender discrimination, 4
general strike, myth of, 196–98
"general will," 56n80
generosity, 58, 68
genetics, 143, 145, 162
genocide, 9n9, 37, 39; Adorno on, 37–38; homogeneity and, 37–38; as method of integration, 37–38
German philosophy, 45, 176, 180
Gobetti, Piero, 196
God as love, in *Les deux sources de la morale et de la religion*, 184–85
Gómez Campos, Rubí de María, *El sentido de sí: Un ensayo sobre feminismo y la filosofía de la cultura*, 187
González Peña, Carlos, 155
good, 55n67, 176, 177, 183–84. See also morality
Greene, Joshua, *Moral Tribes*, 64
Groos, Karl, 178, 190n40
Grosz, Elizabeth, 14, 87, 89, 164, 179; *Becoming Undone*, 143–44
group coherence, 46
group solidarity, 58, 68
Guerlac, Suzanne, 16, 17, 30n1, 34n58, 80, 83, 86, 89
Guilhaumou, Jacques, 74n11
Guillaumet, Paul, 103
Guyau, Jean-Marie, 146–53, 156, 157, 161, 166n34; *Education and Heredity*, 146–47; *Esquisse d'une morale sans obligation ni sanction*, 148–50, 152

habits, x–xi, 45, 62–63; accumulation of, 75n21; acquisition of, 67; changing, 25
Haddox, John, 174, 175, 178–79, 180
the *half-open* (*entr'ouvert*), 6, 15, 29, 30. See also half-openness

half-openness, 18, 28–29, 30
Hampton, Jean, 52–53n26
harmony, 22, 149
Hartmann, Karl Robert Eduard von: 153; *The Phenomenology of the Moral Consciousness*, 148
Hasidic Jews, 15
hatred, x, 65, 72
Havana, Cuba, 150
Haya de la Torre, Víctor Raúl, 208n6
hazing, 126, 127
Hegel, G.W.F., 45, 46, 54–55n57
Hegelians, 150
hegemony, 194, 198, 203–204, 210n30
Heidegger, Martin, 186
Henríquez Ureña, Pedro, 153, 154, 156, 188n2
heredity, 145
heroes, 69
heroic philosophy, 174
hesitation, 28, 45
heterogeneity, 198
Hiddleston, Jane, 97
hierarchy, 15
historical materialism, 202
historicism, 201
history, 5, 196; dialectical understanding of, 197; march of, 195; time and, 195, 200; whitewashing of, 49
Hitler, Adolf, 3
holocaust, 9n9
homogeneity, 6, 37–55; exclusion and, 37–55; genocide and, 37–38
homogenization, 37–38, 44, 46, 49–50; capitalism and, 39–40; nationalism and, 42; as normative, 42–43; "pathological," 38, 39, 49, 50–51; patriarchy and, 41–42; prone to failure, 50; state system and, 39–43; white supremacy and, 40–41

homophobia, 59
Hostos, Eugenio M., 153; *Tratado de Sociología*, 153
Hountondji, Paulin, 91
the human, conceptions of, 163
human animals: adaptability of, 177; empathy for other, 182; nonhuman animals and, 62–63, 178, 186, 190n40; vital energy of, 177
human exceptionalism, 186
humanism, 5, 113, 152, 159–60, 163; Caso and, 175, 187–88; decolonial theory and, 187–88; humanistic studies, 162; materialism and, 143–44; Mexican, 187; new, 143
humanities, 146, 186–87
humanity, 5, 69, 160, 163; open societies and, 69; shared, 29; as social group, 65
human nature: difference and, 144; primordial, 66; war and, 65
human rights, 37, 56n79, 67
human societies, animal societies and, 62–63
Hume, David, 60, 154
humor, 7
Humphrey, John, 2
Hunt, Lynn, *Inventing Human Rights*, 67
Husserl, Edmund, 174, 176, 186
Hutcheson, Francis, 67

Iberian American community, 156
Ibérico Rodríguez, Mariano, 208n5; *La Filosofía de Enrique Bergson*, 155
idealism, 147–48, 153–54, 158, 197; bourgeois, 193; materialism and, 162–65, 201; religious, 154
idées forces, 147, 158
identity, 51n10, 129; hybridized, 132; identity politics, 5; in the metropole, 132–37; oppression and, 29; peoplehood and, 38

ideology: comedy and, 6; ideological mystification, 6
"*idéo-motrices*," 23
ignorance, 4
ijtihad, 19
"imbrication," 18
the "immediate," 155
immobilization, 81
imperialism, 17, 59, 72, 114, 153, 186, 187
Incas, 202
inclusion, laughter and, 125–26
indeterminism, 83
indifference, 23
indigeneity, 188, 191n63
indigenismo, 191n63, 193, 201, 208n2
indigenous groups, 195; indigenous activism, 199; indigenous myth, 205, 206–207; indigenous socialism, 193; in Mexico, 187; mythical timelessness and, 205; in Peru, 200–201, 204–205; resistance and, 204–205; socialism and, 205
individuality, modern forms of, 46
individual rights, 67
inequality, 37, 40, 52n13
infinitesimal calculus, 82–83, 174
Ingenieros, José, 158–59
injustice, 5, 40
insect society, 44–45, 66
"insider/outsider" categories, 39
instinct, 20, 26, 34n40, 63, 65, 104, 177; transcendence of, 178
instinctive society, vs. intelligent society, 44–45
instrumental reasoning, 180, 186, 191n57, 191n59
integration, 49–50. *See also* homogenization
intellect, 85, 104; Bergson on, 81–82, 101; European style of thinking and, 110–12; vs. intuition, 110–12;

intuition and, 86; limitations of, 84–85; particularity of, 179; primary task to think matter, 81; scientific thinking, 83–85
intellectualism, 155
intelligence, x, 45, 63, 66, 104, 176–77; analytic, 155
intelligent society, vs. instinctive society, 44–45
International Commission for Intellectual Cooperation (ICIC), 3
International Congress of Anthropological and Ethnological Sciences, 162
internationalism, 2, 3, 50, 131
interpretation, 19
"intra-action," 165
introspection, 26
intuition, vii–viii, 7, 25, 28; aesthetic, 7, 171–92; aesthetic experience and, 88–90, 102; African style of thinking and, 110–12; as analogous to aesthetic experience, 88–90; art and, 177, 181–82; being and, 87; Bergson's conception of, 87, 179, 180–182; Caso's conception of, 180–181; differences and, 87; double revelation entailed by, 87; duration and, 179; as an ethics, 88; as form of "intellectual sympathy," 88; intellect and, 86, 110–12; intuitionism, 176; "intuitive" concepts, 30; intuitive reason, 106; as method, vii–viii, 87; as method of merging with dynamic flow of being, 87; as mystical vision, viii; Négritude and, 80, 81, 86–90, 104, 107, 155; reason and, 87; vs. science, 86–87; as sympathy, 88; tendencies and, 87; as thought thinking through its own duration, 86; two senses of, vii–viii; value of, 187

Iqbal, Muhammad, 18, 32n22; *The Reconstruction of Religious Thought in Islam*, 18–19
Irele, Abiola, 91, 95–96, 101–102
irrationalism, 109–10
Islamic thought, 8–9n2, 18–19
Italy, 145

James, William, 154, 156, 158–59, 160, 175, 176, 177; *Pragmatism*, 154
Jankélévitch, Vladimir, 15, 26, 29, 34n40, 60
Jaurès, Jean, 196
Jay, Martin, 88
Jesus Christ, 21, 184
Joan of Arc, viii
Jones, Donna, 18–19, 24, 32–33n23, 32n22, 33n24, 93; critique of biological vitalism, 91–92; *The Racial Discourses of Life Philosophy: Négritude, Vitalism, and Modernity*, 18, 91; reading of Senghor, 91–92, 93
"joy of joy," 69–70
Juárez, Benito, 172
Judaism, 29
Jules-Rosette, Bennetta, 94, 96
justice, absolute vs. relative, 4–5, 22

Kant, Immanuel, 150, 174, 176; conception of aesthetic disinterestedness, 181; conception of "free play of the imagination," 177–78; moral law and, 183–84
Kapteyn, Gertrude, 148, 152, 153
Kebede, Messay, 101
Kelley, Robin D. G., 138n4
Kisukidi, Yala, 32n19
knowing: 158; as communion with things, 87; as manipulation of things, 87; two types of, 86–87. *See also* epistemology; knowledge

knowledge, 79–119; accumulation of, 75n21; vs. action, 199–200; intellect's facilitation of, 82; intuition as another source of, 86–90; object of, 104–105; root metaphors of, 107; sources of, 106. *See also* epistemology

Krausistas, 150

Krauze de Kolteniuk, Rosa, 171–72

labor contracts, 41

labor practices, coercive, 200, 202, 204

Laclau, Ernesto, 194, 198, 203, 204, 205–206, 210n30

L'Action Nouvelle, 128

Laïcité, 61

"*la loi de double frénésie*," 26

La Nación, 156–57

Landecker, Hannah, 163

language, 6, 56n77, 191n59; boundaries of, 50; community and, 48–50; construction and, 49–50; difference and, 162; learning, 73; loneliness and, 49; matter and, 164–65; morality and, 49–50; normativity and, 49–50; open societies and, 51; "pathological homogenization" and, 50; peoplehood and, 49; society and, 49

La pensée et le mouvant (Bergson), 16, 29–30

La Plata University, college of Physics and Mathematics, 161

La Revue du monde noir, 132, 133, 136, 137, 137–38n3, 139n36; 6; Bergson's *Le Rire* in, 122–23; "How Should Negroes Living in Europe Dress?," 121–22; internationalist project of, 131; "Question Corner" segment, 122; reclaiming authenticity in, 127–32

Larsen, Neil, 208n2

La Sociedad de Conferencias, 173

latifundios, 202, 204, 206

Latin America: as backwards, 195; Bergson's influence in, 7; racialization in, 151; use of term, 165n3

Latin American philosophy, 174, 189n16

Latin race: Anglo-Saxons race and, 145–46; Darwinism and, 144–51; degeneracy and, 145–46

La Torre, Víctor Raúl Haya de, 150, 208n6

laughter, 121, 122; accompanied by absence of empathy, 125; as act of complicity, 125–26; the black body and, 122–27; the body and, 131; collective identification and, 125–26; dehumanization and, 137; dual function of othering and establishing affinity, 125–26; exclusion and, 125–26; function of, 125–27; inclusion and, 125–26; power and, 130; racialized, 135; social function of, 125, 127; violence and, 127

Laughter: An Essay on the Meaning of the Comic (Bergson), 121, 122–23, 127–28; Caso on, 181–82; comical Negro trope in, 6; Paulette Nardal and, 133–35, 137; racial implications of, 137; read through afrodiasporic lens, 131–32; white viewer in, 129–31

Lawlor, Leonard, 7, 179, 185; *The Challenge of Bergsonism*, 114

League of Nations, 3, 13; International Commission for Intellectual Cooperation (ICIC), 3; mystical intuition and, 3

learning, 153; as starting point for complete sympathy, 73. *See also* education

lebensphilosophie, 93
Lebredo, Joaquín García, 150
Lecky, W. E. H., 74–75n15
Le Dantec, Félix, 176
L'Édudiant noir, 132–36
Lefebvre, Alexandre, 2, 30–31n5, 56n79, 67
leftism, 199
"*le maximalisme bergsonien*," 26
Le Rire: Essai sur la signification du comique (Bergson). See *Laughter: An Essay on the Meaning of the Comic* (Bergson)
Le Roy, Edouard, 155
Les deux sources de la morale et de la religion (Bergson). See *The Two Sources of Morality and Religion* (Bergson)
L'évolution créatrice (Bergson). See *Creative Evolution* (Bergson)
Lévy-Bruhl, Lucien, 16, 23, 31n11, 32–33n23
"*l'humanité primitive*," 25–26
liberal contract theory, 41
liberalism, 195, 202
life, 82, 149–50, 164; dynamism of, 84, 94; as economic, 177; "expansion of," 150; expressed as "closed" and "open" tendencies, 58; flow of, 160, 179; ineptitude of intellect to grasp, 84–85; matter and, 179; plasticity of, 163; as striving, 70; teleology of, 26; tendency toward change and, 47; unconscious vs. conscious, 149–50, 151; "vital impetus" of, 69–70. See also *élan vital*
life force, 160. See also *élan vital*
Lima, Peru, 200
"linguistic turn," social development and, 164–65
Lipps, Theodor, 182
Liu Xiaobo, 69

lived sympathy, 69
living, being and, 176
Llauría, Enrique, 153
local knowledge, method of, 30
Locke, John, 154
loneliness, language and, 49
love, 64, 180; creative emotion of, 21; for humanity, 5, 20–21, 29, 47–48, 58, 69, 71–72, 184; "love of love," 69–70; self-transformation and, 156
Lugones, Leopold, 159
Luxemburg, Rosa, 39
Lycée Schœlcher, 128

madness, mystical vision and, viii
magic, xi, 24
magical thinking, 32–33n23
Malagarriga, Carlos, 154; translation of *L'évolution créatrice*, 154
Malthus, Thomas Robert, 190n32
Malthusianism, 177
Mann, Michael, 38, 51n10
Maran, René, 121
Mariátegui, José Carlos, 7, 193–210; Bergsonism of, 194; cultural studies and, 208n2; death of, 207; *el problema del indio* and, 200; in Europe, 196; "The Final Struggle," 199; indigenous myth and, 205, 206–207; "Man and Myth," 199; myth and, 208n2; "*Pasadismo* and Futurism" ("Pasadismo y futurismo"), 201; *Peruanicemos al Perú*, 202–203; postcolonialism and, 208n2; revolutionary project of, 205; *Seven Interpretive Essays on Peruvian Reality* (*Siete ensayos de interpretación de la realidad peruana*), 201–202, 203, 206; translation of myth of general strike into indigenous activism, 199; "Two Conceptions of Life," 199; vitalism and, 207

markets, commodification of, 49
marriage contracts, 41
Mars, Jean Price, 139n24
Marx, Karl, 9n10, 52n16
Marxism, 97, 98, 194, 198, 200, 204, 208n2, 209n9
masculinization, 49
material idealism, 201
materialism, 95–99, 146, 147, 150–155, 158–64, 194, 200, 202; biological, 148, 161; historical, 202; humanism and, 143–44; idealism and, 162–65; new, 163–64; new materialism, 162–65; philosophical recontextualization of, 144; representation and, 155; scientific, 157
materiality, 157, 163, 164, 165
material phenomena, discursive practices and, 165
mathematics, 80, 82, 83
Matière et mémoire (Bergson). See *Matter and Memory* (Bergson)
matter, 28, 144, 147, 161, 163; language and, 164–65; life and, 179; plasticity of, 163; representation and, 164–65; thinking, 81
Matter and Memory (Bergson), 27–28
McKay, Claude, 121
The Meaning of the War, Bergson, Henri, works of, 68
measurement, 88
mechanistic laws, 157
mechanistic thinking, 105, 153, 154, 163
memory, 1, 28, 160; childhood, 32–33n23; as localized in brain, not as positivist experiences, 27
"mentalité primitive," 32–33n23
Merchan, Rafael, 150
Mercure de France, 159
Merleau-Ponty, Maurice, 86, 186; *Humanism and Terror*, 3

mestizaje, 187, 209n7
mestizos, 188, 195
metaphor of sign and vision, Western epistemology and, 107
metaphors, visual, 107
"metaphysical biologism," 185
metaphysics, 144, 150, 153, 158, 160, 173, 175, 186–87; refounding of, 176; suppression of temporality in, 80–81; violence of, 114; Western, 80–81
methodology, in *The Two Sources of Morality and Religion*, 23–27
metropole, identity in the, 132–37
Mexican philosophy, 7
Mexican Revolution, 155, 171, 173
Mexico, 7, 154, 155–56, 158; Bergsonism in, 171–92; democratization in, 208n6; feminist philosophy in, 187; history of philosophy in, 172; independence movement in, 144; indigenous groups in, 187; modernization of, 172; positivism in, 188n1; women's philosophical relevance in, 187
Mignolo, Walter, 29
militarism, 17
Millet, Jean, 80
Mills, Charles W., 40, 43, 52–53n26
minimalism, 26
minority groups, 39
Mitcham, Carl, 144
mockery, 124, 125–26, 127, 136–37
moderation, 15
modernity, 38, 131, 195, 207; contradictory nature of, 3–4; mask of progress and, 3; Peruvian, 204; thanatocratic nature of, 3–4
Molina, Enrique, *The Philosophy of Bergson*, 154–55
Montalvo, José Rafael, 150
Montoro, Rafael, 150

morality, 64, 67, 148, 150, 152, 153, 154, 171, 180, 186–87; aesthetic intuition and, 178; aesthetics and, 182–83; aesthetic values and, 182–83; Darwinian evolutionism and, 150, 151; language and, 48–49, 49–50; moral imagination, 186; nature and, 150; obligation and, 149; sources of, 20–21, 44–45, 58
moral philosophy, 173, 175; Kantian, 183–84
moral progress, as expansion of responsibility, 74–75n15
moral subject, autonomy of, 153–54
Morocco, 17
motion: duration and, 85; time and, 82–83
Mouffe, Chantal, 198
Mphahlele, Es'kia, 91
multiculturalism, 67
multiplicity, 15, 81, 156; temporal, 29
Munro, Thomas, 103
music and dance metaphors, for African epistemology, 107–108
mystical feeling, 46–47
mystical intuition, League of Nations and, 3
mystical vision, madness and, viii
mystic experience, 70–71
mysticism, 16, 180, 185; art and, 180; Christian, 16; engendering social relation different from fellow-feeling of closed society, 70; pure, 70
mystic/primitive couple, in *The Two Sources of Morality and Religion*, 19–20, 27
mystics, viii, 15, 21, 22, 25, 26, 27, 58; call of, 73; capacity to detach from the particular and attach to the general, 70, 71, 72; complete sympathy and, 69, 71–72; inspiring others, 70; open societies and, 68–69, 70; origins of, 70–71; possibility of conditioned by society, 70; sociality and, 70–72; sociality of call and response and, 72; sympathy and, 70–71
mystic society, 47, 48
mythical timelessness, 205
mythic potential, 206–207
mythmaking, revolutionary role of, 7
myth(s), 194; antagonism and, 193–210; duration and, 198; of the general strike, 196–98; Mariátegui, José Carlos and, 208n2; political survival of, 207; power of, 199; social, 198, 203, 205–206; socialist, 199; social life and, 199–200

Nardal, Jane (Yadhé), 121, 137–38n3
Nardal, Paulette, 6, 121, 122, 139n24; "Guignol Ouolof," 133–37
national identity, arts and, 171
nationalism, 6, 7, 42, 129; capitalism and, 43; colonialism and, 42; homogenization and, 49, 50–51; patriarchy and, 43; Peruvian, 195, 208n2; racism and, 42; white supremacy and, 43
National Preparatory School, 173
nation(s)/nation-state(s): balance of power among, 151; capitalism and, 42, 43; competition among, 152; construction of, 49; exclusion and, 37–55; formation of, 5, 147; global system of, 37, 38, 39–43, 50; homogeneity and, 37–55; national selection, 152; nation-building, 150; as normative concept, 42; representation of, 155; sexism and, 42; state formation, 6; state identity, 38. *See also* state system
nativism, 6
naturalism, 101

natural laws, 62, 158
natural sciences, 159
natural selection, 151, 152, 176
natural sympathy, 58–59, 72; closed societies and, 60–68; vs. complete sympathy, 71–72; obligation and, 63–64; as protective mechanism, 72–73; as source for racism, 72–73; as source for war, 72–73
"natural tendency," 65
nature, 144, 175, 177; duality and, 157; human difference and, 144; morality and, 150; normativity and, 175, 177
Nayar, Pramod, 117n51
Négritude, 6, 13, 18, 88, 121; as active embrace of negative stereotypes of blacks, 94, 95, 96; as antiracist racism, 94–95; *avant la lettre*, 133; Bergsonism and, 6; class conflict and, 95, 99; as critique of colonial and scientific reason, 100; critiques of, 90, 91, 94, 95–99, 100, 114; as distinctive ontological orientation, 91; emotionalism and, 99; epistemology and, 93, 101–102, 104–14; essentialism and, 96–97, 99, 100; Fanon's critique of, 117n51; Fanon's reading of, 95; as form of "political mystification," 98, 99, 100; as ideologically counterproductive, 100; interpretation of, 93, 98; as irrationalism, 95, 96, 98–99; materialist an nonessentialist critiques of, 95–99; myth of black homogeneity and, 98; as myth of religion, 98; as negation of a negation, 94; ontology and, 91, 93; philosophical foundations of, 79–119; as a philosophy, 93; questioning of reason and, 90; as racist, 100; reason and emotion in Négritude epistemology, 109–14; Sartre and, 94–95; Senghor's reading of, 92; subjective and objective poles of, 94–95; as theory of African knowing, 102; as tigritude, 98; vitalism and, 91–92
neocolonialism, 13, 59, 195
neocolonial paternalism, 13
neo-Darwinism, 151–52
neo-idealism, 158–59, 162–65
neo-Lamarckism, 151
new humanism, 152, 159–60
new materialism, 7, 8, 14, 16, 162–65, 186
new physics, 162
Nietzsche, Friedrich, 152, 153, 183, 197, 199
Nodar Manso, Francisco, 187, 192n78
"non-civilized" societies, 24
nonessentialism, 95–99
nonhuman animals, human animals and, 178, 186, 190n40
the noninstrumental, 179
normativity, 43, 45, 46, 175, 186; as general phenomenon of life, 54n50; homogenization and, 42–43; language and, 49–50; nature and, 175, 177
norms: Bergson on, 44–46; establishment and maintenance of, 46

obedience, tendency toward, 65
object: African vs. European approaches to, 104–105; of knowledge, 104–105; subject and, 179; violation of, 104–105
objectification, 104–105
object-subject distinction, 189–90n21
obligation, 23–24, 26, 44–45, 62–63, 65, 66, 148–49; "in general," 63; as general phenomenon of life, 54n50;

morality and, 149; natural sympathy and, 63–64; "totality of," 63; as virtual instinct, 20
observation, 162
Ohana, David, 196, 209n9
Olivares Vargas, Rigel, 176
Oliver, Kelly, *Animal Lessons: How They Teach Us to Be Human*, 186
oneness, 160
ontological pluralism, 189–90n21
"ontologism," 175
ontology, 164; African, 80; of being, 90; epistemology and, 108; European vs. African conception of the world, 106–107; Négritude and, 91, 93; Senghor and, 100; substance, 85
ontology of rhythm, Senghor and, 108–109
the open, 13–35. See also open/closed dichotomy; openness
open/closed dichotomy, 13–35, 50; conceptual shift to the half-open, 29; decolonizing, 27; destabilizing by employing Bergsonian methods, 28; as ill-fitting, ready-made concepts, 30; life expressed as, 58; limits between, 47–48; thermodynamics and, 34n58; in *The Two Sources of Morality and Religion*, 19–20, 22–27, 28
open communities, 49
opening, 20, 23, 26, 29, 50. See also openness
"open love," 30–31n5
openness, x, 5, 15, 21, 28, 29, 70; to all existence, 47; community and, 46–47; in *Creative Evolution*, 22–23; duration and, 23; of the future, xii; tendency to, 16, 25, 26–27, 28; of time, xii; in *The Two Sources of Morality and Religion*, 22–23. See *also* half-openness; the open; open/closed dichotomy; open societies
open societies, 5, 28, 49, 58, 76n53; vs. closed societies, 15; complete sympathy and, 58–59, 60, 68–72; generosity and, 68; humanity and, 69; language and, 51; mystics and, 68–69, 70; sociality in, 71–72
open tendency, 58
opposition, 15
the oppressed, conservation of identity and, 29
oppression, 2, 6; creative possibilities for resistance to, 2; resistance to, 69
optimism, 153, 196
order, 197
Ordine Nuovo, 196
"original nature," 65
Ortega y Gasset, José, 176, 189–90n21
otherness, blackness and, 131–32
ownership, 66

Palma, Ricardo, *Tradiciones peruanas*, 209–10n21
parallelism, asymmetrical, 108
"parasitical" solidarity, 57
Paris, France, black intellectuals in, 122
Paris Peace Conference, 2–3
Parkin, John, *Laughter and Power*, 127
particularity, 5, 178, 179, 188; of human intellect, 179; universality and, 188
pasadismo, 200–201
Pascal, Blaise, 174
past: coexistence and reconfiguration in the present, 29; as continuous immanent transformation of directionality and sense that is tendency, 29; creativity of, 18; dynamic conception of, 18–19; as "half-open," 29; half-openness of,

past *(continued)*
  18; interpenetration of past, present future, 93; survival of, 179; weight of, 14
Pateman, Carole, 41, 43
"pathological homogenization," 38, 39, 49, 50–51; colonialism and, 39–42; language and, 50; nationalism and, 42; patriarchy and, 41–42; race and, 39–42; sexism and, 41–42; white supremacy and, 40–41
patriarchy, 41–42; homogenization and, 49, 50–51; nationalism and, 43; white supremacism and, 43
peoplehood: identity and, 38; language and, 49; organic unity of, 46; in *The Two Sources of Morality and Religion*, 44–45
peoples: construction of, 38; whitewashing of, 49
perception, 23, 186
performativity, racial, 6
permanence, 81
perricholismo, 200, 209–10n21
personalism, 186
personhood, 186
persons, commodification of, 49
perspectivism, 176, 188, 189–90n21
Peru, 7, 155, 193–210; backwardness of, 203; Bergsonism in, 194–95, 208n5; class structure in, 202; colonialism and, 200; contradiction and antagonism in, 203–204; democratization in, 208n6; historic torpor of, 203; history of, 199–203; indigenous groups in, 200, 201, 204–205; intellectuals in, 194–95; "melancholy" national literature of, 200; modernity in, 204; nationalism in, 195; national politics in, 200; national revitalization in, 195–96; positivism in, 195; social relations in, 198
Peruvian history: "change" in, 207; clarifying, 199–203; contradiction and antagonism in, 203–206, 207
pessimism, 152, 153, 163
Petitfils, Brad, *Parallels and Responses to Curricular Innovation: The Possibilities of Posthumanistic Education*, 187
phenomenalism, 158
phenomenology, German, 176
philosophy, 80, 152; abstraction and lack of precision of philosophical systems, 29–30; in Africa, 189n16; African art as, 102–103; aim of being presuppositionless, viii; Bergson's distinct approach to, 44; biology and, 152, 186; creative capacity within philosophical thinking, 7; of culture, 187; discrete approach to, 174; German, 180, 182; heroic approach to, 174; Latin American, 174, 189n16; of love, 180; Négritude and, 93; of physics, 83; science and, 152, 162–63, 186, 187; three fundamental ideas for philosophical thinking, vii–x; of time, 14; two approaches to, 174
physics, 80, 83, 161, 162
Pickety, Thomas, 52n13
Picon, Gaëtan, 110
Pinker, Steven, 55n66
pity, ix. *See also* sympathy
place: (im)possibility of, 121–40; authenticity and, 137; race and, 137
Planck, Max, 161
Plato, 156, 174, 180
Platonism, 158, 180
play, 177–78, 186, 190n36
"pleasing fear," 144

Plotinus, 174, 180
pluralism, 110–12, 113, 189–90n21
poets, 191n59
Poland, invasion of, 3
political life, 174
"political" solidarity, 57
political theory, 14
Ponce, Aníbal, 160–61
Porfiriato, 173
positive science, 149
positivism, 96, 150, 154–56, 158, 171, 173, 175, 179; Caso's critique of, 176; Comtean, 188n1, 189n6; education and, 187; Latin American rejection of, 209n7; in Mexico, 188n1; in Peru, 195; Porfirian, 172; Porfiriato's exaltation of, 186; "superior," 60
possibility, 29, 30
postcolonialism, 14; Mariátegui, José Carlos and, 208n2
postracial present, 14
poststructuralism, 194
power, 51n10, 129; laughter and, 130; race and, 129–30
pragmatism, 151, 176
prejudices, 4; erasure of through humanistic studies, 162
present, interpenetration of past, present future, 93
the "primitive," 15, 16, 17, 18, 23–24, 32–33n23, 33n24, 131, 195
"primitive humanity," 25–26
"primitives," xi, 16, 24, 24–26, 27
"primitive" societies, xi, 24
process, reality as, 83
profits, drive toward, 39–40
progress, 172, 179, 183, 195, 196, 197, 199, 202, 207; bourgeois notions of, 193; in closed societies, 21; mask of, 3; "qualitative," 203;

in *The Two Sources of Morality and Religion*, 21; in United States, 202
proletarian activism, 197
proletariat, collective memory of, 197
Proudhon, Jean-Pierre, 197
Prussia, 145, 146
psychism (*psiquismo*), 160
psychological evolution, 153
psychology, 153, 162; biological, 159; experimental, 154; evolutionist, 159; scientific, 159
public spaces, blackness in, 120–40
public transportation, 124–25

qualitative difference, 197
qualitative multiplicity, vii, viii–ix
quantification, 81, 82, 83, 86, 88
quantitative multiplicity, viii–x
quantum mechanics, 83
quantum physics, 162
Quebec, 31n6
Quijano, Aníbal, 194–95, 208n2
Quranic verse, 18–19

race, 1, 3–8, 59, 159, 188; authenticity and, 137; belonging and, 128, 129, 130, 132; bifurcation into, 40; Darwinian evolutionism and, 145–46; Darwinism and, 144–51; disguise and, 135; dress and, 127, 128–29; drive toward homogenization and, 39–42; as "dynamic essence," 33n24; empathy and, 125; exclusion and, 137; internalist or "noumenal" metaphor of, 33n24; place and, 137; power and, 129–30; racial becomings, 143–70; racial group identities, 8, 133, 137; racial performativity, 6; representation and, 144; as "sociopolitical rather than

race *(continued)*
  biological," 40; state framework and, 37. *See also* racial difference
race consciousness, feminism and, 133
"racial contract," 40–41
racial difference, 159, 162; Bergsonism and, 151–62; biological materialism and, 161
racial hierarchies, 159; evolutionism and, 145–46, 151
racialism, 18
racialization, 159, 160, 163; determinism and, 151; in Latin America, 151; racialized bodies, 160
racism, 2, 4, 6, 59, 65, 68, 72; color-blindness approach to, 5; Darwinian evolutionism and, 145–46; as function of sympathy derived from fellow-feeling, 72–73; nationalism and, 42; Négritude as antiracist racism, 94–95; sexism and, 42; sympathy and, 58, 59; systemic, 5
Rae, Heather, 38–39
Rama, Angel, 208n2
Raney, Magd, 129–31, 132, 136, 139n36
rationalism, 87, 193, 195, 196, 197, 202
rationality, 179, 181, 183–84, 196; Bergson's rejection of Kant's conception of, 176–77
the "real," 90, 162
realism: "agential realism," 165; of the spirit, 158
reality: as becoming, 83; as difference, 83; as process, 83
reason, 105, 149, 153; in African epistemology, 109–10; European tradition and, 105; intuition and, 87; intuitive, 106; Négritude and, 90, 100, 101, 109–14; Senghor's pluralistic view of, 109–11
relative justice, 4, 22

religion(s), 154; dynamic, x–xi, 23–24; origins of, 58; static vs. dynamic, 23–24; of love, x–xi; static, 23–24, 26
religious garb, 31n6
religious idealism, 154
renovation, ethic of, 156
representation, 144, 147, 162, 165; bodies and, 164; materialism and, 155; matter and, 164–65; race and, 144
resistance, 204; indigenous, 204–205, 206; mythical potential of, 206
resistance, collective, 8
Revista de Cuba, 150
revolutionary change, 197
Reyes, Alfonso, 155–56, 173, 188n2
rhythm, 96; African epistemology and, 107–108; of being, 90, 108; ontology of, 108–109; of the real, 90; style and, 108–109; of things, 90
rhythms, ontology of, 108–109
Ribot, Théodule-Armand, 157
rights, 4; equality of, 4
rigidity, comic nature of, 132
Rodó, José, 153; *Ariel*, 152, 153, 157; *Los Motivos de Proteo*, 156
Rojas, Ricardo, 209n7
Rolland, Romain, 196
Romanell, Patrick, 172, 175, 184, 185
romanticism, 144
Rome, 147
Romero, Francisco, 154, 174
root metaphors, 107
Rousseau, Jean-Jacques, x, 40
Royer-Collard, Pierre, 150
rules, 44
Russell, Bertrand, 80

Sajous, Leo, 6, 121
sameness, difference and, 153, 163

Sanguily, Manuel, 150
Sartre, Jean-Paul, 91, 94–95, 113
Satyarthi, Kailash, 69
Scheler, Max, 174, 175, 176
Schiller, Friedrich, 177–78
scholasticism, 158
Scholz, Sally, 57
Schopenhauer, Arthur, 153, 154, 183, 184
science, 104, 151, 152, 159, 160, 162, 171, 179, 186, 189n6; Bergson on, 82–83; cinematographic method and, 83–85; as cinematography, 82; crisis in modern, 100–101; epistemology and, 106; of existence, 174–75; freeze-frame view of world supported by, 83–85; vs. intuition, 86–87; philosophy and, 162–63, 187; Porfiriato's exaltation of, 171, 173; positive, 149; scientific thinking, 83–85, 106; social theory and, 164; view of nature as succession of fixed moments, 82. *See also* positivism; *specific sciences*
scientism, 83, 101
self-interestedness, 180, 186, 191n57. See also *egoísmo*
selflessness, 182–84
self-reflection, 179
self-transformation, love and, 156
Sembène, Ousmane, 100
Senghor, Léopold Sédar, 6, 18, 32n22, 79–119, 121; Afri-centered perspective of, 93; anticolonialist language of, 97; on Bergson, 99–101; colonialism and, 93, 97; on developments in modern European epistemology, 99–101; emotion and, 111–14; epistemology and, 100, 106; on Négritude as epistemology, 104–108; ontology and, 100; ontology of rhythm and, 108–109;

Thiam's Afri-centered reading of, 92–94
sensations, 88–89
sensibilities, acquisition of, 67
Sereqeberhan, Tsenay, 91
sexism, 2, 4, 41–42, 59
"sexual contract," 41–42
sexuality, 49, 59
Sharpley-Whiting, T. Denean, 129
Shepard, Clara, 129, 131–32
Sierra, Justo, 173, 174, 189n9
Sieyès, Emmanuel-Joseph, 74n11
Smith, Adam, 60
social conflict, 198
social conservation, 24
social contracts, 41
social contract theory, 43, 52–53n26
social Darwinism, 189n9, 195
social development, 162, 164–65
social formations: difference of degree between, 24–25; materiality and, 165
social groups, x, 188; cohesion of, 5, 46; sympathy and, 57
social imagination, 8
socialism, 7, 193, 196, 197–98; indigenous, 193; indigenous groups and, 205; myth of, 199; parliamentary, 196; reformist, 197, 204; socialist myth, 199
sociality: of life, 20; mystics and, 70, 71; in open vs. closed societies, 71–72; in *The Two Sources of Morality and Religion*, 20, 27
social laws, 62
social life: myth and, 199–200; organized at intersection of boundary and belonging, 59
social myth, 203, 205–206
"social objectivism," 175
social sciences, 161. *See also* history; psychology; sociology

social theory, science and, 164
Sociedad Científica Argentina, 161
society/societies, 54n55, 64–65; closed, 28, 58–59, 60, 68, 70, 76n53; difference between "primitive" and "civilized," 33n24; human vs. animal, 62–63; inclusive, 59; instinctive vs. intelligent, 44–45; language and, 49; in movement, 25; open, 28, 58–59, 60, 68, 70, 76n53; open vs. closed, 28, 76n53; organization of, 43
sociology, 60, 74n11, 153
solidarity, 68; between and across groups, 73; group, 58; "parasitical" vs. "political," 57; racial, 133
solids, 82
Sorel, Georges, 7, 193–94, 196–98, 199, 203–204, 206, 209n9; *Decomposition of Marxism*, 196; *The Illusions of Progress*, 196; Laclau and, 210n30; *Reflections on Violence*, 196
Soulez, Philippe, 1, 4
Soyinka, Wole, 91, 96, 98–99
space: duration and, 179; as "great unconscious presupposition of Western thought," 81, 86
Spain, 145, 151, 156, 159
Spanish America, 143–70; impact of Bergsonian philosophy in, 154; independence movements in, 144; intellectuals in, 150, 159, 163, 165; use of term, 165n3. *See also specific countries*
Spanish-American War, 151
Spanish art and literature, 159
Spanish colonialism, 200, 202
spatiality, mathematics and, 82
spatialization, 86; of change, 198; of experience, 85; of thought, 81; of time, 82, 83
spatial root metaphors, 81

Spencer, Herbert, 150, 151, 161; *The Data of Ethics*, 148; hypothesis on play, 177–78; "surplus energy theory," 177; "surplus energy theory," 190n36
Spencerian philosophy, 156
"spirit," 194
spiritualism, 150, 154, 158–59
Spivak, Gayatri, 208n2
stasis, x
state structure, closure and, 50
state system, 37; capitalism and, 39–40; doomed to failure, 50; homogenization and, 39–43
static religions, x–xi, 23–24, 26
Stevens, Jacqueline, 53–54n41
Stoler, Ann, 13, 17
"strategic essentialism," 208n2
striving, in *The Two Sources of Morality and Religion*, 70
style, rhythm and, 108–109
subjectivism, Caso's rejection of, 175
subjectivity, 85–86, 160
subject/object relations, 179; African vs. European approaches to, 105
suffering, 50, 73
"surplus energy theory," 177–78, 190n36
surveyor, analogy of, 25
survival, 152, 176, 177, 181
survival of the fittest, 173
"sympathetic communication," 88
sympathy, ix, x, 6, 8, 20, 153, 155; as basis of mutual recognition of the other, 67; belonging and, 58–59; boundary-making and, 58–59; closed societies and, 58–59; community and, 67; complete, 58, 59, 60; in *Creative Evolution*, 73–74n3; deeper source of, 70–71; derived from experience of belonging, not belonging, sympathy, and suffering,

73; exclusion and, 58, 59, 68; as feeling of mutual solidarity between members of a social group, 57; history of the word, 60; intuition as, 88; limitations and possibilities of, 58; lived, 69; as metaphysical explanation for instinct, 73–74n3; mystics and, 70–71; natural, 58, 59, 60, 71–72; natural vs. complete, 58–59, 71–72; open societies and, 58–59; politics of, 57–75; as protective mechanism, 72–73; racism and, 58, 59
syndicalism, 196, 197
synthesis, 196, 197
system-building, rejection of, 19

temporality/time, xii, 1, 6–8, 28, 160–61; Bergsonian, 205; Bergson's embrace of, 80–81; decentered, 29; decolonizing, 29; dynamism of, xii; heterogeneous, 85; history and, 195, 200; homogenous, 85; of indigenous myth, 205; infinitesimal calculus and, 83; infinity of, xii; lived experience of continuous, 82; motion and, 82–83; myth of the general strike and, 197; nonlinear theory of, 29; the open and the closed and, 13–35; openness of, xii; Peruvian history and, 200; philosophy of, 14; as a process or becoming, 83; scientific, 85; spatialization of, 82, 83; suppression of in Western metaphysics, 80–81; temporal multiplicity, 29; thinking in, 82–83; viewed as succession of fixed moments, 82
tendencies, 28; of experience, 27; half-openness of, 28–29; intuition and, 87; to obey, 65; to war, 66
theology, 173, 184–85

theory of relativity, 160, 161, 169n84
Thiam, Cheikh, 91, 92–94; *Return to the Kingdom of Childhood: Re-Envisioning the Legacy and Philosophical Relevance of Négritude*, 92–93
things, rhythm of, 90
thinking/thought: about solids, 82; different styles of, 110–112; in duration, 85, 86, 92, 93, 106; intuitively, 86–90. *See also* spatialization of, 81; in time, 82–83
Thiong'o, Ngũgĩ wa, 111
Tiananmen Square, 69
tigritude, 98
time. *See* temporality/time
Time and Free Will: An Essay on the Immediate Data of Consciousness (Bergson): qualitative vs. quantitative multiplicity, viii–x; Senghor on, 99–100
timelessness, mythical, 205, 209n7
Tolstoy, Leo, 184; *What Is Art?* 177
Towa, Marcien, 91, 96–97
transcendence, 176, 178
Treaty of Versailles, 2–3
The Two Sources of Morality and Religion (Bergson), vii–viii, x, 3, 6, 8, 14–15, 28, 39, 172; analogy to insect society in, 44–45; appeal to Christian mysticism in, 16; aspiration in, 21–23; Caso and, 172; colonialism and, 15, 17–18, 30n1; context of, 32n19, 33n24; critique of imperialism in, 17–18; critique of luxury of spices in, 18; critique of militarism in, 17; disappointment expressed around, 16; foreclosed possibility of decentering and decolonizing temporality in, 29; God as love in, 184–85; human rights theory and, 37; influence on John

The Two Sources of Morality and Religion (Bergson) *(continued)* Humphrey, 2; instinct in, 34n40; international state system and, 37; methodology in, 15, 19–20, 23–27; minimalism in, 26; morality and language in, 48–49; mystic/primitive couple in, 19–20, 27; mystics in, 19–22, 27; open/closed dichotomy in, 15, 19–20, 22–27, 28; political significance of, 185; "primitives" in, xi, 25–26; progress in, 21; question of "peoplehood" in, 44–45; readings of, 16–19; sociality in, 20, 27; sociality of life in, 20; striving in, 70; sympathy in, 57–76; unjust charity in, 185; war in, 47; written in early 1930s, 43

Unamuno, Miguel de, 207
unconscious life, 149–50, 151
understanding, Bergson on, 81–82
United Nations' *Universal Declaration of Human Rights*, 2
United States: actions in Texas and California, 145; Anglo-Saxonism and, 145–46, 151; imperialism and, 153; Mexico and, 173; privileging of STEM fields in education in, 187; progress in, 202
universalism, 188. *See also* universality
universality, 152, 153, 157, 160, 163, 188; of duration, 179; particularity and, 188
Universidad Nacional de Mexico, 173
Universidad Popular Gonzalez Prada, 208n6
Urpeth, Jim, 185
Uruguay, 7, 160, 161, 208n6
U.S. Constitution, 4
utilitarianism, 64, 154
utopianism, 197

Valcárcel, Luis E., *Tempestad en los Andes*, 199
values: aesthetic, 180–81; existence of, 175–76, 180
Varona, E. José, 150
Vasconcelos, José, 155, 157–58, 174, 188n2; *Cosmic Race*, 157, 209n7
Vaz Ferreira, Carlos, 160, 164
Verlaine, Paul, 160
Vico, Giambattista, 154, 199
Villegas, Micaela, 209–10n21
violence, 46, 55n66; colonial, 4, 6; laughter and, 127
virtuality, 28
visual metaphors, 107
vital energy, 177, 179, 183, 190n36
vital force, 69–70, 111–12. *See also élan vital*
vitalism, 7, 152, 163, 177, 195, 198, 208n2; Bergsonian, 176; Bergson's repudiation of, 92; Caso and, 171–72, 188; Mariátegui and, 194, 207; Négritude and, 91–92; Sorelian model of, 194
Vorzimmer, Peter, 190n32

war, x, xi, 20, 43, 46, 47, 58, 61, 62, 68, 72; as function of sympathy derived from fellow-feeling, 72–73; Hegel's view of, 46, 54–55n57; human nature and, 65; as "natural and ineradicable," 47; ownership and, 66; tendency to, 66; war-instinct, 65
weapons, 129
Weismann, August, 152
Western epistemology, metaphor of sign and vision and, 107
Western metaphysics: presupposition of space in, 81; suppression of temporality in, 80–81
Western thought: metaphor of sign and vision and, 107; presupposition

of space in, 81; privileging of spatialization and quantification in, 86; suppression of temporality in, 80–81
White, Melanie, 2
white men, 4
whiteness, 135; as "set of power relations," 40
white spaces, 128; blackness and, 137; black people in, 120–140
white supremacy, 4; homogenization and, 40–41, 49, 50–51; nationalism and, 43; "pathological homogenization" and, 40–41; patriarchy and, 43
wholes, social, 20
will, supremacy of, 153
Wilson, Woodrow, 2
Wiredu, Kwasi, 91

women: biologization of, 192n78; of color, 4; in Mexico, 187
worker conflict, 196
world, European vs. African conception of, 106–107
World War I, 2–3, 68, 186, 195
World War II, 3, 186
Worms, Frédéric, 31n7
Wynter, Sylvia, 187–88

xenophobia, 4, 59, 68, 72

Yadhé. *See* Nardal, Jane (Yadhé)
Yousafzai, Malala, 69
youth, Bergson as philosopher of the, 151, 155, 157

Zea, Leopoldo, 173, 189n8

www.ingramcontent.com/pod-product-compliance
Lightning Source LLC
Chambersburg PA
CBHW030533230426
43665CB00010B/867